THE ROMAN OCCUPATION OF IBERIA

THE ROMAN OCCUPATION OF IBERIA

THE BATTLES FOR HISPANIA, THE JEWEL IN ROME'S CROWN

J. J. HERRERO GIMÉNEZ

FRONTLINE
BOOKS

THE ROMAN OCCUPATION OF IBERIA
The Battles for Hispania, the Jewel in Rome's Crown

First published in Great Britain in 2025 by
Frontline Books
An imprint of Pen & Sword Books Ltd
Yorkshire – Philadelphia

ISBN: 978-1-39903-469-2

Typeset by Lapiz Digital
Printed and bound by CPI UK

The Publisher's authorised representative in the EU for product safety is Authorised Rep Compliance Ltd., Ground Floor, 71 Lower Baggot Street, Dublin D02 P593, Ireland.
www.arccompliance.com

For a complete list of Pen & Sword titles please contact:

PEN & SWORD BOOKS LTD
47 Church Street, Barnsley, South Yorkshire, S70 2AS, UK
E-mail: enquiries@pen-and-sword.co.uk
Website: www.pen-and-sword.co.uk

Or

PEN AND SWORD BOOKS,
1950 Lawrence Road, Havertown, PA 19083, USA
E-mail: uspen-and-sword@casematepublishers.com
Website: www.penandswordbooks.com

CONTENTS

LIST OF ILLUSTRATIONS

LIST OF MAPS

To my parents, Juan & Oris

ACKNOWLEDGMENTS

The writing of this book has been an amazing adventure. And adventures, as the reader knows, are much more fun if they are shared. Of all the historians and archaeologists I have consulted, I must highlight the support, advice and help I have received from Dr Núria Sadurní, who has been very dear to me for several decades now, and Dr Esther Gurri, whose knowledge of Rome is truly encyclopaedic. Both are doing an extraordinary job at the Museum of Badalona, undoubtedly one of the best I have visited in Spain, where visitors can literally walk over part of the urban layout of ancient Baetulo and learn about its astonishing history. I would also like to thank Dr Albert Estrada-Rius of the MNAC (Museu Nacional d'Art de Catalunya) for his help, a truly erudite man whom I deeply admire. I would likewise like to acknowledge the collaboration of different institutions, which have provided me with some of the spectacular images that accompany this book. In this regard, I would like to express my gratitude to Antonio Patiño of the Office of Heritage and Archaeology of the government of Castilla-La Mancha, Ana Mª Bejarano of the Consortium Ciudad Monumental de Mérida and Diana Martín of the Segovia Tourist Office, to name but a few. Obviously, I cannot forget all the support I have received from John Grehan and the rest of the Pen & Sword team: without them you would not have this book in your hands. Last but not least, I would like to thank my family for their constant support. Firstly, my sister-in-law, Mamen Otero, and my brother-in-law, Jose León, for their research assistance. My wife and children have accompanied me on the many journeys I have made across the Iberian Peninsula in search of the traces of the Romans. Without the selflessness and generosity of Yolanda; the unwavering enthusiasm of my son Ferran; and the resigned patience of my daughter Valèria. This book is for them.

J.J. Herrero Giménez
24 November 2023

INTRODUCTION

If we think of two nations whose populations are similar, we are sure to think of many examples on all continents. After all, in many cases, borders are very capricious lines. But surely if you ask us who the Italians are most similar to, the answer is probably the Spaniards. And it is striking, given that they are two countries that do not share a single mile of border, as France, Switzerland, Austria or Slovenia do. In fact, Spain and Italy are separated by almost 350 miles. Obviously, this comment is just a little joke, since there is no single prototype for an Italian, just as there is no single prototype for a Spaniard, Briton or American. However, we cannot ignore the fact that the two nations do share what we might call a certain common ethos. And if we have to go back to a point in history where this symbiosis began, we find it in Ancient Rome. And yet relations started off complicated. It took the Romans 200 years to dominate the entire peninsula. It is true that the resistance of the pre-Roman societies was never coordinated, nor, as we shall see, did they have a feeling, let us call it national, against the invader. We might think that the famous *Divide et impera* (divide and conquer) attributed to Julius Caesar, which worked so well in his conquest of Gaul, did not work in Iberia. There, the Romans encountered a kind of juggling of the Chinese plates, that game in which the artist must see to it that no plate falls to the ground, quelling revolts and uprisings often at far-flung points on a peninsula much larger than the island of Great Britain or California. But in history nothing is black and white, it is made up of nuances, and in this book, we will delve into them. We cannot ignore the fact that there were tribes that welcomed the Romans with open arms; but others fought fiercely against them until their extermination; but there were also many whose interests fluctuated, until total integration with Rome. And when this happened, Iberia became practically a second Italy, an extension of Rome itself. From Iberia came the first consuls and even the first emperors born outside Italy. To give just one example of the similarity between Italy and Hispania, both regions had the same number of circuses, the most complex of Roman buildings, due to their very high construction, and above all maintenance, costs. And if during the next few years, Dr Jiménez Hernández's excavations in Italica manage to locate its Roman circus, we could find that in Iberia there were more circuses than in Italy itself, where fourteen are known. In comparison, in Gaul there were four, to one in Britannia, specifically in Camulodunum (modern Colchester). Iberia's integration into the Roman world was total and seamless until its fall. But what should we call this territory: Iberia, Hispania, Spain? It is necessary to clarify the toponym before proceeding any further. In most works written in English or translations of classical texts, this territory is referred to as *Spain*. But I consider this epithet to be inaccurate: what do we do with Portugal, Andorra and Gibraltar? It is a term that causes unnecessary confusion. On the other hand, as far as we know, the pre-Roman societies of the peninsula did not have a name for that territory either. Although, we will start by talking about Iberia, the name given to it by one of its previous colonisers, the Greeks. Once the Romans entered the peninsula, we will go on to designate the territory as they did: Hispania. But this appellation always had a geographical and, later, an administrative character. In order to better organise the wars of conquest, the Romans divided the territory into two provinces: H. Citerior, i.e. the one closest to Rome, and H. Ulterior, the one furthest away. As we shall see, these designations were merely missions for those in charge of carrying them out (proconsuls, consuls, *propreatores*, *praetores*, etc.). Thus, the first chapter is devoted to the different pre-Roman societies that inhabited Iberia. They were very different to each other, many of them permanently at war, speaking different languages and with very different cultures. It will be a particularly useful chapter to contextualise all the pre-Roman tribes that we will discuss throughout the book. Moreover, in Iberia, two foreign peoples, the Greeks and the Carthaginians, were already present at the end of the 2nd century BC. The power that the latter accumulated in the western Mediterranean was such that Rome provoked what is known as the Second Punic War. And in 218 BC, with the aim of opening a new front of warfare far from Italy, Gnaeus Cornelius Scipio landed at Emporion, as we shall see in the second chapter. And what he found there was a true serendipity. He arrived in Iberia to fight the Punics and found a land of overwhelming wealth. It seemed as if the territory was full of mines: iron, tin, silver, gold . . . And its fertile lands oozed with the typical foods of the Mediterranean triad: wheat, vines, and olives. For an expansionist society like the Romans, Iberia was to become an obscure object of desire. After winning the Second Punic War, it was time to colonise

Iberia and exploit its inexhaustible riches. This process was relatively easy on the coast and in the Guadalquivir river valley. The problem came when the Romans wanted to penetrate inland. The inhabitants, especially the Celtiberians and Lusitanians, fought desperately to maintain their sovereignty, their lands and their freedom. In the third chapter, we will analyse the conquest of that wild European far west, in which the Romans were forced to employ enormous human and material resources, which both sides used with a ferocity and cruelty rarely seen in antiquity. Such was the terror instilled by names such as Viriathus or Numantia that no Roman or Italic wanted to go and fight in such atrocious territory; such were the difficulties in conquering the interior of Iberia that the Romans were even forced to change their calendar, but also to resort to assassinations, treachery and even genocide. Likewise, the occupation and colonisation of Iberia required the best generals of the Republican and High-Imperial periods. Great names of Rome such as Augustus, Julius Caesar, Pompey, Marius, Scipio Africanus, Aemilius Scipio, Cato the Elder, Agrippa, etc. Perhaps with the sole exception of Sulla, there was no Roman of renown who did not begin or forge his political and military career in Iberia. The fourth chapter will be devoted to the civil wars. No major conquests took place during this period, except for Caesar's exceptional and little-known campaign in the west of the peninsula, but the most important aspect of this phase was the integration of the *Hispaniae* provinces into the Roman world. Although we will discuss the term 'Romanisation' in the final chapter, in this period Sertorius managed to get many pre-Roman tribes to accept his leadership, precisely in order to fight against Rome, but at the same time they began to adopt the Roman way of life. Thus, when civil wars broke out between Caesarians and Pompeians, the inhabitants of Hispania sided with one of the two factions. It would no longer be as it was a century earlier during the Second Punic War, when they fought according to their own interests, sometimes supporting the Carthaginians, sometimes the Romans, but always with the aim of safeguarding their sovereignty and independence. In this case, the Hispanians were already fighting as Romans. The end of the civil wars ushered in the principality of Augustus. One of his first objectives was to pacify the frontiers. This is a somewhat paradoxical concept, which we will analyse in the fifth chapter, given that in order to pacify them he was going to carry out the last phase of conquests in Hispania of the tribes that were still independent of Rome, the Asturians and the Cantabrians. Once again, the war was going to be extremely tough. The legionaries would shed rivers of blood to conquer a steep and rugged territory populated by fierce warriors. It was not until the arrival of Agrippa, who carried out a new genocide, that these territories would be incorporated into Rome. To give us an idea of the difficulty of this campaign, we know that the Romans took the same amount of time to conquer Gaul as this territory, except that the lands occupied by the Astur-Cantabrians occupied less than 2 per cent of what Gaul occupied. The final chapter is devoted to the mutual influence that was established between Hispania and the metropolis. Although the Roman contributions to the Iberian Peninsula are practically countless, the Hispanians sent to Rome, in addition to their natural wealth, poets, philosophers, politicians and even some of the best emperors in their history. Rome and Hispania are so intimately intertwined that Philip VI of Spain is, de jure, the legitimate heir to the title of Roman Emperor of the East since its last holder Andreas Palaiologos sold his rights to the kings of Spain in 1502.

The writing of this book has allowed me to dust off my old and beloved books of classical authors from the legendary Spanish publishing house Gredos, but I have also used the English translations, which will be quoted throughout the text. But the primary sources leave many questions open, so I have turned to the work of the best contemporary historians and archaeologists for their work and latest discoveries. Among the classics, Schulten's work, although disputed, remains a reference for all historians of this period. Among the contemporaries, I cannot fail to mention Amela Rodríguez, Peralta Labrador and Jiménez Hernández. His excavations continue to provide us with new answers to the innumerable enigmas that the Roman occupation of Iberia continues to pose. Obviously, we will also find traces of the readings of great historians such as Southern, Goldsworthy or Bearn. And I cannot forget numismatics, one of my personal passions, and one that often gives us historians of the ancient world so many surprises. Of course, the best part of the documentation and research period for this book has been the visits to museums and archaeological sites in Spain and Portugal. I hope, with all this, to have aroused your interest. The Roman conquest of Iberia has all the elements imaginable to be amazed by the rudeness and the desire for freedom of its inhabitants, with epic battles and hair-raising sieges.

Chapter 1

219 BC

A year before the arrival of the Romans on the Iberian Peninsula, this territory was occupied by numerous societies. None of them had established an administrative state that could be compared with the two Mediterranean powers of the time, Rome and Carthage, and the territory was divided into areas of influence of what we might call tribes which, in turn, were organised into clans. Most of these societies could be grouped into three large ethnic groups: the Iberians, the Celts and the Celtiberians. Their lowest common denominator is the scant knowledge that has come down to us about them. The problems we face in getting to know them are the following: firstly, the Roman sources are limited to detailing the wars of conquest over the pre-Roman societies, showing little interest in explaining who they were and how they lived, with the exception of Strabo; secondly, the pre-Roman sources, i.e. the writings of these societies, have still not been deciphered, which is one of the great challenges facing archaeologists today; and finally, the scarce archaeological remains, because, despite the enormous amount of work that remains to be done, the Iberian communities either adopted Roman urban planning models or were destroyed, which means that many questions remain to be answered.

The first name given to the territory occupied by these societies was Iberia, and it was bestowed on them by the Greeks, probably as an extension of the name that the Ebro River, which the Latins called Iberus, would receive. We will see how rivers play a leading role throughout this history, in a country so rich in mountain ranges. The Phoenicians called it Spania, which is usually translated as 'Land of Rabbits', although Javier de Hoz[1] points out that the term derives from the Phoenician *y-spny* ('Northern Coast'), a word that the Romans

1 Hoz (2010), p. 431.

derived in Hispania. A fundamental point for understanding pre-Roman societies is that despite being grouped into communities with common cultural ties (language, religion, socio-economic structures), there was neither a 'supra-tribal' consciousness of belonging to an Iberian or Celtic nation, for example, nor, much less, 'state' power structures. The distribution into tribes, and even into clans, was a system that Eckstein[2] labels for analysing the Mediterranean world prior to the Roman conquest of the known world, i.e., an 'anarchic multipolar system'. Thus, we can apply a correspondence between this system that Eckstein applies to Rome, Carthage and the Hellenic world; in Hispania it could be adjusted to the Iberians, Celts and Celtiberians, whose city-states would compete with each other and, later, against Carthage and Rome, through a system that, to borrow the American historian's words, 'possessed little or no international law, and was regulated only by complex and fluid balances of power (primarily, and very crudely, by military power)'.[3] It is precisely because of these balances of power that, for example, when the Carthaginians fought outside the peninsula, Iberian tribes were hired as mercenary troops, but these never grouped into confederations until Iberia was attacked by a superior power (which destabilised the balances of power) such as Carthage or Rome. As for the social structures of these societies, it seems that there was a strong class stratification. The dominant ones controlled most of the means of production, leaving most of the population to live in impoverished conditions. In more remote times, it seems that the several Iberian societies would have been dominated by a monarch who is believed to have been replaced by a warrior aristocracy between the 5th and 4th centuries BC, in what is known as the crisis of ancient Iberia. These strong social structures were stratified as follows: an aristocracy or warrior elite would oversee the government of small city-states, built around fortresses known as *oppida* (singular, *oppidum*). A second social group would be made up of the people, who would devote themselves to economic activities, changing in each area and, evidently, with a certain evolution over the centuries, from being eminently dedicated to agriculture, livestock, hunting and gathering to gradually moving on to the creation of craft workshops (textile and metallurgical industries) and trade. The feared Iberian warriors came out of this social class, but their service in arms was seasonal, normally from late spring and throughout the

2 Eckstein (2006).

3 Eckstein, op. cit., p. 4.

summer, although this could vary depending on the tribes, as some of them based part of their livelihood on raids against neighbouring tribes, so that their trade of arms would extend throughout the year. In other words, at first, the warfare of these pre-Roman societies would probably not go beyond small skirmishes, or in the event of a pitched battle, the warriors would hardly number more than a hundred. Later, however, with the increase in population, as we shall see in the 2nd and 1st centuries BC, they were able to muster hundreds of men. In the lowest stratum of society, we find the slaves. Another fundamental aspect for understanding pre-Roman societies is the existence of clientelism between the ruling elites and the people, which was based on two institutions: *fides* and *devotio*. The *fides* was an oath of loyalty from an individual to his or her leader; while in the *devotio*, the oath of loyalty was collective. It is believed that, especially in the case of *fides*, the oath must have been ritualised, although the details of what these rituals were like are unknown, as pre-Roman religions remain the great unknowns of these societies. It is important to bear in mind that by means of the *fides*, the Iberian warrior swore that he would fight alongside his leader until death. This meant that if the leader died in combat, his warriors could not survive him. Therefore, they would die either by fighting or by collective suicide, as we will have the opportunity to see on numerous occasions throughout this book. Power in pre-Roman societies was, moreover, largely reinforced by symbolic motifs: the monumentality of the *oppidum* or the presumably magical power of the leaders' weapons could be two examples of this. This idea is reinforced by the fact that these leaders were buried with luxurious trousseaus. Thus, among the everyday objects among which the leaders were buried, we find their weapons, especially their swords. This leads us to the conclusion that they must have had a clear mastery of metallurgy and an abundance of materials to make them, otherwise it would be difficult for their heirs to part with them. The sword as a symbol of power can also be contrasted with the fact that numerous tombs of aristocratic women have been found buried with this type of weapon or other types of military equipment, such as panoply.

Pre-Roman necropolises are one of the best sources of information from which archaeologists continue to obtain knowledge of these societies. Though many necropolises have been excavated, we are only going to highlight a few of them. Among the Iberians, those of Cabecico del Tesoro (Murcia), Cerrillo Blanco (Jaén, Andalusia) and Cabezo Lucero (Alicante, Valencia); among the Celtiberians, undoubtedly that of Castril de Griegos (Guadalajara, Castilla La Mancha); and among the Celts, those of Ulaca (Ávila, Castilla y León) and Monte Bernorio

(Palencia, Castilla y León). The burial system was the cremation of the bodies, but the bones were left behind, which has allowed researchers to conclude that life expectancy in these societies was extremely short, ranging from 30 to 35 years. It was higher among men, as there was a high percentage of women who died in childbirth. It is also estimated that infant mortality was very high and could be as high as 50 per cent. Only 10 per cent were over the age of 50. They tended to be members of the ruling class, whose diet and way of life enabled them to avoid the hardships faced by many of their fellow citizens.

In 219 BC, the Iberian Peninsula was inhabited by the following societies: the Iberians, the Celts, the Celtiberians, the Vascones, the Vettones, the Lusitanians and the Turdetans. Let us take a closer look at each of these societies.

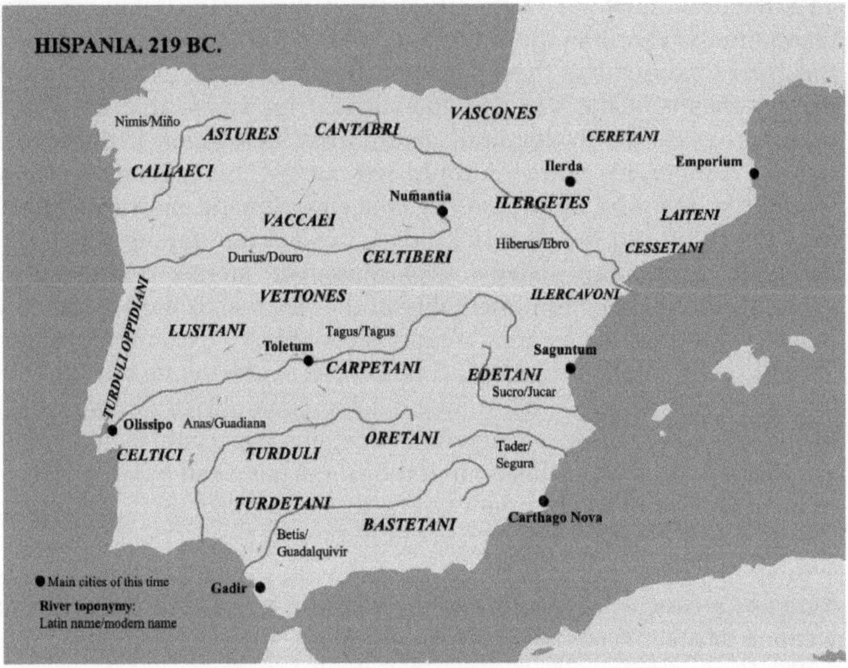

Map 1: Map of the main Pre-Roman societies. Without well-defined borders, they were divided into the following: the Iberians, who lived on the eastern coast; the Celts, who occupied from the north and west coast to the middle basins of the Tagus and Douro rivers; and the Celtiberians, who occupied approximately the centre of the peninsula. We must of course mention other smaller groups, such as the Vascones, the Vettones, the Lusitanians and the Turdetans. In addition, the region from the Guadalquivir River valley to the mouth of the Segura River was under the influence, or political-military control, of the Carthaginians.

As for the Iberians, their exact origin is unknown, although they are believed to be the descendants of the indigenous societies that had lived on the peninsula since the Iron Age. In 219 BC, they occupied practically half of the territory, specifically the Mediterranean strip from the Pyrenees to the coast of what is now Portugal. The most important tribes or tribal confederations from north to south were the Ceretani, who controlled the southern slopes of the Pyrenees; and the Ilergetes, who occupied the interior of what is now Catalonia, located between the rivers Segre, Cinca and Ebro, whose main city was Iltrida, which the Romans would come to call Ilerda, and the most prominent leader was the warlike Indibilis.[4] A little further south, but already on the coast, were the Cossetani, who would become a reliable ally of Rome; in fact, their main city, Kesse, would be the base for the first Roman expeditions, which christened it Tarraco and made it the capital of Hispania Citerior. To the south of the Cossetani and further inland were the Sedetani, in whose territory the Romans founded Caesaraugusta (modern Saragossa). This tribe maintained excellent relations with their southern neighbours, the Edetani, who were probably the first tribe to sign a treaty of friendship with Rome; in fact, one of their main cities was Arse, which the Romans called Saguntum, and whose conquest by the Carthaginians led to the arrival of the Romans on the peninsula. And in the present-day territory of Andalusia, there were two main Iberian tribes: the Bastetani, in the eastern part, and the Oretani, in the central part, who maintained a close relationship with Carthage. An interesting aspect of Iberian culture is the role of women. Once again, archaeology raises questions that the bibliographical sources fail to answer. It is curious, however, that many the tombs found are those of high-ranking women, buried with rich grave goods and even weapons. An example of this is the famous Lady of Baza, whose abundant and rich trousseau leads us to suspect that she was a queen or a high-ranking priestess. However, probably the most famous figure is the Lady of Elche, who is still debated as to whether she was a real woman or an idealisation of a goddess. In any case, the numerous female votive offerings found suggest that upper-class women would have had a social importance similar to that of men.

As for the Celts, unfortunately we are once again left with more questions than answers. It is believed that they arrived in the Iberian Peninsula around the 7th century BC, although it is not known whether

4 Polybius calls him Andobales, a name by which he is also known, and which has been taken by some later sources.

their arrival was peaceful or whether they settled in the territory by conquest. It is likely that it was a combination of both circumstances and that pre-Celtic societies coexisted with the newcomers. In any case, they were relegated to the western part of the territory, losing contact with the rest of the European Celtic tribes. One of their most important characteristics was the fact that they had no writing. In Iberia, the most important were the Gallaecians, which was not a uniform tribe, and located in the extreme north-west of the peninsula. It was a matriarchal society and is described by Silius Italicus in *Punica* (3, 344):

> *Cetera femineus peragit labor: addere sulco semina et impresso tellurem uertere aratro segne uiris. quicquid duro sine Marte gerundum, Callaici coniunx obit inrequieta mariti.*[5]

Among their tribes we can highlight the Albiones, the Bracaros, the Coelernos, the Luancos and the Tamagones. The Oestrimni also lived in this territory, and it is speculated that they must have been an indigenous tribe that lived alongside the Celts. It was a relatively egalitarian society, although it had a military elite. In contrast to the Iberians, there are traces of female warriors here. The military leaders had a priest-counsellor, like the druids, although they were not called druids. To the east were the Austurians, whose main tribes were the Pesicans, Omiacs and Luggoni. Their lands were poor for agriculture, so they focused mainly on livestock. Strabo was struck by the importance of women in this society, which could be described as matrilineal. The Greek geographer details some of their customs, such as couvade, which continued to be practised in the territory until the beginning of the 20th century. They were also excellent warriors. In fact, another of their economic activities was the plundering of the neighbouring territory of the Vaccaei, who enjoyed excellent arable land. The Asturians, as we shall see later on, were excellent horsemen and, subsequently, the Roman Empire took advantage of them. The Vaccaei, to the south of the Astures, had an agriculture based on wheat and barley that made them famous, establishing a rich trade with Celtiberians and Lusitanians. Although it was a society with a clear hierarchy, in which a military elite controlled and dominated society, the Vaccaei were noted for their collectivist system of wealth distribution, which attracted the attention of Diodorus Siculus (5, 34):

---

5 'All other effort is performed by women; the men consider it unmanly to sow seed in the furrow or turn the soil with a plough. But Galician wives, un-resting, perform every task but military service.' English translation by J. D. Duff (1961), p. 139.

Χαριέστατον δὲ τῶν πλησιοχώρων ἐθνῶν {αὐτοῖς} ἐστι τὸ τῶν Οὐακκαίων ὀνομαζομένων σύστημα· οὗτοι γὰρ καθ᾽ ἕκαστον ἔτος διαιρούμενοι τὴν χώραν γεωργοῦσι, καὶ τοὺς καρποὺς κοινοποιούμενοι μεταδιδόασιν ἑκάστῳ τὸ μέρος, καὶ τοῖς νοσφισαμένοις τι γεωργοῖς θάνατον τὸ πρόστιμον τεθείκασι.[6]

Continuing along the coast we come across the Cantabrians.[7] This group of Celtic people played a leading role in the last of Rome's wars of conquest. They were another eminently warlike tribe whose society was based around war. Classical sources, such as Silius Italicus (*Punica*, 3, 325-330) tell us that the elders practised senicide when they were no longer able to fight: 'These people, when disabled by old age, find a strange pleasure in cutting short the years of weakness by an instant death, and they refuse life except in arms. For war is their only reason for living, and they scorn a peaceful existence.'[8] Their main tribes were the Orgenomescos 'the drunkards of slaughter' or 'those who get drunk in the slaughter'[9] or the Concanos, and of whom it is said that the warrior in battle 'opens a vein of his horse to fill his own belly',[10] as we are told both by Silius Italicus (*Punica*, 2, 360) and Horace (*Carmina*, 3, 34).

In the geographical centre of Iberia, surrounded by the Lusitanians to the west, the Cantabrians to the north, the Celtiberians to the west and the Iberians to the south, were the Carpetans. Their language was similar to that of the Celtiberians, i.e., it was an evolution of archaic Celtic. In fact, ancient sources make practically no reference to them until the Battle of the Tagus (220 BC), as part of the Carthaginian conquest of the Iberian Peninsula. In this battle, the Carpetans presented themselves without a clear leader, which leads us to suppose that they were a highly decentralised society. The battle ended in a great Carthaginian victory under Hannibal, followed by the destruction of numerous rebel cities. This caused them to side with the Romans during the Second Punic War, although, as they appreciated their

6 'Of the tribes neighbouring upon the Celtiberians the most advanced is the people of the Vaccaei, as they are called; for this people each year divides among its members the land which it tills and making the fruits the property of all they measure out his portion to each man, and for any cultivators who have appropriated some part for themselves they have set the penalty as death.'

7 Peralta Labrador (2003) has published the most extensive work about the Cantabrians.

8 Duff, op. cit., pp. 137–9.

9 Peralta Labrador, p. 178.

10 Duff, op. cit., p. 141.

freedom, they later fought the Romans during the conquest. Having learned their lesson, this time they chose Hilernus as their leader, but, as we shall see, they were still defeated.

The Celtiberians were the third largest group among the pre-Roman societies of the Iberian Peninsula. The name of their main city, Numantia, made Rome pale in terror for several generations. Together with the Lusitani, they were probably the most warlike people that Rome had to face, at least during the conquest of Iberia. They were located in the Central Plateau. Their origin is not clear, but it is believed that they were societies of Iberian origin that adopted Celtic culture. This mixture can be seen that they spoke a language of Celtic origin, but with an Iberian alphabet. According to the archaeological remains found from the 5th century BC onwards they became an eminently warlike society, although an important part of their economy was still based on the primary sector, as they were settled on very fertile land. Their cereal crops, barley and olives stood out, while their livestock farming included pigs, goats and sheep. They also had an active textile and metallurgical manufacturing industry. As in the case of the Carpetans, the tribes always acted independently of each other, but in certain cases they could form coalitions or federations, but without a single leader to command them. However, there were various institutions of support and mutual aid, such as the *hospitilum* and the *devotio,* which, based on the extended family, like what was known in Rome as the *gens,* established extensive client networks. It is still debated to this day which tribes were part of the Celtiberians. Being on the border between the Iberians and the Celts, they did not all share the same traits and characteristics, some tending to emphasise their Celtic influence, while others have a more Iberian character. However, there is a certain consensus in considering the following tribes to be Celtiberian: the Arevaci, the Titi, the Belli, the Lusones and the Pellendones.

There are other pre-Roman societies that do not fit into the three main groups. These would be the Lusitanians, the Vettones, the Vascons and the Turduli. All of them were the protagonists of important revolts during the Roman conquest. Of these, the Lusitanians, led by the feared Viriathus, were the most important. We should also mention the Turduli, who are believed to be the descendants of the Tartessians. Although this important society had no direct contact with the Romans, it is worth mentioning, as it is considered to be one of the first civilisations in western Europe. It occupied what today would correspond to the western provinces of Andalusia between approximately 1200 and 500 BC. They had very advanced agricultural techniques and great mineral wealth, as well as extensive trade networks that reached as far south as the British Isles. However, their main trading partners were the Phocian Greeks, who established several colonies.

Thus, we have just to mention the last three protagonists of pre-Roman Hispania: the Greeks, the Phoenicians and the Carthaginians, the great powers of the Mediterranean world until the irruption of the overwhelming power of Rome. The arrival of the Greeks was peaceful. Specifically, it was the Greeks from the city of Phocaea in Asia Minor who founded Hemeroskopeion (Valencia) and Mainaké (Andalusia) at the end of the 7th century BC. Around the same time, Greeks from the island of Rhodes founded the enclave of Rhode in the north of present-day Catalonia. Later, this enclave was abandoned by the Rhodians, who were replaced by the Phocians who, a few miles to the north, founded a new colony: Empirion, which means market. In addition, all along the Mediterranean coast they founded small ports for loading and unloading, such as Molybdana, Hyops or Kallipolis. But the astute Greek merchants did not only trade on the coast. There is archaeological evidence that they crossed the Segura River (later called the Tader by the Romans), but also that they penetrated the territory of the Tartessians. However, within a few years of each other, two major defeats of the Phokaioi in other parts of the Mediterranean caused the end of the power of this small city-state in Iberia, particularly after the Battle of Alalia (537 BC) between the Carthaginians and the Phocians. Both societies were in the process of commercial expansion and war seemed inevitable. With its victory, Carthage took control of all trade in the western Mediterranean, leading to the disappearance of virtually all the Greek colonies in Iberia. Actually, it seems that many of the colonies were razed to the ground. The only one that continued with a thriving commercial activity was Emporion, perhaps because the Carthaginians were unable to cross the Ebro River line, or simply because they did not want to.

Several centuries earlier, at the opposite end of the Mediterranean, it is believed that around the 2nd millennium BC, a series of city-states, such as Byblos, Sidon, and Tyre, traditionally grouped under the name of Phoenicians, grew up, although, again, we are dealing with a multipolar system as these city-states acted independently and, despite sharing an identical culture, did not act as a single state. They were a thalassocracy whose wealth was based on a very active trade that led them to found numerous colonies throughout the Mediterranean. It was the Phoenicians from Tyre who founded the city of Gadir (which means 'fortress', modern Cadiz, Andalusia) where they developed a profitable trade with the native Iberians and

Tartessians, especially buying metals from them, such as gold, silver, lead, and copper. The date of the foundation is unknown and, although the date is traditionally accepted as 1110 BC, the truth is that the oldest archaeological remains date from the 8th century BC, which can be explained by the fact that between the two dates there was a pre-colonial stage and, subsequently, the settlement itself was founded. It is also believed that around 814 BC, they founded Carthage, whose Phoenician name was Qart-Ḥadašt (Phoenician for 'New City'). Initially, it was a mere supply port, but the city grew in strength to become a true imperial power. Again, in Iberia, during the 8th century BC the Phoenicians founded new cities on the southern coast and usually at the mouth of a river, allowing them, as a thalassocracy, to receive and send goods by sea and to trade inland via the rivers. Thus, we have the examples of the settlements of Malaka (modern Malaga, Andalusia), next to the mouth of the river Guadalmedina;[11] Las Chorreras (next to the previous one), next to the mouth of the river Algarrobo; a curious colony, by the way, surrounded by mysteries, as it was one of the largest Phoenician cities in the region, but disappeared after a short life, as it remained active between 750–700 BC, and where the famous grave of a Greek mercenary stands out;[12] the colony of Adra, next to the river of the same name; Seks (modern Almuñécar, Andalusia, where, by the way, the local gentilic still is 'sexitanos'), next to the river Verde; that of the Toscanos, next to the river Velez; and we can continue to its northernmost location, in the site known as La Fonteta, at the mouth of the river Segura (Alicante, Valencia). Just over thirty Phoenician sites have been located. Finally, it is believed that around 650 BC the Phoenicians occupied the island of Ibiza, which was an unavoidable stopover for Phoenician ships arriving from Sardinia, Corsica, or Sicily. Incidentally, to put this in context, it was during the period in which the merchants of Tyre founded all these commercial enclaves, at the opposite end of the peninsula, that the Celtic tribes began to penetrate. The golden age of these cities lasted from the 8th to the 6th centuries BC. At that time, a great crisis hit them. The reason for this was probably the conquest of the city of Tyre in 574 BC by Nebuchadnezzar II of Babylon. Without the support of the metropolis, many of these sites eventually disappeared, while others came under the control of Carthage. The Phoenician culture ended up profoundly

---

11 About Malaka: Suárez, Ramón, Mora, Salvago and Chacón (2020).

12 About Las Chorreras and the warrior's grave: Martín, Recio, Ramírez and Macías (2007).

influencing the Iberian culture, developing its economy, improving the productive systems and, especially, being definitive in the creation of the two types of Iberian alphabets that are known, and which would also influence the creation of the Greek and Latin alphabets. In short, Phoenician colonisation was much more important and intense than that of the Greeks.

But the Iberians did not live in isolation on their peninsula. As we have seen, their commercial networks covered a large part of the Mediterranean and even the Atlantic coast of the European continent. But it is easy to deduce that Phoenicians and Greeks, after decades of intense trade, not only on the coast but also towards the interior of the peninsula, would end up knowing well the hard and tough character of the pre-Roman inhabitants, especially that of the Iberians, with whom they established a more intense contact. Therefore, it is not surprising that, thanks to these trade relations, bonds of friendship were established that would eventually lead to the Iberians being hired as mercenaries by the Phoenicians and Greeks. As mentioned above, these local tribes were warrior societies. We can also deduce that warfare between tribes or even clans, in the beginning, would be strongly ritualised, with strict rules that would not allow the fight to lead to a generalised slaughter that would harm the community. These early battles may have been duels between warriors chosen between the two contenders, as we have found in other parts of the Mediterranean arc, or the war may have been limited to a certain number of casualties and, once this figure was reached, a ceasefire was declared. Here we draw on Social Anthropology to point to the cases of the Yanomami societies in the Amazon or the inhabitants of Papua New Guinea. Likewise, greater demographic density would end up making these primordial laws of war more flexible and, finally, repealing them. We must also assume, as happened at the time in the Italian peninsula, that the inland tribes, especially those living in mountainous areas, based a large part of their economy on the theft and plunder of the more prosperous communities living near the coast. For all these reasons, the Iberians earned a well-deserved reputation as warriors in antiquity, and we will see them fighting as mercenaries in the various conflicts that shook the central Mediterranean from the 5th century BC onwards. Hence, the first references are found in the context of the Sicilian Wars.[13] It is Herodotus (*History* 7, 165) who, when he recounts

13 The Sicilian Wars pitted Greeks against Carthaginians for control of Sicily. It was the longest war in antiquity, lasting 335 years (from 600 BC to 265 BC). In the end, the

the First Battle of Himera in 480 BC, lists the Iberians among the mercenary troops of the Greeks:

> Τήριλλος ὁ Κρινίππου τύραννος ἐὼν Ἱμέρης ἐπῆγε ὑπ' αὐτὸν τὸν χρόνον τοῦτον Φοινίκων καὶ Λιβύων καὶ Ἰβήρων καὶ Λιγύων καὶ Ἐλισύκων καὶ Σαρδονίων καὶ Κυρνίων. [14]

The nature of the Iberian mercenary army in Sicily raises several questions that neither the ancient sources nor the archaeological remains allow us to answer: was their presence on the island permanent from then on? Did they travel with their families, did the trade of arms pass from father to son? How did they adapt? The point is that we find them again in the context of the Peloponnesian Wars. In 415 BC, the Athenian general Alcibiades, nephew of Pericles, arrived in Sicily to help Segesta in its war against Selinus. There he met the Iberian mercenaries whom he did not hesitate to take to Athens to fight alongside the Athenian armies, as Thucydides tells us (*The Peloponnesian War*, Book 6, 90, 3), where they took part in the Coup of the Four Hundred in 411 BC:

> εἰ δὲ προχωρήσειε ταῦτα ἢ πάντα ἢ καὶ τὰ πλείω, ἤδη τῇ Πελοποννήσῳ ἐμέλλομεν ἐπιχειρήσειν, κομίσαντες ξύμπασαν μὲν τὴν ἐκεῖθεν προσγενομένην δύναμιν τῶν Ἑλλήνων, πολλοὺς δὲ βαρβάρους μισθωσάμενοι καὶ Ἴβηρας καὶ ἄλλους τῶν ἐκεῖ ὁμολογουμένως νῦν βαρβάρων μαχιμωτάτους.[15]

In the Second Sicilian War (410–340 BC), according to Diodorus Siculus, the Iberians were once again called upon to fight, but this time they were hired by the Carthaginian general Himilco. Although it could well be said that the Iberians were their natural allies, since in the 4th century BC Carthage's influence on the Iberian Peninsula was intense. The military campaign from 409 BC to 405 BC was a complete

---

Carthaginians prevailed, expelling the Greeks from Sicily, and remaining on the island until the end of the First Punic War.

14 'Terillus son of Crinippus, the tyrant of Himera. This man, who had been expelled from Himera by Theron's son of Aenesidemus, sovereign ruler of Acragas, at this very time brought against Gelon three hundred thousand Phoenicians, Libyans, Iberians, Ligyes, Elisyci, Sardinians, and Cyrnians.' English translation by A. D. Godley. Cambridge. Harvard University Press (1920).

15 'In the event of all or most of these schemes succeeding, we were then to attack Peloponnese, bringing with us the entire force of the Hellenes lately acquired in those parts, and taking a number of barbarians into our pay, such as the Iberians and others in those countries, confessedly the most warlike known.'

success for Himilco and his army, winning the Battle of Selinus, the Siege of Akragas, the Battle of Gela and the Battle of Camarina, which ended with the surrender of Dionysius I of Syracuse, who accepted Himilco's appointment as king of Sicily in exchange for his recognition as lord of Syracuse. However, the peace was to last only a few years. In 395 BC, Dionysius rebelled and declared war on Himilco, who besieged Syracuse in 396 BC. But on this occasion, the Carthaginian troops were decimated by fevers, so Dionysius took advantage of the situation to attack and defeat the besiegers. The Carthaginian general Himilco negotiated a way out for himself and his compatriots, leaving his allied Sicels, the island's native inhabitants, and his mercenaries behind. Many of them were captured and executed, but the Iberians fared better. Diodorus Siculus tells us about it (14, 75):

> Οἱ μὲν ἐν ταῖς ὁδοῖς {καὶ} ταῖς προφυλακαῖς ἐμπίπτοντες συνελαμβάνοντο, οἱ δὲ πλεῖστοι τὰ ὅπλα ῥιπτοῦντες συνήντων, δεόμενοι φείσασθαι τοῦ βίου· μόνοι δὲ Ἴβηρες ἠθροισμένοι μετὰ τῶν ὅπλων ἐπεκηρυκεύοντο περὶ συμμαχίας. Διονύσιος δὲ πρὸς μὲν τούτους σπεισάμενος κατέταξε τοὺς Ἴβηρας εἰς τοὺς μισθοφόρους, τὸ δὲ λοιπὸν πλῆθος ἐζώγρησε καὶ τὴν {λοιπὴν} ἀποσκευὴν ἐφῆκε τοῖς στρατιώταις διαρπάσαι.[16]

But the war did not end there. Himilco returned to Carthage and admitted he was responsible for the defeat. He locked himself in his house, boarded up the doors and windows and let himself starve to death. The new Carthaginian general in Sicily was Mago, who took with him a new contingent of Iberian mercenaries. But there was no final battle. At Cabala (ca. 377 BC), the Carthaginians won; but at Cronium (376 BC), the Greeks were the victors. Eventually, the Carthaginians would gain control of Western Sicily. But the Sicilian Wars did not end until 307 BC, when the Carthaginians gained full control of the island. The Carthaginians were eventually triumphant, but the island came to the attention of a new Mediterranean power: Rome.

In the 1st century BC, Marcus Terentius Varro established that the city of Rome was founded in 753 BC, and the Roman calendar was henceforth fixed as *Ab urbe condita*. Over the course of those centuries, the metropolis had grown from a tiny village growing up under the

16 'Some were taken captive as they fell in with the guards on the roads, but the majority threw down their arms, surrendered themselves, and asked only that their lives be spared. Some Iberians alone massed together with their arms and dispatched a herald to treat about taking service with him. Dionysius made peace with the Iberians and enrolled them in his mercenaries.'

river Tiber (again, a river at the establishment of a city) in the middle of the Latium region to become by 264 BC one of the great powers of the Mediterranean. Along the way, Rome had been a monarchy, which had become a republic, had absorbed the peoples of the Italic Peninsula and, with a fearsome army and a powerful naval fleet, could now match the great power of the western Mediterranean: Carthage. It was only a matter of time before war broke out between the two cities, which shared a warlike and expansionist spirit. And the perfect excuse, or *casus belli*, as you prefer, came in 265 BC, in the city of Messana (now Messina). That city had been occupied by Mamertine mercenaries and they were being pressured by Hiero II of Syracuse to abandon the city. The Mamertines sought the protection of Carthage and Rome. At that time, the island was occupied by the Carthaginians, although the eastern part of the island was dominated by the city of Syracuse. The relationship between the two was peaceful and cooperative. Nevertheless, the Punics sided with Hiero II. Moreover, among the many treaties of friendship that had been signed between Rome and Carthage, one of them stated that 'the Romans were obliged to keep away from the whole of Sicily, and the Carthaginians from the whole of Italy' (Pol., *Hist.*, 3, 26). But would the virtuous Romans be capable of breaking a diplomatic pact? Let us have no such illusions. We shall see that they did. And it was neither the first nor the last time. It is true that, up to that point, Rome had never really looked at the island south of its peninsula. But most of the city's rulers felt strong enough to prevail over Carthage and finally demonstrate Roman supremacy in the western Mediterranean. In 264 BC, the consul Appius Claudius Caudex landed near Messina, which he occupied, starting the First Punic War, which, lasting 23 years, was the longest of the three conflicts between Rome and Carthage, being especially a naval war. Although there were also numerous land campaigns, in which the Carthaginians used a huge number of mercenary troops, including Iberians, it is believed that a large part of their infantry was made up of troops from Hispania and the Balearic Islands. As Polybius indicates (*Hist.*, 1, 18): 'Accordingly, they enlisted mercenaries from over sea – a large number of Ligurians and Celts, and a still larger number of Iberians – and dispatched them to Sicily' or 'There were in the army Iberians and Celts, men from Liguria and the Balearic Islands, and a considerable number of half-bred Greeks, mostly deserters and slaves; while the main body consisted of Libyans' (*Hist.*, 1, 76). From this point on, Polybius no longer differentiates between them by their region of origin and limits himself to citing them as 'Carthaginian mercenaries'. It is not the purpose of this book to detail the events and battles that made up the First Punic War, other than the actions of the Iberian and Balearic mercenaries who took part in it, forming part of the infantry units and fighting both on the island of Sicily and in North Africa. Suffice it to say that it was a very hard war, a war of attrition. The historian Laura Valiani[17] has calculated the cost in human lives of the war on the Punic side that in the sea alone (between naval battles and storms), the Carthaginians must have lost approximately 200,000 men, of whom she calculates that 10 per cent were Punic and the rest mercenaries. Bearing in mind that the population of Carthage at that time was around 200,000, the losses were very heavy. And that is not counting the land battles that took place during the 23 years of war. Thus, a Carthage exhausted by the tremendous effort it had to face, had no choice but to surrender and sue for peace. In 241 BC the Treaty of Lutatius[18] was signed, which, among other clauses, established that Sicily and the northern islands as far as Africa would remain free of Carthaginian control (*ergo*, under Roman control) and that the defeated Carthaginians would have to pay an indemnity of 3,200 Euboean talents of silver to Rome, of which 1,000 would be payable immediately.[19] This was a fabulous amount of precious metal, of which there was little left in the exhausted coffers of Carthage, emptied after such a long war. Finally, the city was able to meet the first and urgent payment, but in return they was left without funds with which to pay the large army of mercenaries they had hired for the battle. When the Carthaginian Suffetes explained to the mercenaries' representatives that they had no money with which to pay for their services, they rose up in arms, laying siege to Carthage and initiating what is known as the Mercenary War, or the Truceless War, which lasted from 241 BC to 237 BC. The sources do not detail the presence of Iberians among the rebels, but by all logic, they must have been part of it, given that, as we have seen, they formed part of the Carthaginian army. Although it is true that no warrior from Hispania is known to have been among the leaders of this revolt, who were the Celts of Gaul, Spendius and Autaritus, we should also note the support of the Libyans who were living in subjugation under the power of Carthage, and who were led by Mathos. It was a cruel and bloody war that ended with the extermination of practically

17 Valiani (2016).

18 Named after Gaius Lutatius Catulus. Together with Aulus Postumius Albinus he was the consul of the republic in 242 BC and had led the Roman fleet in the decisive Battle of the Aegates (241 BC).

19 If we follow the calculations of Kroll (2008), p. 43, the total figure would be around 74 long tons.

all the mercenaries. But Carthage's troubles were far from over. A secondary chapter of the Mercenary Wars took place on the island of Sardinia, where local mercenaries had also taken up arms against Carthage, which had managed to maintain control of this island and Corsica. Thus, as the Carthaginians were forced to send a small army to Sardinia, the Romans accused them of preparing an invasion of the Italic Peninsula, forcing an 'amendment' in the Treaty of Lutatius in 237 BC whereby they lost control of Corsica and Sardinia, which became occupied by Rome, and added an additional 1,200 Euboean talents as war reparations. The situation for Carthage was catastrophic. Not only was Carthage without two sources of revenue, but the debt it had to pay was increasing. Faced with this desperate situation, Hamilcar Barca convinced the Carthaginian Senate of the need to conquer new territories. And his victim could be none other than Iberia. The Punics were aware of the riches offered by the Iberian Peninsula, and, at the same time, they had seen how in recent decades the colonies that they had 'inherited' from the Phoenicians had been losing importance. The time had come to occupy the territory militarily and subjugate it to the imperious (and imperial) needs of Carthage.

But before we start detailing the Punic campaign over Iberia, it is worthwhile to look at who Hamilcar Barca was, the founder of the legendary dynasty that made Rome tremble and of whom Polybius stated that 'we must credit the Carthaginians with the best general of the day both for genius and daring. I mean Hamilcar Barca' (*Hist.*, 1, 64). Polybius' opinion influenced later classical authors, although it is really an exaggeration to claim that Hamilcar was a general on a par with his son Hannibal. In a detailed analysis of his military career, the historian Gómez de Caso,[20] concludes that Hamilcar's campaigns during the First Punic War were, in most cases, a real disaster, as for example the Battle of Mount Erice (249 BC); in his campaigns against the Libyans, he managed to prevail due to his overwhelming superiority in men and material means. It was not until the Battle of the Bagradas River (255 BC), during the Mercenary Wars, that Hamilcar proved himself to be an excellent general.

The Carthaginian Senate was divided into two factions, led by two political rivals. On the one hand, we have Hanno II, whose private interests inclined him to extend the conquests in North Africa; on the other, Hamilcar Barca, who advocated a conquest of the Iberian Peninsula. Its occupation would have some advantages. For instance,

20 Gómez de Caso (2001).

many of the cities in the south of the peninsula had been founded by the Phoenicians or even by the Carthaginians themselves, which allowed them to establish a series of bases and allies in a territory that could be hostile. Thus, in 237 BC, Hamilcar landed at Gadir and began a series of military operations against the Turdetans, who were supported by Celtiberian mercenaries, whose leaders included Istaletius and Indortes. After defeating them, the Carthaginians consolidated their position in the rich territories located between the valleys of the Guadiana and Guadalquivir rivers. A Numidian revolt forced Hamilcar's son-in-law, Hasdrubal (known as Hasdrubal the Fair), to move to North Africa with part of his troops. The young Carthaginian general put down the revolt and immediately returned with his father-in-law, with whom he continued to conquer new territories. In this new phrase, the Carthaginians moved eastwards in an attempt to gain the eastern coastal areas of Iberia. Near the present-day city of Alicante, Hamilcar founded Akra Leuke, which gave him a base close to the rich silver and iron mines of Castulo, the capital of the Oretans. Around 229 BC, Hamilcar was taken by surprise by death. Its circumstances are unclear, but according to Diodorus (25, 10, 3-4), he died during the siege of the city of Helike. It seems that Hamilcar's local allies included a small Oretan army under the command of Orison, but they surprisingly switched sides and attacked the besiegers. In the fighting, Hamilcar was killed. For the next eight years, the leader of the Carthaginians in Iberia was Hasdrubal. His first decision was expeditious: to eliminate Orison and all Oretani who dared to dispute Carthage's power. In a swift campaign, he subdued the twelve resistant cities. He then embarked on a policy of alliances and diplomacy that brought him a host of local allies. Apparently, it all started after he married the princess of an ancient Tartessian city, Mastia. His wife's name is believed to have been Titayu (we do not know the fate of Hasdrubal's first wife, who was Hamilcar's daughter and therefore Hannibal's sister; we do not know whether she died prematurely, or for political reasons, he had divorced her; in any case, it does not seem that the Carthaginians contemplated bigamy). As a result, Hasdrubal's intelligent policy allowed him to consolidate and even peacefully increase the territories controlled by Carthage. Although it is true that he did not renounce military campaigns when necessary. He also founded what was to be his new capital: Qart-Ḥadašt (as the Romans would literally translate it, Carthago Nova or, in other words, New Carthage). Located in modern Cartagena (Murcia), the new city had many advantages: it was closer to Carthage than Gadir and it had a magnificent port, easily defensible. Such was Hasdrubal's power that he behaved practically as a king independent of his metropolis, but, although classical authors would have it that way, he never actually created a kingdom of his own. What seems undeniable is that he acted with great autonomy, as in 226 BC, when he signed a treaty with the Romans without the permission of the Senate of Carthage. This was the famous Treaty of the Ebro. Incidentally, one of the consuls that year was Lucius Apustius Fullo, who, coincidentally, was a client of the Cornelia family, a detail of essential importance, as we shall see. What was Rome's attitude from Hamilcar's landing at Gadir (237 BC) to the foundation of Qart-Ḥadašt (227 BC)? Apparently, the Romans regarded the Punic advances in Iberia with a certain indifference. After all, they had more pressing problems on their nearest frontiers: to the north, in Cisalpine Gaul, from 234 BC a new land distribution promoted by Rome at Licenum caused unrest among the Celts north of the river Po, which resulted in the Celtic tribes uniting in a coalition that led to a war in 225 BC, in which the Gauls defeated a Roman army at the Battle of Faesulae, but were beaten a few months later at the Battle of Telamon. On the other hand, the Romans were also concerned about their positions in the Adriatic Sea, as the Illyro-Roman Wars (First Illyrian War, 228–229 BC; Second Illyrian War, 220–219 BC) took place at this time. But the expansionist policies of the Barquids must have worried the Roman Senate at some point, as they sent representatives to Qart-Ḥadašt with whom they negotiated a treaty that would divide the areas of influence in Iberia. It is important to note that traditionally, it has been believed that the line demarcating the separation of the two areas of influence would be the line marked by the river Ebro, but this location raises many doubts. And this is an important point since, as we shall see, we are facing the future *casus belli* of the Second Punic War and the subsequent Roman invasion of Iberia. To begin with, there are 270 miles between Qart-Ḥadašt and the mouth of the Ebro. And the Romans were not generous enough (especially not to the Punics) to grant them such a vast territory for nothing in return. A more logical location would be to delimit the frontier at the mouth of the river Segura (or Tader, as the Romans called it), which was 40 miles from the capital of Hasdrubal. Moreover, Saguntum was 170 miles north of Qart-Ḥadašt. That is, above the Segura but below the Ebro. In fact, Titus Livy himself indicates, transcribing an alleged speech by Hannibal, that to attack Saungutm he had to cross the river Ebro (21, 44, 6), so the most likely rivers would be the Segura or the Júcar. Hannibal's subsequent attack on Saguntum was not immediately responded to by Rome. If the line of the river Ebro was the one that marked the areas of action of the two powers, the Romans had no excuse to act, since, as T. A. Dorey[21] showed, there is no previous treaty of friendship between Rome and Saguntum that obliged the former to act in favour of the Edetan city. But let us not get ahead of ourselves any further than necessary, for an event of momentous importance took place in 221 BC: the assassination of Hasdrubal. Apparently, the Carthaginian leader had asked for the submission of the Olcades tribe, probably located in the upper river Segura basin. His refusal probably provoked a military campaign and the subsequent execution of their king, Tagus. Silius Italicus (*Pun.*, 1, 165-180) tells us how one of his servants, subject to *devotio,* stabbed Hasdrubal in the chest and subsequently endured torture and crucifixion with a smile on his face, happy to have been able to avenge his lord. The death of the Punic general had as a direct consequence the coming to power, by acclamation of the army, of Hamilcar's eldest son: Hannibal Barca. He was only 26 years old, but he had already earned the respect of his soldiers, who saw in him a brave and expeditious general who had also sworn eternal hatred for Rome. And Hannibal's first decision was ruthless: to annihilate the Olcades. Once he had succeeded, he continued his military campaign against the Vaccaei, attacking their capital, Helmantica, in the Douro valley. In doing so, he wanted to gain access to the fertile lands of what are today the northern regions of modern Extremadura and western Castile. Incidentally, it should be noted that he did not abandon the diplomatic actions that had been so successful for his brother-in-law, and in imitation of the latter, he married another Iberian princess, Himilce, daughter of the king of the Oretani, thus sealing an alliance that would be beneficial for both parties. She was also the mother of his only son, Aspar, but we know little more about him, not even if he reached adulthood. What is certain is that Himilce died in Qart-Ḥadašt during a plague epidemic, shortly after Hannibal left for Italy. Finally, in 219 BC, Hannibal ordered the siege of Saguntum, whose Iberian name was Arse. The world was about to change.

21 Dorey (1959).

Chapter 2

THE SECOND PUNIC WAR

Why did Hannibal attack Arse/Saguntum? Ancient sources speculate that there may have been two factions among the city's elites, one pro-Carthaginian and the other pro-Roman, with the latter gaining the upper hand. Moreover, it is also cited that the Edetani were gaining great power by attacking their neighbours, probably the Contentani, situated roughly between Qart-Hadašt and Arse/Saguntum, or the Turdoleti, their western neighbours, both allies of Carthage. So, Hannibal had no choice but to put an end to the threat. At the time, it is not really known what the status of Arse/Saguntum was towards Rome. While classical sources claim that the city was an ally of Rome, Dorey showed that there is no evidence that this was the case. In fact, Livy (21, 6) does mention the existence of a treaty, but if it is the Treaty of the Ebro, it would reinforce the idea that the agreed border was not marked by the river as commonly believed, and if it was a pact between Rome and Arse/Saguntum, it was signed during the first weeks of the Punic siege, which must have begun in the spring of 219 BC. The Edetani diplomatic mission to Rome must have been that the Iberians would offer a *deditium*, whereby they would submit in exchange for protection. But the longed-for help did not come. In recent years, the Roman Senate had been dominated by the Fabian faction, whose personal interests were far removed from overseas adventures and who preferred to consolidate power in territories closer to home, such as Cisalpine Gaul or Illyria. In contrast, the Cornelians and Emilians, with a mass of clients in the Mediterranean islands (Corsica, Sardinia, and Sicily), feared that Carthage's power in Iberia would be used as a springboard to declare a new war and put in check all the power that Rome had gained during the First Punic War.

While the Roman Senate debated how to respond to the Edetani embassy, Hannibal wasted no time in attacking the city. In the first attempt, he tried to storm the city, on three different fronts. But the assault was thwarted by the fierceness with which the Edetani defended their walls, and, in addition, they attacked the Carthaginian left flank with a brave sortie that disorganised the assault. At that moment, a shower of javelins and darts were hurled from the defensive towers. One of the darts (Livy, 21, 7, 10) struck Hannibal's own thigh. Bewilderment and fear fell like a slab among his troops. The Carthaginian general had no choice but to order a retreat. Other authors claim that the wound must have been to the face, which is why Hannibal is often depicted as one-eyed in later engravings. But his troops maintained their camps near Saguntum. When he had recovered (given the extent of the wound, Hannibal would probably be lame for life), siege work resumed, building more and better siege machines and preparing for a fight that would be much slower and more costly than expected.

The Romans, on the other hand, sent a diplomatic delegation to Qart-Ḥadašt months later, led by a former *praetor*, Quintus Baebius Tamphilus, and a former consul, Publius Valerius Flaccus, to demand that Hannibal lift the siege of Saguntum, but the Carthaginian general ignored them. His victory did not seem far off, and, before a final assault, he offered the Saguntines surrender: they were to leave the city with only two pieces of clothing per person and unarmed. For an Iberian man, such a proposal was impossible to accept. For them, carrying arms was part of their identity as a man. Not to bear arms was to take away their manhood, their honour. Not to mention that they would be totally exposed to attack by other tribes as soon as they crossed the border of their territories. In some societies today, something similar is happening. Even in societies that seemingly have nothing to do with each other, such as, for example, among the men of Yemen, where every man must carry his own dagger, or even in the United States, with the staunch defenders of a conservative view of the Second Amendment to the Constitution. As the legendary actor Charlton Heston said: 'I'll give you my gun when you pry it from my cold, dead hands'. Therefore, the Saguntines could do nothing but refuse and fight to the bitter end. Thus, when they saw that all was lost, that the Romans were not going to send them the requested help and that the Carthaginians were going to make the final assault, they built a great pyre in the centre of the city into which they threw all their valuables, mixing the gold and silver with worthless metals, so that the Carthaginians could not take advantage of them. For their part, Hannibal's troops managed to demolish some of the defensive towers and open breaches in some of the walls. The fighting was fierce, and both sides suffered heavy casualties. But the superiority of the assailants finally prevailed, and they managed to penetrate into the city. While some Saguntines, in desperation, threw themselves onto the great pyre, others committed suicide and many others continued to fight in the streets of the city against the invaders, who mercilessly massacred all the Edetani they came across. Finally, a small group of Saguntines survived. A minority almost unbelievably managed to flee, but almost all the survivors were sold as slaves to neighbouring tribes. Saguntum had fallen.

The fall of Saguntum gave sufficient grounds to the senatorial faction of the Cornelians and Emilians to force the Senate to send a diplomatic delegation to Carthage to demand reparations for the capture of the city. It should come as no surprise that the consuls of that year were Tiberius Sempronius Longus and Publius Cornelius Scipio, both of whom were in favour of starting a new war against the Punics. The Romans could hardly have found any higher ambassadors: headed by the former *praetor* Quintus Baebius Tamphilus, who had already been one of the ambassadors to Hannibal at Saguntum, and the former consuls Gaius Licinius Varus, Marcus Livius Salinator, Lucius Aemilius Paulus and Quintus Fabius Maximus Verrucosus Cunctator. That is, the two outgoing consuls of 217 BC (Livius Salinator and Aemilius Paulus) and probably one of the most influential men in Rome of his generation, Fabius Maximus, several times consul and several times *dictator*. Before the Carthaginian Senate a truly undiplomatic discussion began in which the Roman emissaries demanded that Hannibal be handed over to them if he had acted without their approval, since the conquest of Saguntum violated the Treaty of the Ebro, but the Punics replied that Hasdrubal had signed that treaty precisely without their permission, so they did not recognise it and, therefore, did not consider that Saguntum had violated any treaty binding on them.[1] Although, again according to Livy (21), Fabius Maximus, wrapped in his pompous patrician toga, raised one hand and then the other: 'Here we offer you peace and here we offer you war, Carthaginians, which do you want?' To which one of the Punic Suffetes defiantly replied that the Roman should be the one to choose, so Fabius concluded: 'Then you shall have the war'. To which the Carthaginian senators shouted back: 'War, war, war!'. As we can see, subtlety was not a defining quality of diplomacy at the time.

On the return to Rome of the diplomatic delegation, the Senate gave the consuls of 219 BC consular armies and entrusted them with the protection, or conquest, of two regions: Tiberius Sempronius Longus

---

1 We will see that this argument will often be used by the Roman Senate in the future during the conquest of Hispania.

was given the island of Sicily, important because of its proximity to Africa, which would prevent a Carthaginian landing on the island and its subsequent passage to the Italic Peninsula, and could be used as a platform for a future attack on Carthage itself; while the other consul, Publius Cornelius Scipio, was given the province of Hispania.[2] The consul embarked with his army at Pisa and travelled to Massalia,[3] trying to prevent Hannibal from crossing the river Rhône. But the Carthaginian general had already beaten him to it. The Punic, who had learned warfare on land from his father, carried out a bold plan: to conquer Rome by taking his army on a journey from Iberia to the heart of Rome. He hastily assembled a large army at Qart-Ḥadašt. By taking advantage of the *devotio* of his Iberian allies or by forcing the chiefs of other tribes to hold hostages in the most important cities under their control, he managed to raise an army that was supposed to be close to 100,000 men in addition to his own Carthaginian troops and his Numidian and Libyan allies. Not all of them would make the journey to Rome. He left two armies in Iberia under his brothers Hasdrubal and Mago Barca, and with about 60,000 men, a large contingent of cavalry and his famous 37 elephants, he crossed the Pyrenees. Some of his Iberians deserted at the gates of the mountain range, as they refused to advance into Italy. In any case, Hannibal had enough skill to attract new Gallic allies to his cause, not only gaining new troops, but also being able to cross the Rhône with a speed that surprised Cornelius Scipio himself, who on reaching Massalia discovered that Hannibal and his army had already crossed it and were heading with great speed towards the Alps. Yet, he had no choice but to turn back and return to Italy. However, he did not want to neglect his province (mission), so he sent his brother Gnaeus Cornelius Scipio Calvus, as legate, to Emporion to occupy north-eastern Iberia and thus cut off any logistical support Hannibal might expect. Publius' decision could not have been more correct. Gnaeus, his elder brother, was no newcomer to the military field, having been consul in 222 BC, the year in which he had fought the Insubres of Cisalpine Gaul and conquered the city of Mediolanum (modern Milan).

2 It should be clarified that, from an administrative point of view, Hispania was not a Roman province. At that time, the term 'province' designated the mission that a consul had to carry out under his mandate, and which was not necessarily linked to a territory, since the creation and maintenance of a fleet or ensuring the supply of grain from a foreign territory could also be 'consular provinces'.

3 Modern Marseille was an ancient Greek colony and, for decades, a loyal ally of Rome.

The exact day is unknown, but it must have been in late summer. What is certain is that in 218 BC, for the first time a Roman army disembarked in Iberia.[4] Gnaeus Cornelius Scipio, accompanied by 20,000 men, comprising two legions, two *alae* and 2,200 cavalrymen, and 60 quinqueremes, landed at Emporion. From there, he headed south, which was relatively quiet. The settled tribes tended to be pro-Roman, although those inland tended to favour the Carthaginians, so the Romans would have some minor skirmishes against the Ilergetes, Ilercavones and Ausetani. However, the clear Roman superiority crushed any Iberian attempt to sweep through. For his part, Hannibal had left in the territory an officer named Hanno[5] in command of some 10,000 men, along with a few hundred Ilegertian allies. The Punic commander waited for the Romans near a city known as Kesse (or Cissa). It was at the end of September that Gnaeus arrived with his troops in its vicinity. Cornelius quickly deployed his troops according to the classic Roman positioning: in the centre, the two legions; flanked by the two *alae* units; at the ends the Roman cavalry and some allied Iberian units; and finally, in reserve, Iberian infantry units and crew members of the Roman fleet. The fighting should not be difficult, Gnaeus' troops were twice as large as Hanno's, who set up his troops in a narrow but long line, in which he placed the Ilergetes, under the command of Indibilis, on the right flank. The legionary troops began to march against the Punics, who remained static. After hurling their spears, they turned to hand-to-hand fighting. Hanno's infantry soon collapsed and began to disband. Only the Ilergetes held firm, against whom Gnaeus threw the reserve of his Iberian infantry. It was an excellent situation to see how his allies, whom he hardly knew, would fare in combat. As the Carthaginians fled, the Ilergetes were surrounded by Romans and Iberians. Gnaeus gave them two options: surrender or die fighting. They chose to capitulate. The legions then reached the Punic camp, where they managed to capture most of the survivors of the battle and, more importantly, the baggage that was ready to leave for Cisalpine Gaul for Hannibal. With over 6,000 dead, plus some 2,000 prisoners, including Indibilis and Hanno himself, the Carthaginian army disappeared north of the river Ebro. It was never to be regained. Shortly afterwards, the Romans entered the city of Kesse, which welcomed them with open arms. Gnaeus would turn it

---

4 It is true that we must suppose that the first Roman to arrive in Hispania must have been some anonymous trader at an undetermined date in the past, but for its conquest, the first was the eldest of the Scipio brothers.

5 Smith (1867), p. 344.

into Tarraco (modern Tarragona, Catalonia), and it would become one of the main cities of Roman Hispania. Meanwhile, Hasdrubal arrived with his army of some 12,000 men in the vicinity of Kesse. The battle was already lost, but he won a pyrrhic victory by sinking part of the Roman fleet before retreating south of the Ebro.

In 217 BC, Hasdrubal set out to drive the Romans out of Iberia, so he received a large number of reinforcements from the metropolis, especially quinqueremes. With them, he advanced along the Mediterranean coast, very close to his land army. Gnaeus set out to meet them with part of his navy (half of his ships had sailed to Rome for reinforcements) and with the help of some twenty quinqueremes sent by the Massalian allies. The naval battle took place at the mouth of the river Ebro, where the Punic navy, commanded by Himilco, was stationed. The Roman fleet waited at the mouth of the river for Himilco's ships to sail out to sea, which were attacked by surprise. One after the other, as they reached the sea, the Punic quinqueremes were sunk. Hasdrubal's debacle was complete, and he had no choice but to retreat. It seemed the moment to strike the final blow against the Carthaginians, so Gnaeus organised an expedition to hunt down Hasdrubal's troops. He was very annoyed with the Turdetani for their lack of fighting spirit and dismissed them, causing them to revolt in his territory. The Romans headed south along the coastal road, closely supported by their fleet. The pursuit of the Cornelius ended at Saltus Castulonensis (modern Despeñaperros, northern Andalucia), just as Hasdrubal was entering Lusitania. The Ilergetes had rebelled again and the Roman positions north of the river Ebro were in danger. Gnaeus was forced to return to the battlefield to face the stubborn troops of the Iberian leader Indibilis, whom he had liberated shortly after the Battle of Kesse.

In 218 BC, we had left Hannibal at the gates of the Alps. It took him three months to cross it, in hellish (well, more like Arctic) weather conditions, in which he lost a third of his men and almost all his cavalry and his intimidating elephants. But to the terror and astonishment of the Romans, he succeeded. The Punic general's first mission was to find food and shelter for his exhausted men. The first tribe contacted were the Taurini, who refused to help, and in response Hannibal massacred them, sending a message as clear as it was strong to the other Celtic tribes of Cisalpine Gaul. Publius Cornelius Scipio was in the region, trying to recruit troops among the Celts. He would soon have the opportunity to face Hannibal at the Battle of Ticinus at the end of November of that year, which ended in a Roman debacle in which Publius himself was wounded and almost captured. His life was saved that day by his eldest son, a teenager barely 16 years old, named after him Publius

Cornelius Scipio. This young patrician showed promise. He seemed to have the makings of a warrior. With the consul convalescing from his wounds and his army decimated, the Senate ordered the other consul, Tiberius Sempronius Longus, to return from Sicily to face Hannibal. It was not long before he had his chance, between 18 and 22 December, at the Battle of the Trebia, where the Carthaginians defeated their opponents, achieving a great victory that not only caused terror among the Romans, but also great admiration among the Celts of Cisalpine Gaul, who began to see in the Carthaginian general the man who could free them from the Roman yoke. Soon, thousands of Gaulish Celts joined the ranks of the Carthaginian army. Meanwhile, new consular elections were held in Rome. Gnaeus Servilius Geminus and Gaius Flaminius were elected, taking office on the Ides of March 217 BC. The latter received Cisalpine Gaul as his province. Flaminius faced his second consulship as one of the most prestigious Roman politicians. New legions were recruited, and the consul hurried north to confront Hannibal. Spotting the invading army, Flaminius ordered him to be intercepted in the vicinity of Lake Trasimeno (about 110 miles north of Rome), but a thick fog helped the Romans to fall into the trap set by Hannibal. Attacked on three different flanks and with the lake at their backs, it was one of the worst days of the Roman army, which lost 21,000 men on the battlefield: some 6,000 prisoners and 15,000 dead. Among those who died fighting was the consul Gaius Flaminius himself, whose body was never found, perhaps being drowned in the lake, like many of his men, although both Polybius and Livy recount his death by the sword on the battlefield.

The terrible defeat unleashed terror in Rome. The Senate appointed Quintus Fabius Maximus Verrucosos as *dictator* who, aware of the Roman inferiority to Hannibal, practised a war of attrition in which he pursued the Carthaginians or allowed himself to be pursued, but without engaging in any decisive battle. This tactic proved to be effective, as it slowly wore down the Punic army which, as it travelled along the Italic Peninsula, was unable to receive reinforcements from either Carthage or Iberia. But what would later become known as the Fabian Strategy, so far removed from the *virtus* of the Roman soldier, was not understood by many of his fellow citizens. His enemies grew daily, accusing him of being a coward and even a traitor. His attitude earned him the nickname of *Cunctator* ('the delayer'). In fact, even his *magister equitum* Marcus Minucius Rufus, at the first opportunity, attacked the Carthaginians at Geronium in the autumn of 217 BC. But the troops under his command were quickly surrounded by Punic warriors and the *magister equitum* nearly died at the head of his troops had it not been for the swift intervention of Quintus Fabius who burst in with his troops to save his life. Amidst criticism, but keeping Hannibal at bay, the legal period of Quintus Fabius' dictatorship came to an end and new consular elections were held. Gaius Terentius Varro and Lucius Aemilius Paullus were elected. Rome prepared for the great battle. They recruited the largest army in their history. It is estimated that the Romans fielded about 90,000 men, infantry and cavalry, on the battlefield. It was an army equal to the danger they faced. Hannibal, on the other hand, had approximately 55,000. The consuls took turns each day commanding the army. On 2 August 216 BC[6] the command fell to the impetuous Gaius Terentius Varro, who formed his men in battle array, even though his consular colleague had advised against it. The battle began with the advance of the Roman legions and the first battles of the cavalry, placed on the wings of each formation. The Roman right-wing cavalry was soon outnumbered by the powerful Carthaginian and Numidian cavalry. The Roman horsemen were dispersed, while the Carthaginians went to pound the left wing. There a fierce battle had broken out between the Roman horsemen and the Celtic and Iberian cavalry. The arrival of the Carthaginians and the Numidians finally tipped the balance. Shortly after the battle began, the Romans had run out of cavalry. However, they had the spectacular strength of their infantry and overwhelming numerical superiority. Hannibal had some 800 Balearic slingers, placed in a second line in the centre of the battle, which he hoped would stop the advance of the legions. They failed. The Romans advanced undeterred until they were within throwing distance. It did not take long for the melee to begin. Deftly, Hannibal ordered his disciplined troops in the centre to retreat slowly and orderly. The Roman legionaries gradually lost their orderly formation, not realising that they were entering a cauldron of Carthaginian soldiers (and their allies). The drama really began when they were attacked from the rear by Punic cavalry. Suddenly, they were completely surrounded. No space to move. No space to attack. No space to defend. On that day the Iberian mercenaries shone especially bright. Their sword proved to be particularly suited to slaughtering the enemy in hand-to-hand combat. The Romans would take good note of this after the massacre, making that sword, called *gladius hispaniensis*, the standard weapon of the legions for the next five centuries. The battle was a real catastrophe for the Roman army,

6 Sir William Smith (Vol. II, p. 336) indicates that the Roman calendar in those years was very advanced and that the battle took place in mid-June. In any case, for history, the date was fixed by the Roman historian Quintus Claudius Quadrigarius on 2 August 216 BC.

one of the greatest defeats in its history. Livy lists the number of dead at 50,000 men, although contemporary estimates put the figure slightly lower. Looking at the list of the men who died in that battle gives us a sense of the magnitude of the tragedy. Falling with their swords were: the consul Lucius Aemilius Paullus (who was also pontiff), as well as the former consuls Gnaeus Servilius Geminus (c. 216 BC), Marcus Minucius Rufus (c. 221 BC, who had also been *magister equitum* the previous year with Quintus Fabius). The latter two were among the forty-eight military tribunes who took part in the battle and of whom twenty-nine (more than 60 per cent) were killed in action; and eighty senators.[7] Hannibal's army lost, according to Titus Livy, 8,000 men, of whom Polybius details that 1,500 were Iberians. The Punic general gave his weary men several days' rest while they enjoyed the extraordinary spoils of the battle. However, Maharbal, the head of the Numidian cavalry and one of the general's closest collaborators, urged Hannibal to lose no time and head for Rome. After his refusal, Maharbal replied: 'Of a truth the gods have not bestowed all things upon the same person. You know how to conquer, Hannibal; but you do not know how to make use of your victory' (Liv. 22 51).

Some of the survivors of the debacle managed to retreat to Canusium. Among the military tribunes were Gaius Octavian (Augustus' great-grandfather), Quintus Fabius Maximus (the son of the *Cunctator*), Appius Claudius Pulcher and Publius Cornelius Scipio (son and nephew of the proconsuls fighting in Hispania). Apparently, there was a heated debate about the next step to be taken. Many young Roman nobles, seeing the war as lost, advocated fleeing Italy and being hired as mercenaries in foreign armies. When Cornelius Scipio heard of these machinations, he presented himself at the lodging which housed Lucius Caecilius Metelus (leader of those who wanted to flee) and, drawing his sword, exclaimed:

> With sincerity of soul I swear that neither will I desert the cause of the Roman republic, nor will I suffer any other citizen of Rome to desert it. If knowingly I violate my oath, then, O Jupiter, supremely great and good, mayest thou visit my house, my family, and my fortune with perdition the most horrible! I require you, Lucius Caecilius, and the rest of you who are present, to take this oath; and let the man who shall not take it be assured, that this sword is drawn against him.

---

7 Hervé Danton has managed to list them in: 'Who are Roman Senators dead in year -216?'

Thus, all the soldiers assembled in Canusium returned to Rome under the command of Appius Claudius Pulcher and Publius Cornelius Scipio. This decision is striking, since Cornelius was the youngest of the military tribunes. However, it was already evident that the 19-year-old already exuded a charisma and leadership that was to make him one of the greatest generals in the history of Rome. The consequences for the survivors of the battle were mixed. Those who had fought bravely and shown their *virtus* on the battlefield, including Varro himself, were spared. The young men who had conspired to leave Italy were demoted to the status of *Aerarii*,[8] and when a delegation of the prisoners captured at Cannae, led by Lucius Calpurnius Piso, arrived in Rome to set out the terms of the ransom, the Senate refused to receive them. The three senators who were part of the delegation, instead of taking advantage of the circumstances to stay in Rome, returned with the rest of the prisoners to southern Italy.

At that time, three Carthaginian armies were stationed in Hispania, those commanded by: Hasdrubal Gisco, Hasdrubal Barca and Mago Barca, the latter two brothers of Hannibal; faced by two of Romans, commanded by the brothers Gnaeus and Publius Cornelius Scipio. However, the balance of power over the territory was determined by the number of allies that both armies were able to recruit for their cause from among the native populations. Shortly after the Battle of Cannae, Hasdrubal Barca was ordered to take his army to Italy to support Hannibal. To do so, he recruited a large number of Iberian troops and set out across the Ebro River. But in the vicinity, he was informed that an army under the command of Gnaeus Cornelius Scipio was besieging the city of Ibera, an ally of the Carthaginians. Instead of coming to their aid, Hasdrubal went to besiege Dertosa (modern Tortosa, Catalonia), an ally of the Romans. On hearing this news, Cornelius lifted his siege and went to rescue his allies. The two armies met near this city and, after five days of harassment and skirmishing, arrayed their armies for battle. The Romans had approximately 28,000 infantrymen, including Roman legionaries and Italic allies, plus about 2,000 Iberian allies; by about 2,500 Roman and Italian horsemen and about 400 Hispanians. Hasdrubal's infantry contingent numbered some 24,000 men, of whom a third were Hispanians and nearly 5,000 horsemen in all, plus 20 war elephants. Hasdrubal's plan was to use the same tactics as his older brother had used the previous year at Cannae. He therefore placed the Iberian infantry in

8 They were the lowest social class in Roman society. The *Aerarii* lost many of their rights, including citizenship, and were forced to pay a special tax.

the centre of the battle line, leaving his fearsome Libyan spearmen on the wings. However, the battle did not go according to plan. At first, the forcefulness of the legions pushed the thin line of the Hispanians back, but on this occasion neither the Carthaginian cavalry nor the elephants managed to dislodge the Roman cavalry, which, despite its numerical inferiority, resisted the onslaught of the enemy. On the wings, it seemed that the Libyans managed to push the Italians back, but the situation remained relatively stable. It all came to an end when the Iberian troops in the centre were unable to resist the pressure of the legions and fled the battlefield. The Romans moved to the wings, in support of their Italic allies, slaughtering the Libyan spearmen. In view of the situation, the Punic cavalry withdrew from the battlefield. The Roman victory was complete. But the importance of that day was that it deprived Hannibal of much-needed reinforcements to continue the war in Italy.

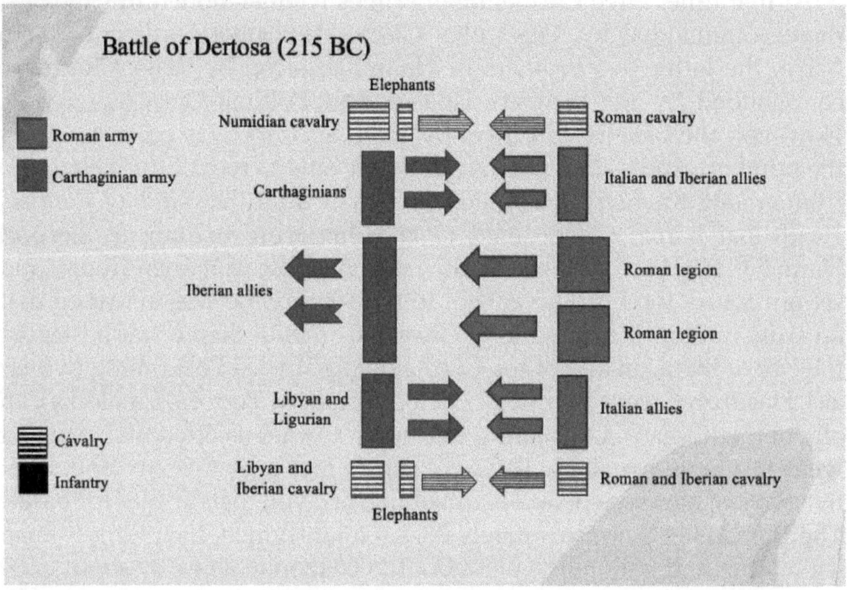

Map 2: In the spring of 215 BC, Hasdrubal Barca moved to the outskirts of the mouth of the river Ebro to confront the Scipio brothers. His intention was to win a decisive battle that would enable him to drive the Romans out of Iberia. Hasdrubal used a tactic identical to that employed by his brother Hannibal at Cannae. On this occasion, however, the less well-trained and more inexperienced core of his troops failed to stop the thrust of the Roman legions. The result was a crucial victory for the Scipios, who were able to consolidate a strategic line north of the river. The Romans would hold this position until the end of the Empire.

The following two years, from 214 BC to 212 BC, 'nothing very memorable had been done in Spain', in Livy's words (25, 32), although at another stage of the narrative the same author points out various campaigns in the Guadalquivir valley, which historians such as Schulten claim to be mere inaccuracies or exaggerations, since to enter that territory, Saguntum or Qart-Ḥadašt would first have to be controlled, and both cities were still firmly in Punic hands. Both armies suffered from a shortage of troops and were content to hold on to the territories they had conquered, while trying to add (and keep) as many Iberian and Celtiberian allies on their side as possible. At the end of the day, both armies maintained their strategic objectives: the Romans, to prevent Hasdrubal from crossing the Pyrenees with his army to help Hannibal; the Carthaginians, to preserve the mining basins of the Guadalquivir valley, which were essential to continue financing the war. During this period, the Carthaginians' lack of military resources was alleviated by the arrival of new reinforcements from Africa, and they managed to gather three armies under the command of Hasdrubal Barca, Mago Barca and Hasdrubal Gisco. Despite this, they show no intention of crossing the Ebro. It may be a good time to describe the role of the Iberian tribes, especially during the Second Punic War. *Vae victis*, in the end, the only version of what happened, both for the Carthaginians, but also for the Iberians and Celtiberians, comes from Roman sources. In some cases, such as Polybius, closely linked to the family of the Cornelius Scipio. Thus, the Iberians, more than mere puppets in the hands of the two armies in contention during the Second Punic War, participated in their own political game. Hence, far from being merely Iberians, as Latin authors point out, their social reality (as we have seen in the previous chapter), was much more complex, they were Olcades, Carpetani, Ilergetes, Vaccaei, etc, whose main objective was not to help Rome or Carthage win the war, but rather to maintain their own independence and, surely, to hoard enough power to conquer the lands of a weaker neighbour. For this reason, both the Iberians and the Celtiberians changed allies many times. It was not that they betrayed one or the other. It is that they followed their own political criteria as the third players on the game board.

The situation changed in 212 BC. The Scipio brothers found themselves for the first time strong enough to launch an expedition against the Punic armies, whose passivity towards the Romans can be explained by the fact that they had to face a revolt of the Turdetani. On this occasion, moreover, and for the first time in the history of Rome, they had hired an army of Celtiberian mercenaries, at that time the strongest tribes. These new allies allowed them to cross the Ebro and reach the gates of Saguntum without having to fight. Hasdrubal had left that territory under the command of an officer called Bostar. However, he presumably did not have sufficient forces to face two Roman armies and the new Celtiberian contingent, so he quartered himself near Saguntum. Once there, Polybius (98-99) and Livy (22, 22) tell us an anecdote about a Hispanian leader called Abilyx (according to Polybius) or Abelux (according to Livy), a former ally of the Carthaginians who, seeing that the Romans could end up winning, decided to change sides and, to ingratiate himself with Cornelius, plotted a trick to get the hostages that Hannibal had left in the city months earlier. To this end, Abilyx persuaded Bostar that in order to gain the trust of the Iberian peoples who were keeping their relatives in Saguntum as hostages, it would be a good idea to free them and return them to their homes, which Abilyx himself would take care of. A somewhat childish ploy, but according to the Latin authors, Bostar believed it and handed the captives over to Abilyx, who, in the middle of the night, as agreed with the Romans, took the hostages to his camp. Cornelius, instead of keeping them, entrusted Abilyx with the mission of returning them to their homes, along with the message that it was the magnanimous Rome who was returning their relatives. Shortly afterwards, the Romans took the city and continued into the interior of the mainland. This meant they could establish a solid base from which to push inland and attack the Carthaginians. In their westward advance, the Scipios succeeded in attracting the cities of Iliturgi (modern Mengíbar, Andalusia) and Castulo (modern Linares, Andalusia), separated by about 15 miles and controlling rich mining territories, through diplomatic agreements. The Scipio brothers then made a fateful decision. With the aim of destroying the three Carthaginian armies, they decide to divide their forces: Publius, with two-thirds of the Roman army, would march against Hasdrubal Barca; while Gnaeus, with one-third of the Roman army and the 20,000 Celtiberian mercenaries, would attack the forces of Mago Barca and Hasdrubal Gisco. The Scipio brothers would never meet again. News reached Publius that a large Ilergete contingent led by the stubborn Indibilis was to join the armies of Mago and Gisco. The Roman general knew that he could not face so many enemy forces at once, so he set out with part of his men to face Indibilis' troops, leaving a contingent under the legate Titus Fonteius in his camp near Iliturgi. Thus, while Publius' vanguard clashed with Indibilis' troops, his rearguard was surprised by the Numidian cavalry, led by a young prince named Masinissa. Engaged on two fronts, the Romans fought fiercely, but the situation became dramatic when the troops of Mago and Gisco appeared. Surrounded, Publius' men were being wiped out.

The only way out was to try to break through one of the fronts and, from there, attempt to retreat. But when the Roman general was trying to organise his men, a spear knocked him off his horse. Livy (25, 34, 11) recounts his epic death:

> *pugnanti hortantique imperatori et offerenti se ubi plurimus labor erat latus dextrum lancea traicitur; cuneusque is hostium, qui in confertos circa ducem impetum fecerat, ut exanimem labentem ex equo Scipionem uidit, alacres gaudio cum clamore per totam aciem nuntiantes discurrunt imperatorem Romanum cecidisse.*[9]

The death of their general plunged his men into confusion, and they were exterminated, except for a small group who managed to flee and join Titus Fonteius who, on hearing the news, tried to meet with Gnaeus. On his side, he had already suffered the disaffection of his Celtiberian mercenaries. One morning, they raised their banners and, with the excuse that their territory was under attack (Livy, 23, 33), left the Roman camp, without Gnaeus being able to do anything to prevent it. This is a controversial point in the narrative, since other authors, such as Appian, do not mention this betrayal. According to Salinas de Frías.[10] the story could be false, and an invention of authors close to the Cornelius circle to justify the death of Publius and Gnaeus and the subsequent repression that the Celtiberians suffered by their descendants (the Scipio Africanus and Aemilius Scipio). Be that as it may, there are two versions of the end of Gnaeus.[11] According to Livy, shortly afterwards, the arrival of the armies of Mago and Gisco must have made him fear that his brother had been defeated. He had no choice but to retreat. But on his way, he was constantly harassed by Masinissa's Numidian cavalry. Therefore, he had to stop and try to defeat it before the Carthaginian infantry joined him, taking up a hill as a defensive position. As misfortune would have it, this was practically a bare rock, with no trees and hardly any earth on which to dig trenches

9 'The general, while fighting and encouraging his men, exposing himself wherever the strife was the hottest, was run through the right side with a lance; and when the party of the enemy, which, formed into a wedge, had charged the troops collected round the general, perceived Scipio falling lifeless from his horse, elated with joy, they ran shouting through the whole line with the news that the Roman general had fallen'. Livy. *History of Rome by Titus Livy, books nine to twenty-six. Literally translated by. D. Spillan. and. Cyrus Edmonds.* York Street, Covent Garden, London. Henry G. Bohn. John Child and son, printers (1849).

10 Salinas de Frías (2011), pp. 97–118.

11 For an extensive and detailed analysis of the death of Gnaeus Cornelius Scipio, see Latorre Molina (2017), pp. 194–211.

or build palisades. Although they were able to hold off Masinissa's attacks, they did not prevent the arrival of the Punic infantry, who had no difficulty in assaulting the weak Roman defensive lines, causing them to be slaughtered. It is believed that the Roman general managed to make his way to a nearby tower with some survivors, where the Carthaginians managed to break down the gates, enter and massacre the defenders, including Gnaeus Cornelius Scipio. Appian (*Ib. Wars*, 4, 16) reports another version. In it, the Roman general was unaware of his brother's fate. He had sent soldiers to collect wheat, but they have been attacked and killed. Gnaeus went in pursuit with part of his army and was surprised by the bulk of the Carthaginian army. The Romans took refuge in a tower where its occupants, led by Gnaeus, were burnt to death. In any case, the disaster was complete. Only two small Roman contingents remained in the territory. One took refuge in the city of Ilorci, a city that had only recently switched to the Roman side. But with the arrival of the Punic army, the population changed sides again and, faced with the danger of being razed to the ground by Hasdrubal's troops, it is not known whether they surrendered the Romans or killed them inside the city walls. The other contingent consisted of the troops that Publius had left in the camp under the command of Titus Fonteius. In view of the critical situation, the centurion Caius Lucius Marcius Septimus was acclaimed by the troops to command their return journey north of the river Ebro, where they could hope to find a safe place to take refuge. He secured the defences and asked to be appointed *proprietor* of the territory, but as he was a mere knight, the Senate refused, and to head the Roman army in Iberia they sent Caius Claudius Nero, who arrived with a reinforcement of some 10,000 soldiers and about 1,000 horsemen. The period from 211 BC to 209 BC may be the most mysterious period of the Second Punic War. It is striking that Hasdrubal Barca did not force his way through the Pyrenees. According to Livy, both Marcius Septimus and Claudius Nero inflicted heavy defeats on the Carthaginians (in one of them, he speaks of over 37,000 Punic dead), which seems to be an exaggeration or invention, since other authors do not mention it. Moreover, it is unlikely that with the weak force of his 11,000 men and the survivors of the disasters of the 211 BC campaign, Claudius Nero went as far as Baetica, as the famous historian from Patavium claims. What is striking is that Claudius Nero landed with his troops at Tarraco and the following year, in 210 BC, while Publius Cornelius Scipio, son and nephew of the dead generals, arrived at Emporium, 150 miles further north. The triumphal exploits recounted by Livy are called into question by this fact, since, if Claudius Nero had so much control over the territory, it would have been natural for the new proconsul to land in the main city of Roman Iberia, Tarraco. But the truth is that, by this point in the war, almost all the Iberian allies of the Romans had changed sides. Defeat seemed obvious and the Romans' time in Iberia was numbered. Even in the Senate it was feared that, faced with the dwindling army sent, Hasdrubal would manage to cross the Pyrenees and that the most sensible thing to do would be to evacuate Iberia and focus all resources on defending Italy. But I have jumped the gun a little. In 210 BC, Rome was still looking for a proconsul to accept the mission of leading a new army in Iberia. One of the conditions for the post was that he had previously been consul. No candidate offered himself. It was Publius Cornelius Scipio, the eldest son of the dead general, who stepped forward. He did not meet the requirements and was only 24 years old. How could he be given command of a proconsular army? By a fiery speech, overwhelming charisma, and popular acclaim. The Senate could not refuse him. Surely, the Senate did not want to deny him. Of course, the young and impetuous patrician was to be accompanied by Marcus Junius Silanus, and as Fernández Rodríguez notes,[12] it is not clear whether with an *imperius minus* or a *par potestas*. Likewise, Cornelius Scipio was accompanied by his younger brother Lucius (who was 21 years old) and Gaius Laelius, according to Polybius, a close childhood friend of the young Roman general, with whom he had shared various vicissitudes on the battlefields.[13] It is interesting to mention that it was his son, Gaius Laelius Sapiens, who told Polybius about his father's military campaigns. Both were intimately linked to the *gens Cornelia* and, in fact, both accompanied Scipio Aemilianus on his campaigns in Iberia. With a new reinforcement of 11,000 men, the young Cornelius was to land at Emporium. Before him was the enormous challenge of defeating three Carthaginian armies three times his number in a territory that was totally hostile to the Romans. And to everyone's surprise, he was going to succeed. His first step was

---

12 Fernández Rodríguez (2005), p. 40.

13 Polybius, 10, 3, 2: 'ὧν εἷς ἦν Γάιος Λαίλιος, ἀπὸ νέου μετεσχηκὼς αὐτῷ παντὸς ἔργου καὶ λόγου μέχρι τελευτῆς, ὁ ταύτην περὶ αὐτοῦ τὴν δόξαν ἡμῖν ἐνεργασάμενος διὰ τὸ δοκεῖν εἰκότα λέγειν καὶ σύμφωνα τοῖς ὑπ᾽ ἐκείνου πεπραγμένοις ἔφη γὰρ πρώτην γεγονέναι Ποπλίου πρᾶξιν ἐπίσημον, καθ᾽ ὃν καιρὸν ὁ πατὴρ αὐτοῦ τὴν ἱππομαχίαν συνεστήσατο πρὸς Ἀννίβαν περὶ τὸν Πάδον καλούμενον ποταμόν'. Translated: 'Of such Gaius Laelius was one. He took part in everything he did or said from boyhood to the day of his death; and he it was who convinced me of this truth: because what he said appeared to me to be likely, and in harmony with the achievements of that great man. He told me that the first brilliant exploit of Publius was when his father fought the cavalry engagement with Hannibal near the Padus.'

to move with the bulk of his army to Tarraco and summon the former allies of the region to warn them that Rome had returned.

Meanwhile, in the south, the three Carthaginian armies were wintering in their barracks. Near Saguntum, the largest of all was quartered under Hasdrubal Barca, with about 30,000 men. To the east, at Saltus Castulonensis, controlling the mining region of the Guadalquivir valley, the youngest of the Barca brothers, Mago, had 20,000 men. Near Gadir, Hasdrubal Gisco had another 20,000 men. In spring, a new revolt in Carpetania forced Hasdrubal to move the bulk of his army from the eastern coast to suppress it. Although some authors claim that this may have been due to Cornelius' skilful diplomacy, it is more likely that it was simply because the Carpetani wanted to maintain their independence (as would happen once the Romans had prevailed in the war). The same must have happened in Lusitania, since Gisco had to move there, while the position in Gadir was occupied by Mago, so we deduce that he must have the least combative army. In any case, the three armies were still only a few days apart. If Cornelius Scipio had decided to attack any one of them, he would have been exposed to having to defend himself against a second or even a third, as had happened to his father and uncle. During the winter he had spent in Tarraco, the Roman general had been gathering information about his enemies. He knew where they were located and even that there were certain rivalries and disagreements between them, for example when dealing with their Iberian allies. Thus, it seems that Gisco was ruthless, forcing them to pay heavy taxes and to hand over many hostages, such as the daughters of Indibilis, who took it as an insult, and many of them were imprisoned in Qart-Ḥadašt. And the Punic capital in Iberia could be the key to the war. Cornelius Scipio had surely been thinking about this plan since he had been in Rome, so he had also gathered information about its defences and planned a tactic to conquer it. The plan was extremely risky, but Cornelius Scipio never tired of repeating that it was Neptune himself who had revealed it to him, and therefore victory was guaranteed. The young patrician was indeed a deeply religious man. But the assault on the city would have to be completed in record time, before one of the Carthaginian armies reacted and the Romans were caught in the crossfire. In Qart-Ḥadašt, the Carthaginians held their greatest treasure in Iberia, as well as controlling a territory that had important silver mines; it held numerous hostages from local tribes; and, finally, it was the most important communication junction between Iberia and Carthage. The city's defences were commensurate with its importance. On the one hand, a series of natural obstacles favoured its defence: the city was located on an isthmus, to the south having the sea on one side and to the north a lagoon called Estero. In addition, the city was surrounded by five hills, some of which were inside the city (on one of which stood the lavish palace of Hasdrubal the Fair), but others were part of its fortifications and were virtually impossible to climb, especially those on the eastern side, which protected the gateway to the city. In addition, it had several defensive towers, numerous war machines and a garrison of some 1,000 experienced soldiers, under the command of an officer named Mago (not Hannibal's brother, but a namesake), to which could be added the city's men of fighting age, although it had weapons for only about 2,000.[14] The first two decisions Cornelius Scipio took were: on land, to build a palisade around the city, to prevent the city from being helped from the outside, either by food or by the arrival of Hasdrubal Barca's army, the closest to the city (it was in the vicinity of the future Toletum, capital of the Carpetani, about ten days' march away); and from the sea, he blockaded it with the thirty quinqueremes captained by Gaius Laelius, a remarkable responsibility for a young man of Cornelius Scipio's age, which he performed with extraordinary efficiency. Soon, he prepared for the first assault. But to his surprise, just as the Roman vanguard was beginning to march towards the eastern wall, the city gates opened and Mago's 2,000 armed citizens poured out to meet the Roman troops. Enthusiasm and motivation (they were fighting for their city, to defend their families) helped the militiamen who, at first, were able to hold off the attacking troops. However, it did not take long for the tables to turn. The discipline of the Romans eventually prevailed and the citizens of Qart-Ḥadašt were pushed back to the ramparts. Suddenly, the retreat turned into a rout, which resulted in the defenders being trapped in the funnel before the city gates. The legionaries massacred them. They also took the opportunity to begin the assault on the city. But the high walls, defended by Mago's professional soldiers, caused the Romans to fail. Cornelius Scipio did not seem to be too concerned and that same afternoon he organised a new assault on the eastern wall. While fierce fighting raged on that section of the wall, Gaius Laelius' sailors launched an assault on the southern wall. But the key to the assault came at the Estero lagoon. Fishermen from Tarraco had told Cornelius Scipio that this lagoon, in which small boats fished, was wadeable at certain points under certain conditions of wind and tide. The Roman general chose 500 elite soldiers

14 For these figures we follow Polybius (10, 12). Appian increases the number of defenders to 10,000 men (10, 19).

and assured them that Neptune (probably he himself was convinced of this) would allow them to cross the lagoon without any problems. The northern wall, which was the lowest and had hardly any defenders, was stormed by the 500 men, who spread panic among the defenders who were holding their ground in the southern and eastern sectors. They had no difficulty in breaking through to the city gate, which they managed to open and then, following the orders of Cornelius Scipio, a great massacre of the Carthaginian citizens began. Mago, with about 500 men, took refuge in the palace of Hasdrubal, where he eventually surrendered. The Roman victory was overwhelming and the booty unprecedented. Gaius Laelius went to Rome by sea to announce the great victory and hand over Mago and the captured notables of the city. In addition, Cornelius Scipio freed the city's Iberian hostages, including the daughters of Indibilis, which brought many tribes, including the warlike Ilergetes, to the Roman cause. Dominated by the Romans, the city was refounded as Carthago Nova, the name we will use hereafter, which is a literal translation of its Punic name, Qart-Ḥadašt.

After spending the winter in that city, Cornelius Scipio could no longer delay attacking the Carthaginian armies. He had used the winter to increase the number of his Iberian and Celtiberian allies, but he was still clearly outnumbered. The key again was speed: to locate and attack the Carthaginian armies separately. And the closest was that of Hasdrubal, which in the spring of 208 BC was in the vicinity of Baecula, some 170 miles as the crow flies west of Carthago Nova.[15] This time, the Romans had numerous Iberian contingents, including the fearsome Ilergetes and the Edetani. It is believed that it was in mid-June that the two armies met in the vicinity of the *oppidum* of Baecula. It is estimated that Hasdrubal had about 25,000 men, while Cornelius Scipio must have had just over 30,000, including the newly-incorporated Ilergetes. The course of the battle, narrated by Polybius and Livy, leaves us with a few questions. According to Roman authors, after two days of skirmishing, Cornelius Scipio ordered his *velites* (Latin for 'skirmishers'; singular, *veles*) to charge uphill towards the Carthaginian camp. The attack surprised their enemies, who opposed them with Balearic slingers and Numidian cavalry. However, the Romans continued to advance up the hill, causing the rest of the Carthaginian army to panic, as there was no time to form up for battle. Only Hasdrubal, with a few

---

15 Bellón et al. (2016), after a detailed study, concluded that Baecula would have been located on the Turruñuelos hill, in the vicinity of the modern city of Úbeda, in the province of Jaén (Andalusia).

men, managed to flee. According to Roman authors, some 8,000 men were killed and another 10,000 were captured. However, I believe that this is yet another exaggeration by Roman authors, always so benign towards the *gens Cornelia,* since what is certain is that Hasdrubal Barca managed to flee. Not only that, but he managed to cross Iberia, Gallia Narbonensis and Gallia Cisalpina (including the dangerous crossing of the Alps) to reach northern Italy. In other words, a feat that would have been impossible with only 10,000 men and hardly any cavalry. If we follow the course of history, Hasdrubal reached the vicinity of Metauro with about 40,000 men. Although he was able to convince several Celtic tribes of Gaul to accompany him on the way, it does not seem feasible that a virtually annihilated and morally bankrupt army was capable of such a feat. What is more likely is that, after the attack by the *velites* and seeing the impossibility of deploying his army on the battlefield, Hasdrubal ordered a general retreat and the Romans only faced the Punic rearguard, which they eventually defeated. Be that as it may, the fact remains that, after the battle, the main Iberian and Celtiberian leaders swore allegiance to Cornelius Scipio and proclaimed him their king, an office to which a good Roman republican had a tremendous revulsion, and which the young patrician was quick to reject. Incidentally, the battle was followed by an event which, beyond the anecdotal, had important consequences. One of the Numidian horsemen who fell prisoner was Prince Massiva, Masinissa's own nephew, who had fought in secret that day, against his uncle's wishes. When he was brought to Cornelius Scipio and his identity was revealed, the Roman general not only treated him with the utmost respect, but gave him a golden ring, rich clothes and a horse and ordered some of his horsemen to escort him to the Carthaginian camp (Livy, 27, 19, 8-12). If we refer again to Hasdrubal's army, we do not know why Cornelius Scipio did not pursue his enemy and stayed in the Guadalquivir valley, since one of his main strategic objectives was precisely to prevent Hasdrubal from reaching Italy and joining his brother Hannibal. The news of his arrival caused consternation in Rome (and great anger against Scipio for having allowed it), who sent a powerful army to the hands of the two consuls of that year, Marcus Livius Salinator and Gaius Claudius Nero, the former *propraetor* who had arrived in Iberia in 211 BC. Although the two consuls were sworn enemies, the victory over Hasdrubal was absolute: his army was destroyed and even he died during the battle. Few days later, his head was thrown into Hannibal's camp. This caused great consternation for the great Carthaginian general. Not only had he lost one of his brothers, but all hope of receiving help from Iberia. Eight years had passed since the Battle of Cannae and the situation seemed to have reached a strategic impasse. Secluded in southern Italy, controlling the Apulia region and with incursions into Campania, where he had allies, Hannibal was unable to repeat the feat of 216 BC, despite important victories such as that of Silarus in 212 BC. Even when the Romans laid siege to Capua (211 BC), Hannibal marched, this time to the gates of Rome, but had to retreat before the arrival of a Roman army from outside. This situation, in which Romans and Punics alternated victories and defeats without any decisive battle, continued until 203 BC, when Hannibal urgently returned to Africa, as we shall see below.

Back in Iberia, the 207 BC campaign began with the arrival of a new Carthaginian army from Africa under the command of Hanno the Elder, which joined that of Mago, who had travelled to the Balearic Islands to recruit a new contingent of mercenaries. Then the two Punic generals also went into Celtiberia to recruit more men. Cornelius Scipio ordered Marcus Junius Silanus, with some 10,000 men, to follow and attack them, which he did successfully, forcing them to retreat south, despite being clearly outnumbered. While Mago Barca managed to flee, Hanno the Elder was captured (and executed in 204 BC). Silius Italicus, in his poem *Punica* (16, 45-65), recounts how among Mago's mercenaries was a detachment of Cantabrians, whose leader was Larus, a warrior of enormous size and strength. Seeing that the battle was lost, they decided to fight to the death. Larus, whose weapon was a formidable double-edged axe, approached the position of Lucius Cornelius Scipio, who accepted the challenge and engaged in hand-to-hand combat with the Cantabrian giant, from which the young patrician emerged victorious, having managed to cut off his arm.

The 206 BC campaign would be conclusive. Mago and Gisco, aware that the situation had taken a radical turn, knew that they had to face Cornelius Scipio in a decisive battle, and so they managed to gather an army of around 50,000 men. The Romans, after spending the winter in Tarraco, returned to the Guadalquivir valley with an army of some 45,000 soldiers, which included new Iberian allies, such as 3,000 Turdetani under the command of their king Culcas. Although to understand the complexity of the situation among the pre-Roman societies, the Carthaginians also had a small army of Turdetani under the command of Attenes, another of their king-tribesmen. The two armies met in the vicinity of the city of Ilipa (near of modern Alcala del Río, Andalucia). Gisco camped on a hill on the north bank of the river Guadalquivir, the Romans built their redoubt on a hill opposite. The time had come for the great battle. For some days, the two armies formed up in attack position in the morning, but no one seemed willing to take the first step into battle. Gisco and Mago arranged their troops in the classical way: in the centre, the small Carthaginian contingent, together with their allies and Libyan and Ligurian mercenaries, trained like Hellenic hoplites, were their shock force, the elite infantry; at their sides, the two contingents of Iberian allies; and at the ends, in the front line, the elephants and, behind them, the Numidian cavalry. As for the Romans, Cornelius Scipio used the classic Roman disposition which, in general terms, did not differ from the Punic one: in the centre the legions, on the sides the newly-incorporated Iberian allies and, finally, in the wings, the cavalry. During those first days, the armies did not move. The generals studied each other, looking for the enemy's weak point. But one morning, everything changed. Cornelius Scipio had it all planned. He ordered his men to wake up earlier than usual, served them breakfast and changed the formation. This day they would not be arranged as usual. In the centre, the Iberian allies were placed; next to them, the legions and the *velites*, the skirmishers; and on the wings, the cavalry. Then, they began to march. It was so early that the manoeuvre surprised the Carthaginian army. Gisco and Mago ordered their men to form up immediately in the same formation as usual, without realising, in their haste, that the Romans' formation had changed. Suddenly, the groups of *velites* began to fall on the elephants. Pachyderms can be phenomenal war machines, especially in their psychological effects on the enemy, but an out-of-control elephant can cause more damage in its own ranks than in the enemy's. And that is what happened that day. The elephants, finding themselves under surprise attack, backed off and caused chaos at the ends of the Carthaginian line. It was a bad start to the day for Gisco and Mago. The *velites* then began to fight against the disorganised lines of the local allies, gradually being replaced by the legions. The fighting was fierce, but the Roman superiority was clear. In the centre, the Romans' Iberian mercenaries pinned down the hoplites in the centre of the Punic line. Meanwhile, both cavalries clashed in a fierce fight. The theoretical superiority of the legionaries did not become apparent until midday, when fatigue and hunger began to take its toll on the Punic men, who, let us remember, had not had time for breakfast in the face of the impetuous Roman advance. In the end, the Punic's Iberians retreated, leaving the hoplites alone on the battlefield. While some of the Romans slaughtered their retreating enemies, others moved towards the centre of the line, where the Carthaginian, Libyan and Ligurian infantry, who had not yet taken part in the battle, were holding their ground. Gisco had no choice but to order their retreat, which was carried out in good order. And yet they were lucky that, when they were at the gates of the

Punic camp, an unexpected storm broke out and forced the Romans to retreat. But the victory was complete. During the night, the Iberians who had supported the Carthaginians deserted en masse. Some returned home, others, like the Turdetani kinglet Attenes, went over to the Roman side. This defeat meant, *de facto*, the end of the Carthaginian presence in Iberia. After the loss of Carthago Nova, they had lost the economic resources provided by their rich mines; now, with the loss of the Upper Guadalquivir regions, they had just lost the rest of the mines that were essential to maintain their war machine. Not to mention the fact that they had been abandoned by practically all their local allies. If, in addition, we consider that the previous year, in Italy, the Battle of Metauro had taken place, it could be said that the situation of the Punics, in general, was desperate.

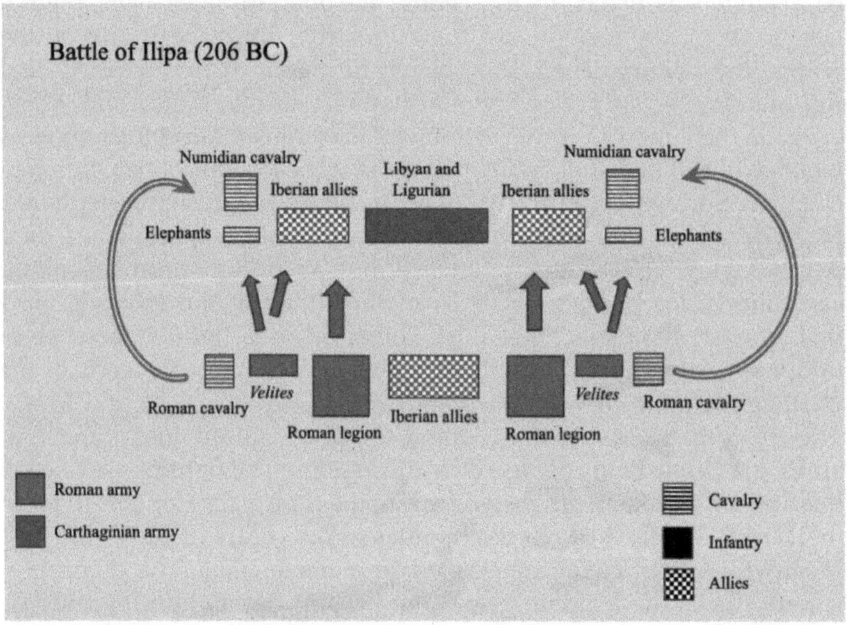

Map 3: In 206 BC, Mago and Gisco faced Scipio Africanus in the vicinity of Ilipa (modern Alcala del Rio, Andalusia). The two armies faced each other for several days, but without fighting, until Scipio decided to change the classic disposition of his army, with the legions in the centre, replacing them with his Iberian allies. That day, the Romans went on the attack and, while the Iberian allies contained the powerful Libyan and Ligurian infantry, the Roman infantry and cavalry crushed the wings of the Punic army. Scipio Africanus' decisive victory meant *de facto* Roman victory on the Iberian front in the Second Punic War.

In the following days, Cornelius Scipio could not prevent Gisco, Mago and a small number of his men from embarking for Gadir, a city which the Romans advanced towards, but did not besiege. We return to Livy (28, 35, 8-13) to narrate another episode that was to be of great importance. Its protagonist is Masinissa, the Numidian prince and commander of the Carthaginian cavalry. He had suggested to Gisco that he should go out and plunder the area around Gadir to obtain food. The Punic general thought it was a good idea, but in fact Masinissa went straight to meet Cornelius Scipio to thank him for returning his nephew safely to him without asking for a ransom and to express his willingness to join the Roman side. Masinissa would prove to be a loyal ally of Rome for the next 60 years and was instrumental in the final Roman victory in Africa. But for the time being, so as not to arouse suspicion, he ravaged the territory around Gadir and returned to the city. Shortly afterwards, he set sail for Africa. The historicity of this encounter may raise some doubts, since it is not clear that the Romans arrived at that time. Furthermore, sources reveal a revolt among the Ilergetes, which forced Cornelius Scipio to travel with part of his army to Tarraco, leaving Silanus in control of the territory. With the Carthaginians defeated, it was time to settle accounts with the Iberian cities that had betrayed the Romans. Thus Cornelius Scipio, accompanied by his faithful friend Laelius, marched with two-thirds of his army on Iliturgi (the city which in 211 BC had surrendered to the Roman soldiers who had taken refuge there after the hecatombs of the Roman general's father and uncle), while Lucius Marcus marched on Castulus with the rest of his forces. At Iliturgi, the attack came from two different points, one commanded by Scipio and the other by Laelius. The city was heavily fortified, and it seems that the first assault must have failed, as Scipio himself threatened his men that he would climb the scaling ladder himself if they failed in storming the city. But in the end, they succeeded, and a terrible slaughter ensued, in which neither women nor children were spared (Liv. 28, 20, 6-7). After the massacre, the city was razed to the ground. In fact, it was not until 2019 that the exact site of the original city could be established.[16] When news of the destruction of Ilturgi reached Castulus, its king, Cerdubelus, beg to surrender without resistance, praying that the Romans would show mercy. To this end, he ordered the arrest of the Carthaginian garrison. Scipio returned to Carthago Nova, leaving part of his army in Turdetania under the command of Marcius Septimus with the order to

16 Tiberius Sempronius Gracchus later re-founded it at a location nearby.

suppress the cities that had supported the Carthaginians. One of these was Astapa (modern Estepa, Andalusia), which on seeing the Roman troops arrive closed its gates and refused any kind of surrender. The tribal council met and chose fifty warriors. Their mission was to kill all the inhabitants of the city in case the Romans conquered it. The rest of the men made a desperate sortie that took the Romans by surprise, causing them considerable casualties; but once Septimus was able to organise them, the Turdetan warriors were slaughtered. At that moment, a column of smoke appeared from inside the city. In the centre of Astapa a large pyre had been set up on which its citizens threw their valuables. Some even threw themselves into the fire. Others committed suicide in their homes, while the fifty warriors took the lives of the survivors. When Septimus entered the city, he found only death and destruction. Another notable event of this period is the foundation by order of Cornelius Scipio of the first Roman city in Hispania, Italica (modern Santiponce, Andalusia), in the territory of Turdetania, to house the soldiers wounded in his military campaign, according to Appian (*Ib. Wars*, 38):

> Καὶ αὐτοῖς ὁ Σκιπίων ὀλίγην στρατιὰν ὡς ἐπὶ εἰρήνῃ καταλιπών, συνῴκισε τοὺς τραυματίας ἐς πόλιν, ἣν ἀπὸ τῆς Ἰταλίας Ἰταλικὴν ἐκάλεσε: καὶ πατρίς ἐστι Τραϊανοῦ τε καὶ Ἀδριανοῦ τῶν ὕστερον Ῥωμαίοις ἀρξάντων τὴν αὐτοκράτορα ἀρχήν.[17]

While the Romans settled in Turdetania, Hasdrubal Gisco returned to Africa, where he managed to get the Numidian king Syphax to ally with the Carthaginians. However, the arrival of Cornelius Scipio on the African continent meant that the Punics suffered a series of military setbacks. In 203 BC, after the Battle of the Great Plains, Gisco was again defeated and, although he managed to flee, he ended up committing suicide in Carthage when a mob threatened to lynch him. As for Mago Barca, he took refuge in Gadir and then went to the Balearic Islands to hire mercenaries, leaving Hanno in command of the Punic army in Iberia, who recruited some 4,000 Celtiberian warriors, with whom he faced Roman troops in 206 BC in the Battle of Carteia (also known as the Battle of the Guadalquivir). On that

17 'Scipio left them a small force suitable for a peace establishment and settled his sick and wounded soldiers in a town which he named Italica after Italy (and this was the native place of Trajan and Hadrian, who afterwards became emperors of Rome).' Tarraco was founded earlier, but as a military camp. The peculiarity of Italica is that it was the first Roman settlement founded as a city.

occasion, the Romans were commanded by Marcius Septimus (the man who had taken command after the death of the Scipio brothers in 211 BC) and won a crushing victory. While the surviving Celtiberians returned home, the Carthaginian soldiers set sail for Africa. Shortly afterwards, Mago Barca tried to return to Gadir, but found that the Gaditans were already negotiating their new alliance with Rome and would not allow him to enter the city. Mago then moved to northern Italy, where he managed to control the region of present-day Genoa for about three years. In 203 BC, after several military defeats in Africa, he was ordered to return to Carthage and died during the sea crossing.

The war in Iberia was over. But it continued in Africa. The climax of the conflict took place on 19 October 202 BC. On the plain known as Zama, the Roman and Carthaginian armies, commanded by Publius Cornelius Scipio and Hannibal Barca respectively, clashed in the final battle. At last, the two generals were facing each other. In the Punic army there was still a small group of Iberian and Balearic mercenaries fighting. They were the survivors of Hannibal's Italian campaigns and formed part of the third line of infantry of the Carthaginian general. They were tough, hardened men, loyal to their leader. Not in vain had they fought at his side in Iberia; with him, they had crossed the Alps, in an epic journey that had led them to victory at Cannae and in dozens of battles in Italy. All of them ended up as pyrrhic victories, of no avail. With more than 20 years of war behind them, the battle was hard fought. At the climax, the Roman *Triarii,* along with what was left of the *Principes* and the *Hastati,* clashed with Hannibal's veterans once the newly-hired mercenaries and Carthaginian citizens had already been defeated. The veterans held their own, it even looked as if they might win in hand-to-hand combat against the elite Roman legions, but the arrival of the Numidian and Roman cavalry finally tipped the balance in favour of Scipio's army, which from then on earned the nickname Africanus. Rome had won. The Second Punic War was over.

But the Hispanians did not only fight in the Second Punic War on their own territory and in Africa or Italy. Another point of conflict was the island of Sicily. There we meet a Celtiberian leader who deserves to be part of our history: Mericus. He was a kind of Lord of War who fought in the service of Hiero II of Syracuse. Despite pressure from his trusted men, the old ruler remained loyal to Rome, even after the hecatomb of the Battle of Cannae. A few weeks later, however, Hiero II died and was succeeded by his young grandson Hieronymus, who was swept along by his grandfather's advisors and declared war on Rome, which responded by sending an army under the command of the consul Marcus Claudius Marcellus. But the complicated topography of the area, the magnificent city walls and the ingenious inventions of the legendary Archimedes meant that all Roman attempts to conquer the city failed. In addition to numerous mercenaries, such as those commanded by the Celtiberian Mericus, who was one of those in charge of defending the strategic position of Achradina. In the absence of progress, Marcellus decided to send an embassy led by a nobleman named Belligenes from Iberia[18] to convince Mericus to betray Hieronymus and allow the Romans to enter through the Achradina gate. Subsequently, Mericus himself would meet secretly with Marcellus and they agreed on a plan of attack. Days later, the assault was carried out as planned, allowing the Romans to enter Syracuse and depose Hieronymus. In the sacking that followed, the murder of Archimedes is to be regretted. In the summer of 211 BC, Marcus Claudius Marcellus led a parade in the city (the Senate did not grant him a triumph, but an ovation). As Livy (25, 26) tells us, the parade consisted of a model of Syracuse, numerous war machines, part of the city's treasury and eight elephants. In addition, preceding the consul were:

> *Et non minimum fuere spectaculum cum coronis aureis praecedentes Sosis Syracusanus et Moericus Hispanus, quorum altero duce nocturno Syracusas introitum erat, alter Nasum quodque ibi praesidii erat prodiderat. his ambobus civitas data et quingena iugera agri.*[19]

In other words, Mericus was the first Hispanian to receive Roman citizenship. But it was not only the Lord of War who was rewarded, but also the diplomat Belligenes:

> *Moerico Hispanisque qui cum eo transierant urbs agerque in Sicilia ex iis qui a populo Romano defecissent, iussa dari id M. Cornelio mandatum ut, ubi ei*

---

18 Livy tells us (*History of Rome*, 24, 49) that the Romans had brought 300 Hispanian nobles to Italy to try to persuade their compatriots to leave the Carthaginian ranks and join the Roman army.

19 'Sosis, the Syracusan, and Mericus, the Spaniard, who preceded him with golden crowns, formed not the least interesting part of the spectacle; under the guidance of one of whom the Romans had entered Syracuse by night, while the other had betrayed to them the island and the garrison in it. To both the freedom of the city was given, and five hundred acres of land each.' Translated by D. Spillan and Cyrus Edmonds. York Street, Covent Garden, London. Henry G. Bohn. John Child and son, printers (1849).

> *videretur, urbem agrumque eis adsignaret. in eodem agro Belligeni, per quem inlectus ad transitionem Moericus erat, quadringenta iugera agri decretal.*[20]

Mericus and his men were given the Sicilian city of Morgantina, which had also rebelled against Rome. To conclude the story of Mericus, it is interesting to note that the mercenary leader minted bronze coins with the term HISPANORVM. In other words, they already named their territory of origin after the Romans, using the Latin alphabet and language, instead of specifying whether they were Celtiberi or Iberi, as was still common in the literature of the time. These rare coins are a numismatic treasure and are the first to refer to Hispania.[21]

20 'Mericus and the Spaniards who had come over with him were ordered to have a city and lands assigned to them in Sicily, which had belonged to some of those who had revolted from the Romans. It was given in charge to Marcus Cornelius to assign them the city and lands wherever he thought proper. [14] In the same country, four hundred acres of land were decreed to Belligenes, by whose means Mericus had been persuaded to come over.' Translated by D. Spillan and Cyrus Edmonds. York Street, Covent Garden, London. Henry G. Bohn. John Child and son, printers (1849).

21 Amela Valverde (2013), p. 35.

Chapter 3

THE CONQUEST OF A WILD FAR WEST

Auferre, trucidare, rapere falsis nominibus imperium,
atque ubi solitudinem faciunt, pacem appellant.

Tacitus[1]

While the Second Punic War entered its final phase in Africa, the Roman army remained in Iberia. On the one hand, the Romans wanted to make sure that the Carthaginians did not think of reopening that front; but, on the other hand, they had also realised that they had at their fingertips the enormous riches that the Iberian Peninsula offered: mines of gold, silver, iron, tin; rich harvests of vines, wheat, oil . . . Although they faced an essential problem in their exploitation: the pre-Roman societies. Iberians, Celtiberians and Celts were not going to welcome them with open arms. We have already seen in the previous chapters that many of these societies were truly warlike and unyielding, with a pronounced sense of freedom.

The first major revolt took place in the territory of the Ilergetes. The rebel Indibilis wanted to drive the Romans out of his territory. With Cornelius Scipio in Africa, accompanied by most of his best officers, such as Laelius and Silanus, the *praetores* Lucius Lentulus and Lucius Manlius Acidinus were left in Iberia to control the territory. Indibilis apparently argued that his oath of friendship had been sworn to a man, Cornelius Scipio, and not to an entity ('Rome'). Without Scipio

1 'To ravage, to slaughter, to usurp under false titles, they call empire, and where they make a desert, they call it peace.'

in his territory (moreover, rumour had it that the general had died of an illness), Indibilis felt free of his oath. In addition, alongside the Ilergetes, their neighbours, the Ausetani, whose leader was called Mandonius, also rebelled,[2] together with some other (unspecified) tribes. Both armies occupied the territory of the Sedetani, allies of the Romans, provoking their reaction. At first, the Romans tried to resolve the conflict diplomatically, while the armies of the two *praetores* were assembled. But when the Iberians refused to withdraw, the Romans prepared for battle. The two armies met at an undetermined point in Sedetania, although it is thought to be near their capital, Celsa (modern Velilla del Ebro, Aragon). The Iberians numbered some 30,000 warriors, forming into three blocks: the Ilergetes on the right, the Ausetani in the centre and the coalition of allies on the left. As for the Romans, they had about 25,000 men. The *praetores* organised their troops as follows: Legio XII was placed in front of the Ilergetes; Legio V, in front of the Ausetani; and Legio VI,[3] in front of the Iberian coalition allied to the Ilergetes, with Legio XIII remaining in reserve. The battle started well for Indibilis' men, who were overpowering Legio XII. Lucius Lentulus had to send part of Legio XIII and the Roman cavalry to stabilise the Roman left wing. Indibilis sent his own cavalry which, as was the custom at the time, fought dismounted to support his infantry. After fierce fighting and moments of confusion, the Roman heavy infantry began to gain the upper hand, causing confusion among the Iberian front line, which could no longer count on the support of its cavalry. In an attempt to tip the balance in his favour, Indibilis himself led a counter-attack with his personal escort. But his unit was mowed down by the legionnaires' *pila*. Livy recounts that Indibilis himself was left wounded and standing surrounded by his dead men, and that he fought until he was cut down by the Romans. The death of their leader caused panic and disbandment, which spread to the rest of the Iberian formation, who fled back to their camp. Lentulus and Manlius gave the order to pursue and exterminate them. The legionaries carried out the order to the letter. According to Livy, some 13,000 men were killed and 8,000 captured in the battle, more than a third of the troops Indibilis had put on

2 Traditional historiography claims that they were brothers, but this is not possible, as they led different tribes. However, it is thought that they may have had some kind of kinship or alliance, and it is suggested that they may have been brothers-in-law.

3 Although Livy does not mention them specifically, they were the two legions that Cornelius Scipio had left behind in Iberia. After the campaigns of the Second Punic War, they would have been severely depleted.

the battlefield. Subsequently, a delegation from the Ilergetes went to visit the Roman *praetores* to negotiate peace terms. Lentulus and Manlius, in addition to imposing a large sum of money as a penalty, demanded the surrender of Mandonius and the rest of the Iberian leaders who had encouraged the revolt. The Iberian emissaries accepted the conditions and Mandonius and other Iberian leaders were seized and handed over to the Romans. They were sent to Rome as part of the conquered booty and were crucified. The Iberian tribes of the Ebro River valley, including the Ilergetes and Ausetani, signed a peace treaty with Rome. Now was the time when Iberia would become Hispania.

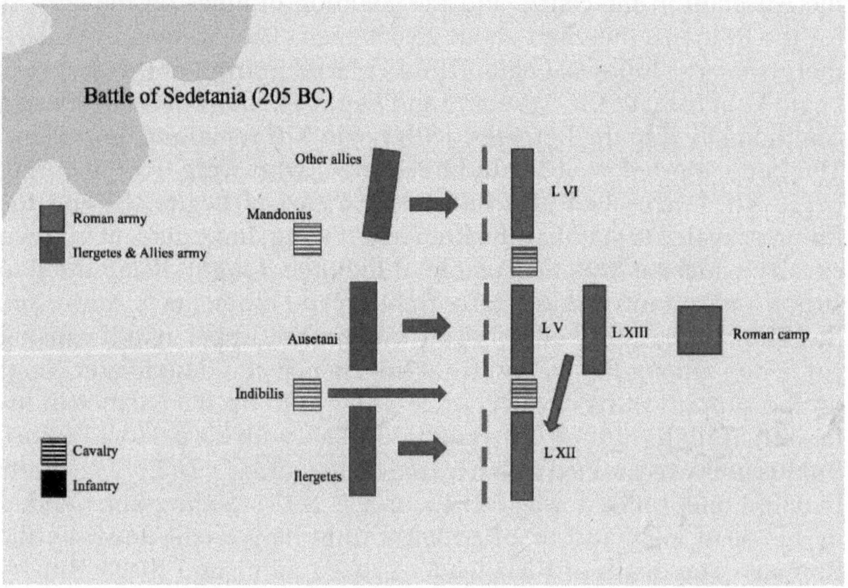

Map 4: The battle began with an Iberian attack on the Roman lines. On the Roman left wing, it seemed that Legio VI would not be able to hold the Ilergetes, so L. Lentulus sent the cavalry and part of Legio XIII to reinforce that sector. The tables were turned and the Ilergetes began to retreat. Indibilis then led a counter-attack with his cavalry. The king of the Ilergetes died on the battlefield and his troops finally disbanded.

The Campaigns of Cato the Elder

After the revolt, the situation was relatively calm. But in 197 BC, the Roman Senate agreed to create two provinces in Hispania, Citerior and Ulterior. The former was to control the valley of the

Ebro River and the rich region of Carthago Nova, while Ulterior was responsible for the Guadalquivir valley, which was no less rich in mines and natural resources. In order to exploit the natural resources and control the territory, the Senate sent two *praetores*: Gaius Sempronius Tuditanus[4] for Citerior and Marcus Helvius Blasius for Ulterior. The change of administrative regime brought with it fiscal reforms and greater pressure on the tribes recently incorporated into the Roman orbit, which caused the social situation to become tense, to the point of provoking a general revolt in the two provinces. To complicate matters further, at the time, the Senate's attention was focused on both the final stages of the war against Carthage and the Second Macedonian War (200–197 BC), so that the *praetores*, despite having some 8,000 men and 1,500 horsemen, most of them auxiliary troops with a minimal percentage of legionaries. Before the end of the year, Gaius Sempronius Tuditanus had been killed in battle by the Ilergetes (Livy, 33, 25, 8-9). His colleague Helvius Blasius, meanwhile, had to deal with a revolt in Turditani led by the kings Culcas, who had fought alongside the Romans at the Battle of Ilipa, and Luxinus. After the death of Sempronius Tuditanus, moreover, he had to take charge of the administration of both provinces until the arrival of the following year's *praetores*, Quintus Minucius Thermus, for Citerior, and Quintus Fabius Buteo, in Ulterior. No news has come down to us of what happened during that year, except through a letter to the Senate sent by Minucius Thermus in which he narrates his victory over Iberian troops in the vicinity of a city called Turda (unknown location, but in Turdetania) in which he claims to have killed 12,000 enemy soldiers and captured Budar, apparently a Celtiberian leader who had been hired by Culcas and Luxinus, who managed to flee. It should be noted that Minucius Thermus was a Roman general with combat experience, having served as a military tribune in Africa under Scipio Africanus, gaining his friendship and trust.

4 Probably brother of Marcus Sempronius Tuditanus, military tribune with Publius Cornelius Scipio, who performed brilliantly during the capture of Carthago Nova in 209 BC.

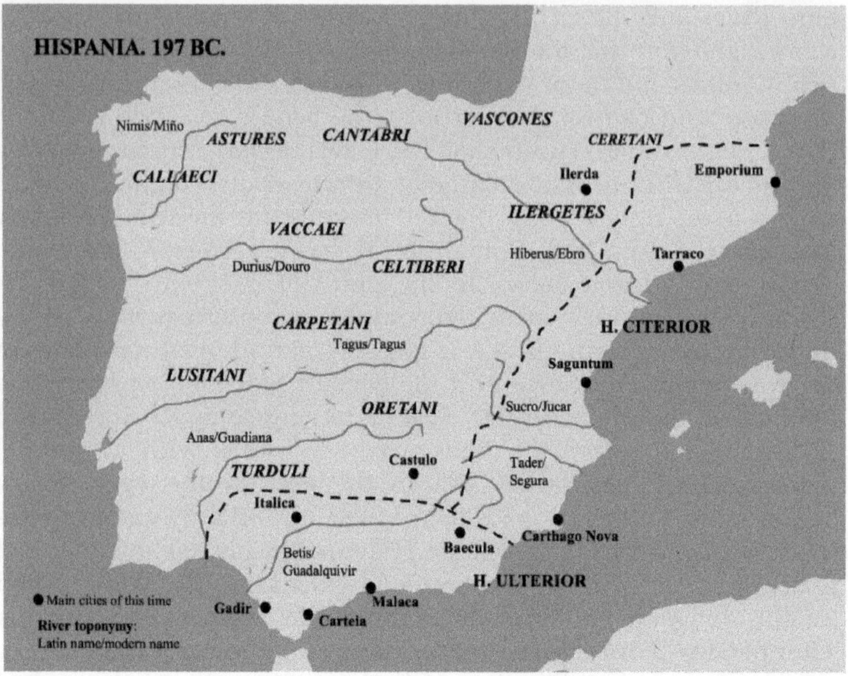

Map 5: The situation in Hispania in 197 BC. The Roman Senate divided the areas occupied by its army into two provinces: Hispania Citerior and Hispania Ulterior.

In the consular elections of 195 BC, Marcus Porcius Cato was designated together with Lucius Valerius Flaccus, who was also his client.[5] In the drawing of lots for the provinces, Cato was given Hispania. This time, it seems that the Roman Senate took the Hispanian revolt seriously and the *praetores* sent together with Cato were Publius Manlius Vulso for Citerior and Appius Claudius Nero[6] for Ulterior, two generals of great prestige and proven ability for military

5 Williams (1969), pp. 16–17, notes that for a new man like Cato, who, moreover, was of very humble origins, his own qualities were not enough to get a consulship: the patronage and help of some influential family was needed. Thus, just as Scipio Africanus helped his friend Gaius Lelius to get it, Valerius Flaccus also helped his client and friend Cato the Elder.

6 He was the nephew of Gaius Claudius Nero, the victorious consul at the Battle of Metauro and whom we have seen how he was appointed *propraetor* in Hispania after the death of Publius and Gnaeus Corenlius Scipio. His brother, Tiberius, was consul in 202 BC. It is very likely that Cato the Elder forged a loyal friendship with the Claudius Nero family during the Battle of Metauro and hence influenced the election of Gaius as *praetor* for the province in which he served as consul. From this legendary branch of the Claudius Nero family would emerge the dynasty of the successor emperors of Augustus.

command. But then, so was Cato himself, who, although he has gone down in history for his diatribes from the Senate and for his extreme conservatism of Roman traditions, his remarkable military skills have been forgotten. He was initiated into the art of war during the Second Punic War, under the orders of Quintus Fabius Maximus, who saw in him a promising general. He took part in the Battle of Cannae, where he was almost captured, but was saved at the last moment by the consul Lucius Aemilius Paulus. His most notable actions were during the Battle of Metauro, where he acted as military tribune, and at the siege of Tarentum. It is said that he proudly wore the many scars caused by the numerous wounds he received on the battlefields. The generals were accompanied by four legions, one for each *praetor* and two for the consular army. During his first weeks in Emporium, Cato spent his time training his troops, most of whom were inexperienced. He soon had the opportunity to put them on the battlefield, facing a coalition of local tribes near Emporium, and to recapture the port of Rodhe, which had been taken by the enemy. After his conquest, Cato ordered his army to head south. Before doing so, however, he received Bilistages, the new leader of the Ilergetes, who came to offer an alliance with the Romans and to ask for soldiers for a war in his territory. Cato readily accepted the new alliance and promised to send them help, ordering his men to prepare to proceed to the Ilergetes' territory, but when the ambassadors had left, Cato ordered his men to stay with him (Livy 34, 11, 1-13). On their way south, the Romans would re-establish their alliances with the coastal peoples, such as the Laietani (in the region of modern Barcelona, Catalonia) or the Cessetani, whose capital was Tarraco. He would follow his steps towards Ulterior, where his friend Claudius Nero had asked him for help to put down the revolt in southern Hispania. Following the coastal route, Cato and his army would pass through Carthago Nova and from there into Turdetania. Cato was informed that the local tribe had hired an army of some 10,000 Celtiberian mercenaries. This combination of forces would make the Turdetani a formidable enemy. As these allies were in separate camps, Cato sent a delegation to the Celtiberians to try to convince them to return home. But as the Celtiberians demanded payment of 40,000lb of silver, a veritable fortune. In response, Cato ordered an attack on their own territories, such as the city of Saguntia, where they kept their impedimenta. These attacks were convincing enough for the Celtiberians to abandon the Turdetani. Without their mercenaries, the rebels suffered a massacre at the hands of Cato's men. On this occasion, Culcas and Luxinus were captured and executed. With the region pacified (at least for a while), the consul decided to return to H. Citerior via Celtiberia, rather than retrace his steps by the coastal route. In doing so, he was not only the first Roman to set foot in that territory, but also showed Roman power among the potentially dangerous populations. He crossed the territory of the Arevaci and, according to Aulus Gellius (*Noctes Atticae*, 16, 1, 3-4), he passed through Numantia, but did not have time to stop. His *imperium consularis* came to an end and he had to return to Rome. He did have to face a revolt by the inland peoples of what is now Catalonia, such as the Bergistani and the Austeni, whom Cato crushed with sufficient cruelty to prevent them from ever again rising up against Rome. His arrival in Rome was an apotheosis, as he brought with him a fabulous booty, which aroused the admiration (and greed) of the people and the Senate of Rome and which consisted of (Livy, 34, 46. 2):

> *tulit in eo triumpho argenti infecti viginti quinque milia pondo, bigati centum viginti tria milia, Oscensis quingenta quadraginta, auri pondo mille quadringenta.*[7]

If anyone had any doubts about whether Hispania was worth conquering, they disappeared at that moment. He also claimed that during his stay in Hispania he had killed more than 10,000 of Rome's enemies. He was granted a triumph, and at last Cato the Elder had the satisfaction of placing himself on the same military level (or at least close to) that of his rival Scipio Africanus.

In 194 BC, the *praetores* elected were: for Hispania Citerior, Sextus Digitius; and for Ulterior, Publius Cornelius Scipio Nasica, son of Gnaeus Cornelius who died in Hispania in 211 BC and cousin of Africanus. If they thought they would find a pacified territory, as Cato the Elder proudly proclaimed, they were wrong. That year was hell for Sextus Digitius, who had to face numerous revolts in which, although Livy (35, 1) states that they were of little importance, the same author claims that the *praetor* lost half of his army in the fighting. In Ulterior Scipio Nasica fared somewhat better. He dealt with the peoples of the area with an iron fist, but he also had to face the incursions of the Lusitani and Vettones into Turdetania. In fact,

---

7 'He carried in his triumph twenty-five thousand pounds of silver bullion, one hundred and twenty-three thousand silver denarii, five hundred and forty thousand silver coins of Osca, and one thousand four hundred pounds of gold.' Livy. Books 31-34 with an English Translation. Cambridge. Cambridge, Mass., Harvard University Press; London, William Heinemann, Ltd. (1935): no copyright notice.

in one of his cities, Ilipa, Nasica intercepted an army of Lusitani returning home with immense booty. The Roman *praetor* attacked them, winning a remarkable victory in which it was claimed that 12,000 warriors were killed and 540 captured, returning to Rome at the end of his *imperium* with the requisitioned treasure. In the following year, 193 BC, the *praetores* chosen were Caius Flaminius, son of the consul who died in the Battle of Lake Trasimeno, for Citerior; and Marcus Fulvius Nobilior, for Ulterior. Such was the situation in Citerior that Caius Flaminius complained so bitterly about the state of the Roman troops in his territory that the Senate gave him permission to recruit a new legion and discharge the survivors of Sextus Digitus' army. The climate of revolt was widespread throughout the province and the two *praetores* saw their imperium extended for another year. Their most notable achievements were for Caius Flaminius, the conquest of Licabrum (modern Cabra, Andalusia), where he managed to capture its king, Corribilius; and, for Fulvius Nobilior, the conquest of the capital of Carpetania, Toletum (modern Toledo, Castilla la Mancha), against a coalition of Carpetani, Vettones, Vaccaei and Celtiberians, led by Toletum's sovereign, Hilernus, apparently an able and charismatic leader. In 193 BC, heavy fighting between the two armies ended in a Roman victory near the city, which, however, could not be conquered, although Hilernus was captured. In 192 BC, Fulvius Nobilior returned with his army to the city, which was only supported by a contingent of Vettones. On this occasion, the Roman eagles completed the victory of the previous year by conquering the city, a strategic point for dominating the Tagus River basin. In 181 BC, Caius Flaminius was renewed as imperium for the Citerior, while Lucius Aemilius Paullus, a member of the renowned *gens Aemilia*, took over as *praetor* for Ulterior. His father, of the same name, was the consul who died at Cannae, while his sons were Quintus Fabius Maximus Aemilianus and Scipio Aemilianus, whom he gave up for adoption to two other prominent Roman families, and he was also the father-in-law of Cato the Elder, who had married his daughter, Aemilia Secunda. Although this Aemilius Paullus will go down in history as the victor of the Third Macedonian War, for which he earned the nickname Macedonicus, he will be important in our history because he left what is the first Roman inscription in Hispania, the so-called Bronze of Lascuta found in the excavations of Hasta Regia (modern Mesas de Asta, Andalusia). During his *imperium*, he focused on quelling various insurgencies in Bastetania, on the southern coast of the Ulterior, but the Romans were unable to stop the climate of generalized insurrections.

The First Celtiberian War

During the following decade, the Romans had to face the so-called First Celtiberian War, with many reinforcements from Rome and with some very capable *praetores* such as Aulus Terentius Varro, son of the other consul of Cannae, and Lucius Calpurnius Piso. But victories followed defeats and the Celtiberians continued to resist. In 188 BC the *praetor* of Ulterior, Gaius Atinius, was killed in battle. In 183 BC, in other parts of Europe, Cornelius Africanus, his brother Lucius, and Hannibal died.

The situation changed radically in 180 BC, when Tiberius Sempronius Gracchus was appointed *praetor* of Citerior. He came from an old senatorial family, was married to Cornelia, the daughter of Africanus, and was the father of Tiberius and Gaius Sempronius Gracchus. He was possibly the first Roman to understand the situation in Hispania. Or at least one of the first not to want to squeeze pre-Roman societies by taxation and exploitation of their natural resources. In Ulterior, the *praetor* was Lucius Postumius Albinus, a member of one of the oldest and most prestigious patrician families in Rome. They had an army of 8,000 infantrymen and some 5,000 horsemen. Their first actions should be focused on defeating the Celtiberians, who were in the interior of the Ebro valley (in what would be today the region of Aragon and La Rioja). Some years earlier, in that region, Cato the Elder had managed to pacify it and signed or renewed alliances with some cities, such as Calagurris or Caravis. It was precisely in the latter city that he carried out one of his first military actions. According to Appian (*Ib. Wars*, 43), the city was under siege by an army of some 20,000 Celtiberians. Following Gracchus' orders, Cominius, a cavalry prefect, dressed as a Centiberian and managed to enter the city and ask its defenders to hold out for a few more days, as the Roman army was only a few days away. As the *praetor* had foreseen, his arrival caused the besiegers to flee. He subsequently conquered the rebel cities of Complega and Ervica. Another of Gracchus' important campaigns was the conquest of Carpetani (Livy, 40, 49), who, after the capture of Hilernus, now faced the Romans under the leadership of their new king, Turrus, and a contingent of Celtiberian mercenaries. Pacifying this territory, located in the centre of the Iberian Peninsula, was key to control and exploit the economic resources of the Guadalquivir valley. The Roman army was expeditious, and the Carpetani cities fell one after the other. At Arce, Gracchus even captured two sons and a daughter of Turrus. The cruelty of the Roman army and the lack of combativeness shown by the Celtiberian mercenaries made him inclined to negotiate peace with Rome. Gracchus, once again, was generous to the vanquished. The agreement benefited both sides and that is why it was to be so long-lasting. On the one hand, Rome would receive taxes and, when necessary, soldiers; its new allies agreed not to fortify their cities, in return for receiving farmland and Rome's protection from outside enemies. Rome succeeded in making Turrus a loyal partner for many years. However, his greatest victory, and indeed the one that ended the Celtiberian revolt, was at the Battle of Mons Caunus, a battle that Livy details as lasting three days and in which both armies suffered heavy casualties, estimated at 22,000 dead in the Celtiberian side, an exaggerated figure by any standards. Livy also informs us of an expedition of Postumius Albinus into the territory of the Vaccaei, fighting in various battles that caused them some 35,000 dead. It could now be said that Hispania was pacified, at least the territories comprising Citerior and Ulterior, however diffuse their borders might be. The conquered tribes accepted the same conditions as the Carpetani. A period of more than two decades of peace began in which Rome was able to begin to administer the territories with a certain degree of calm. It is a period in which we can say that the process of the Romanisation of Hispania really began. In 179 BC, Gracchus founded Gracchurris (modern Alfaro, La Rioja); the same *praetor* rebuilt Iliturgi; and the settlement of Carteia (modern El Rocadillo, Andalusia) obtained the title of *Colonia Libertinorum Carteia* in 171 BC, being the first city to receive this title outside Italy. All these enclaves were occupied by veterans of the various wars that had ravaged Hispania in recent years. It was not long before new cities were founded in which Roman and Italic colonists settled, as was the case of Corduba (modern Cordoba, Andalusia) in 169 BC, founded by the *praetor* Marcus Claudius Marcellus. In 178 BC, Gracchus and Albinus both celebrated triumphs in Rome. The former paraded with a fabulous booty of 20,000lb of silver, the latter with 40,000lb. In addition, they distributed a generous amount of *denarii* among their troops. During these almost 25 years of peace, relationship between Romans and Hispanians was intense. The former exploited the natural resources of the region, bringing with them such a wealth that Rome was surprised; the local elites, who began to be treated fairly and justly, saw in the arrival of the Romans an opportunity to enrich themselves and live in peace. At least in theory. What is true is that hardly any information has come down to us from that period. We do know that in 170 BC, a delegation of Hispanian leaders went before the Senate of Rome to complain about the tyrannical ways of some of the *praetores* of the previous years, who were more concerned with personal enrichment than just government. Among the accused were Marcus Titinius,[8] Publius Furius Philus[9] and Marcus Matienus.[10] All of them were patricians and from ancient Roman families, so it should come as no surprise that they were acquitted in the trials in which they were accused. This predatory attitude may help us to understand why, from time to time, some tribes took up arms against the Romans. Thus, in the same year, Canaleius suffered an attack by king Olyndicus, who according to Florus '*qui hastam argenteam quatiens quasi caelo missam*'.[11] The rebel leader was killed and the Celtiberians completely defeated. The government of Canaleius was indeed an eventful one. Another delegation visited the Roman Senate. These were Hispanians born of Roman or Italic parents asking for a land. The Senate decreed that they should settle in the aforementioned Carteia, which obtained the distinguished title of *Colonia Libertinorum Carteia,* with the privileges that the title of Colonia meant, without distinction of origin among its inhabitants (Hispanians, Romans, Italians or, even, Punics). In the future, Carteia would stand out among the most faithful of the cities to Rome. Again, the sources are silent about what happened in Hispania until the middle of the 2nd century BC. From then on, a period began in which two of the bloodiest wars that the Romans had to face in Hispania took place. Moreover, these two wars were practically parallel in time and plunged the metropolis into a deep crisis. They were the First Lusitanian War, in Ulterior, and the Second Celtiberian War, in Citerior. For a better understanding of the events, we will begin by describing the Lusitanian revolt, and then go on to detail the Celtiberian wars. It all started around 154 BC.

Viriathus and the Lusitanian Wars

Traditionally, the Lusitanian tribes raided the territories of the Turdetani or Oretani in the Guadalquivir valley, whose fertile lands and rich mines allowed these societies to live in comfort that the Lusitanians could not even dream of because their arable land was very poor and did not allow for the development of agriculture, which made many of those tribes semi-nomadic. But the attack of that year, 154 BC, went a step

8 *Praetor* of Citerior from 178 to 176 B.C.

9 *Praetor* of Citerior from 174 to 173 BC.

10 *Praetor* of Citerior in 173 BC.

11 'Who, waving a silver spear, seemed heaven-sent.' Lucius Annaeus Florus, *Epitomae Historiae Romanae,* 33, *Res in Hispania gestae,* 14.

further. The number of Lusitanian warriors was unusually large; on this occasion, moreover, they were accompanied by a large contingent of Vettones warriors. The warlord who led them, Punicus, was particularly ambitious. And the enemy they faced was not the Turdetani farmers: it was Rome. The forcefulness of the attacks surprised the *praetor*, Manius Manilius, who suffered numerous defeats, losing more than 5,000 men in battle. The Lusitanian army ravaged not only the Guadalquivir valley, but also reached the southern coast of Hispania, even attacking, according to Appian (*Ib. Wars*, 56), the Bastophoenicians.[12] However, in one of the battles, Punicus fell and was replaced by Kaisaros. Later, he also defeated the new *praetor* Calpurnius Piso.

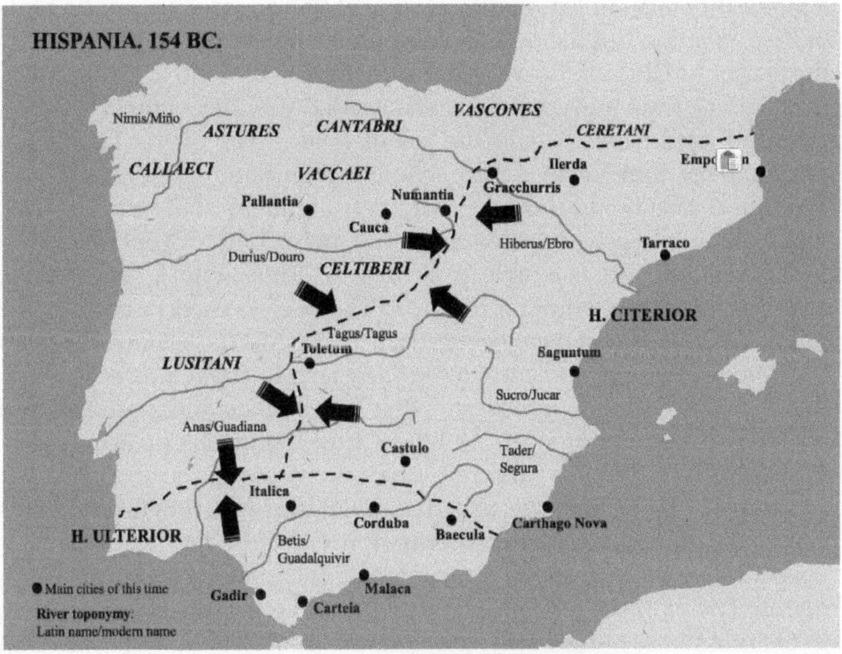

Map 6: The situation in Hispania in 154 BC. From the end of the Second Punic War until the middle of the 2nd century BC, Rome advanced towards the interior of the peninsula. It managed to pacify the territories of the Ilergetes, Carpetans and Oretans. On its borders were the Lusitanians and Celtiberians, with whom it spent the next 70 years fighting almost uninterruptedly.

12 It is interesting to note how populations of Phoenician origin continued to settle in this area. In fact, we have already seen how in the case of Carteia, where part of its inhabitants came from Libya or Carthage. This phenomenon was studied by Domínguez Monedero (1995).

The outbreak of the Second Celtiberian War, which we shall see later, and the intensification of the war in H. Ulterior must have caused such terror in Rome that the Senate decreed a change in the calendar, so that the new *praetores* could arrive in Hispania in the middle of winter and thus be ready in their provinces when spring began, and military campaigns could be organised. Until then, the Roman year officially began on the *Ides* of March (15 March). From then on, in 153 BC, the start of the year was changed to the *kalendae* of January (1 January). A decision that has survived to the present day. Moreover, to put an end to the war once and for all, the year's *praetores* did not travel alone. They were again accompanied by a consul, in this case Quintus Fulvius Nobilior, and an army of 30,000 men, made up of the *praetor*'s legions, the consular legions, the *alae* of the Italics, as well as contingents of Iberian allies. But the defeats continued, such as the one suffered by the *praetor* of Ulterior, Lucius Mummius Achaicus, who lost 9,000 men, his baggage train and numerous standards. After his victory, Kaisaros attracted new tribes to join the revolt. Then, part of the Lusitanian army moved into North Africa, where it plundered numerous towns. Mummius decided to pursue them, trapping them in the city of Ocile, where he apparently defeated them and, according to Appian, caused 15,000 deaths, and was able to return to Rome with a large booty, allowing him to celebrate a triumph. The war seemed to be over the following year, when the new *praetor*, Marcus Atilius Serranus, entered Lusitanian territory and conquered their largest city, Oxthracae. After this victory, he made peace with the Lusitanians and Vettones and retired to his winter quarters. But these tribes soon took up arms again. Probably, the Romans did not keep their promises and the war continued. The next *praetor* to arrive in Ulterior was Servius Sulpicius Galba, the namesake of a future emperor with close ties to Hispania. It was not long before he was confronted by the Lusitanians, after a long march. The battle began before his men could enjoy the necessary rest. In the first phase of the battle, the Romans seemed to be victorious and began to pursue the fleeing Lusitanians. But suddenly, the Lusitanians turned and charged the disorganised Roman lines. The legionaries, exhausted after the march and the battle, were easy prey for their enemies and were exterminated. It is believed that over 7,000 of Rome's soldiers died that day. Galba was able to organise the survivors of his army and retreated to the allied city of Conistorgis (somewhere in the southern Portugal). The following year, he attacked the Lusitanians again, this time with the help of the *praetor* of Citerior, the sinister Lucius Licinius Lucullus. They won a remarkable victory that led the Lusitanians to sue for peace and to respect the agreements that had been reached with Atilius two years earlier. Galba agreed, at least outwardly. He offered the Lusitanians land on which to settle and divided them into three large groups. Later, as a gesture of goodwill, he asked them to disarm. The Lusitanians, in good faith, obeyed. But they were suddenly surrounded by legionaries who began to massacre them with impunity. It is estimated that on that day, Galba ordered more than 15,000 men, women and children to be killed. And those who did not die were captured and sold into slavery. Very few were able to escape indiscriminate slaughter or enslavement. But one of them would soon make Rome tremble. It was Viriathus. That action was considered an outrage in Rome and, on his return, Galba was brought to trial, accused not only of betraying the Hispanians but also of having kept a share of the booty that belonged to his soldiers.[13] His accuser was none other than the octogenarian Cato the Elder. However, Galba, whom Cicero considered the best orator of his generation (*De Oratore*, 1, 40), defended himself. But he based his speech on the gimmicky (if shabby) ploy of speaking to the jury with his children in his arms and showing concern for the fate of his offspring if he was convicted. In the end, Galba was acquitted. Moreover, a few years later, he obtained the consulship. What is certain is that the treachery of Galba (who would not be the only Roman to use this tricky stratagem, as we shall see later), served to pacify Lusitania. Rome could focus its efforts on its new conflicts: the Third Punic War and the Fourth Macedonian War. Thus, it is likely that the Lusitanians took advantage of that period of relative calm, when the best legions and the most impetuous generals set their sights on North Africa or Greece. All seemed to begin to change in 147 BC, when some 10,000 Lusitanians reoccupied land in Turdetania. The *praetor* of Ulterior of that year, Gaius Vetilius, went immediately with an army of about 10,000 men. Some Lusitanians wanted to negotiate a cession of land with the *praetor*; but another faction, led by Viriathus, opted for confrontation. Finally, Viriathus prevailed and, selecting about a thousand warriors, met the Roman legions near a city called Tribola (location unknown, probably near Ronda, Andalusia). At first, the Romans seemed to gain the upper hand and the Lusitanians retreated. But this was just a tactic of Viriathus, who lured the Roman troops into a gorge. There, he ambushed them. The Romans, with no favourable place to deploy, were stabbed, thrown off a cliff or captured. Vetilius not only lost more than 4,000 men that day, but he also lost his life. Captured by a

13 Muñiz Coello (2004).

Lusitanian warrior, he did not believe that the fat old man was the Roman general, and slit his throat. The lucky legionaries who managed to escape took refuge in Carteia. In addition, he also killed some 5,000 Celtiberian allies of the Romans. Hispania Ulterior was again in flames. In 146 BC, the Lusitanians ravaged Carpetania and retreated westwards. The *praetor* of that year, Gaius Plautius Hypsaeus, again faced them with an army of 10,000 infantry and 2,000 horsemen, but suffered a series of terrible defeats in the territory that today corresponds to the Portuguese region of Coimbra. In fact, the defeats were of such magnitude that, on his return to Rome, Plautius was condemned to exile (Diodorus Siculus, 33, 2). In the same year, Viriathus faced the *praetor* of Citerior, Claudius Unimanus, who had an even larger army. But the result was another humiliation for the Roman eagles. Orosius (*Historiae Adversum Paganos* 5, 4) tells us that, at the time, Viriathus collected Roman banners and nailed them to a mountain. In 145 BC, after the wars in Greece and North Africa were over, Rome decided to put an end to the Lusitanian war and sent the proconsul Quintus Fabius Maximus Aemilianus, who arrived in Hispania with an army of 17,000 men[14] on a mission to capture Viriathus. An experienced general, Fabius Aemilianus spent the first year of his rule training his men in the type of warfare Viriathus was waging. It was a war of low-intensity guerrilla warfare, of constant ambushes, of small groups of warriors emerging from nowhere to strike the Romans and disappear. His *imperium* extended for a year, so Fabius Aemilianus went on the attack in 144 BC, conquering two cities held by the Lusitanians, but was unable to capture Viriathus. That year, the *praetor* of Citerior, Gaius Laelius Sapiens,[15] also fought the Lusitanians. Finally, the *imperium* of Fabius Aemilianus came to an end and he had to return to Rome, with the bittersweet feeling of having won the first victory over the Lusitanians in almost a decade, but without having been able to capture their leader. In 144 BC, Viriathus also married a woman whose name is unknown. We do know the name of his father-in-law, Astolpas, a nobleman from the Turdetani city of Tucca (probably modern Tocina, Andalusia).[16] The following year, he defeated the new *praetor* of

---

14 At that time, a consular army should have consisted of some 30,000 soldiers, but Rome had already lost many men, not only in Greece and North Africa, but also in Hispania. New recruits were difficult to find.

15 Son of Gaius Laelius, general and close friend of Scipio Africanus. Friendship that had been passed on to the next generation of the families.

16 The wedding episode is described by Diodorus Siculus, 33, 8. In it, the Greek author does not hide his admiration for the austerity and wisdom displayed by Viriathus. He scorns

Citerior, Quinctius (although this name may be a mistake, according to scholars such as Schulten and Kornemann[17]). Anyway, the year was another disaster for the Romans, who suffered heavy casualties. In 142 BC, H. Ulterior saw the arrival of a new consular army, some 18,000 strong. This time under the command of Quintus Fabius Maximus Servilianus.[18] The first major battle took place in the vicinity of the Roman-allied city of Itucci (near modern Baena, Andalusia), but with no clear winner, both armies withdrew. Shortly afterwards, Servilianus received 300 horsemen and 10 elephants as reinforcements from his Numidian allies. In the next battle, at an undetermined place, the Romans lost 3,000 men. Constantly harassed by the Lusitanians, Servilianus had no choice but to come back to Itucci. The campaign of 140 BC was more favourable to the Romans. Servilianus, instead of pursuing Viriathus, set about ravaging the cities allied to the Lusitanians and managed to capture Connoba, one of his lieutenants, along with 500 of his men, whom he freed after cutting off their hands (Appian, *Ib. Wars*, 14, 68). Servilianus then attacked the city of Erisana. In a manoeuvre that surprised the Romans, Viriathus arrived with his army, leaving Servilianus' men surrounded and at his mercy. But this time, instead of slaughtering them, Viriathus offered them a peace treaty, which Servilianus accepted. After negotiations, Rome recognised the independence of Lusitania, Viriathus as its king and that they could keep the occupied territory. Viriathus, for his part, declared himself a friend of Rome. Why did Viriathus simply not annihilate the Roman army as he had done for the past eight years? Probably because, after almost 15 years of war, the Lusitanians would demand the end of the war. No matter how much they defeated the *praetores*, every year a different one came along; no matter how much they destroyed their armies, every year they had to face a new one. The Lusitanians probably understood that they could not defeat the Romans. The least bad solution would have been to come to an agreement with them. But this pact was not to Rome's liking. The new consul of H. Ulterior in 140 BC was Quintus Servilius Caepio,[19] the uterine brother of Servilianus. On learning of the terms of the peace treaty, Caepio complained to the

---

the riches that his father-in-law has displayed at the wedding.

17 Schulten (1937), p. 116; Kornemann (1904), p. 117.

18 He was the adopted son of Quintus Fabius Maximus and the biological son of Gnaeus Servilius Caepio. Interestingly, both had served as *praetors* in Hispania in the past. Fabius in Citerior in the period 188–186 BC and Servilius in Ulterior in 174 BC.

19 The other cónsul was Gaius Laelius Sapiens.

Senate, which asked him to provoke Viriathus to make the Lusitanians break it. But since the Lusitanians did not fall into the trap, the Senate gave him permission to openly attack their positions. He soon penetrated the Lusitanian territory and ravaged villages and towns with ruthless cruelty. He was no kinder to his own soldiers either. In fact, Cassius Dio (22, 78, 3) tells us an anecdote that reflects the extent to which his own soldiers hated him, when on one occasion, as a punishment, he ordered soldiers to go and collect firewood without an escort, which was extremely dangerous considering the guerrilla tactics of the Lusitanians. When they returned, they piled the wood around Caepio's tent and set fire to it. The consul was spared because he was not inside his tent at the time. However, his policy of terror led the Lusitanians to despondency and disaffection. Moreover, Caepio managed to get the Senate to extend his *imperium* in Ulterior for an additional year and, in addition, he received the support of the new consul Marcus Popillius Laenas, who had received H. Citerior as a province. Popillius, who, as we shall see, had also broken a peace agreement with the Numantines, added to the expeditious tactics of his colleague Caepio. The Lusitanians, fed up with the relentless war and destruction, demanded that Viriathus sue for peace. Viriathus agreed and sent three of his closest collaborators to Caepio's camp. They were Audax, Ditalkon and Minuros.[20] But instead of negotiating the pacification of Lusitania, they were corrupted by Caepio, who promised them land and wealth in exchange for killing Viriathus. Thus, when they reached his camp, they entered his tent at night and killed him, fleeing immediately to the Roman general to announce that their plans had been successfully carried out and, of course, to claim their reward. It seems that they never received it, although we do not know their fate either. The Roman Senate disapproved of the treachery and denied Caepio the triumph he claimed. This ended the war of the Lusitanians. It is true that some of them continued to take up arms under the leadership of Tautalos, but he soon surrendered to Caepio's army and accepted the peace terms offered to him. In classical sources, Viriathus was regarded as the most capable leader of the Hispanians, showing respect and even admiration for his austere and generous nature and his military abilities, which brought him close to the ideal of a republican general, defining him as Romulus of Hispania or the Hannibal of the barbarians. For example, Frontinus in his *Strategemata*

---

20 Appian (*Ib. Wars*, 15, 74). Diodorus Siculus (33, 21), claims that their names were Audas, Ditalces and Nicorontes, and were relatives and friends of each other, from Urso, a Turdeani city.

mentions him on up to four occasions,[21] being one of the most frequently cited enemies of Rome in his book. Viriathus was the only Hispanian leader with the capacity and charisma to unite different Hispanian tribes and to be able to fight against the Romans for eight years, forcing them to send various consular armies, causing thousands of casualties. Hispania would not see another leader with his characteristics.

The Second Celtiberian War

While these events were taking place in H. Ulterior, in H. Citerior the Romans had to face the no less bloody Celtiberian Wars. It all began around 154 BC in the territory of the Celtiberian tribe of the Belli (today, in the central and southern areas of Aragon). Since the time of the peace treaties promoted by Sempronius Gracchus, the territory had remained fairly calm. But at that time, the Romans began to worry about the preponderance that the charismatic king of the Belli, Carus, was gaining among their neighbours.[22] The perfect excuse to start the war was the refurbishment of the walls of the Belli capital, Segeda (near Mara, Aragón). The Romans interpreted that the new walls were violating the terms of the peace treaty of 179 BC. The Segedians sent a delegation led by one of their nobles, Kakyros, who claimed that the peace treaty forbade them to found new cities, but the Romans did not accept this interpretation and declared war on them.[23] The reasons for the resumption of a new war in H. Citerior, especially when we consider the instability of H. Ulterior, are suggested by Richardson,[24] would be related to the will of the Roman Senate faction of the *nobilitas* who pressed for further wars, after the victories of Publius Cornelius Scipio Nasica Corculum[25] in Dalmatia (155 BC) and of Quintus Opimius in Liguria (154 BC). Thus, the consul who received the province that year was Quintus Fulvius Nobilior, a member of the influential *gens Fulvia*, strongly linked to Hispania, where, for example, we have already seen that his father had served as *praetor* in H. Citerior (193-192 BC), but other members of the *gens Fulvia* had also served, either as *praetores* or as military tribunes, in the conquest of Hispania. Therefore, in 153 BC,

---

21 Book 2, On Ambushes, 7 and On Retreating, 4. Book 3, On Setting Traps to Draw out the Besieged, 6; and On Pretended Retirements, 11.

22 García Riaza (2002), p. 63.

23 Diodorus Siculus, 33, 39: Ἡ δὲ ἔλυσε τὰς συνθήκας καὶ πόλεμον ἐπήνεγκεν.

24 García Riaza, op. cit., p. 66.

25 Son of Publius Cornelius Scipio Nasica, whom we have already seen as *praetor* in H. Ulterior in 196 BC.

the year the Roman calendar moved forward, Quintus Fulvius Nobilior arrived in H. Citerior with a consular army of 30,000 men, ready to exterminate the threat that the Celtiberian tribes of the Belli and its allies, the Titii might pose in the future. The appearance of the Roman contingent, with two legions (of about 5,000 men each), two Italic *alae* (totalling about 10,000 men) and auxiliary Iberian allies (estimated at another 10,000 men), alarmed the Belli, who had not yet finished building the new walls of Segeda. They moved on to the other great Celtiberian city of H. Citerior, Numantia, the capital of the Arevaci, who were initially unwilling to go to war with Rome, but the timely arrival of the Roman banners that the Lusitanian general Kaisaros had captured in H. Ulterior convinced the Arevaci to join the coalition against Rome. The first encounter between the two armies took place on 23 August and is known as the Battle of Vulcanalia.[26] That day, the Romans marched towards Numantia in their usual marching order: a vanguard composed of light cavalry units and a first contingent of Iberian allies; followed by the bulk of the Iberian allies, the Roman legions and, finally, the Italic allies, in a column that could have been seven miles long; the rest of the cavalry, together with the baggage train, took an alternative route. As the army passed through the vicinity of a ravine called Valdano (near of modern town of Soria, Castilla y Leon), they were surprised by the Celtiberian army under the command of Carus. The Roman vanguard was totally annihilated and the Celtiberians fell upon the second group, formed by the rest of the Iberian allies and the Roman legions. The fighting was fierce, but the terrain favoured the Celtiberians. Nobilior ordered the withdrawal of his men, who managed to retreat to a nearby hill, a manoeuvre that was made possible by the arrival of the cavalry that had been protecting the baggage train. In that fighting Carus was killed, which led the Celtiberians to retreat in the direction of Numantia. But the disaster for the Romans was complete. Appian acknowledges the death of more than '6,000 Roman citizens', i.e., legionaries. It is estimated that the total number of Roman dead must have been at least twice as high. The Celtiberians also lost many men, although it is impossible to quantify, but it is thought that there may have been around 4,000. But the most sensitive death was that of Carus, an energetic and charismatic leader, who Schulten claims, had he survived, could have been a match for the Romans on a par with Viriathus.[27]

26 Roman festival in honour of the god Vulcan, which was celebrated by lighting bonfires on which small live animals were thrown as a sacrifice in honour of the god of fire.

27 Schulten, op. cit., p. 12.

In any case, 23 August was declared by the Senate of Rome as *dies atri* (unlucky day), so that Roman generals were henceforth forbidden to engage in battle on that day. Nobilior reorganised his troops on the hill of Gran Atalaya, four miles east of Numantia. It was an exceptional place to build a camp, which allowed him to keep watch over the city, but also very close to the river Douro, through which he could receive food, weapons and, above all, reinforcements. And these did not take long to arrive. Masinissa sent 300 horsemen and 10 elephants from North Africa. Nobilior prepared to assault Numantia, which had chosen as its new leaders Ambon and Leucon, probably a Bellus and an Arevacus. It seems that the Celtiberians again asked Nobilior for an end to the war, but he proposed peace terms that were totally unacceptable, so they prepared for a new battle. This time, the two armies stood on the plain to the east of Numantia, i.e., the Romans fought with their camp on the Gran Atalaya behind them. At first, it seemed that the Romans were going to prevail, as the elephant charge caused the Celtiberians to flee to Numantia. The elephants and the rest of the army chased them and began to receive all kinds of projectiles from the city walls. As bad luck would have it (or good luck, depending on your perspective), a large stone hit the head of one of the elephants, which, frightened, turned around and began to charge the Roman troops. The rest of the elephants followed suit, creating great confusion among the legionaries. The Celtiberian troops took advantage of this moment to break out of the city and attack the Romans, whose formation had been broken. They lost more than 4,000 men and had to withdrawal to their camp at full speed. The rest of the year was a nightmare for the Romans. Every time they left their camp they were ambushed. On one occasion, Nobilior sent a detachment under his cavalry commander, Biesius, to negotiate some kind of alliance with cities around Numantia, but they were ambushed, and much of the detachment was wiped out, including Biesius himself. In addition, the city of Occilis (modern Medinaceli, Castilla y León), where the Romans kept much of their impedimenta, rebelled, switching to the Celtiberian side. Nobilior decided to attack the city of Uxxama (near modern Burgo de Osma, Castilla y León), in the territory of the Belli, but suffered another heavy defeat, losing most of his men. His last weeks were of real hardship. Constantly harassed by the Celtiberians, in one of the coldest regions of Hispania, his men began to drop like flies, victims of hypothermia, disease and ambushes. Nobilior must have been comforted when his *imperium* was over, and he returned to Rome.

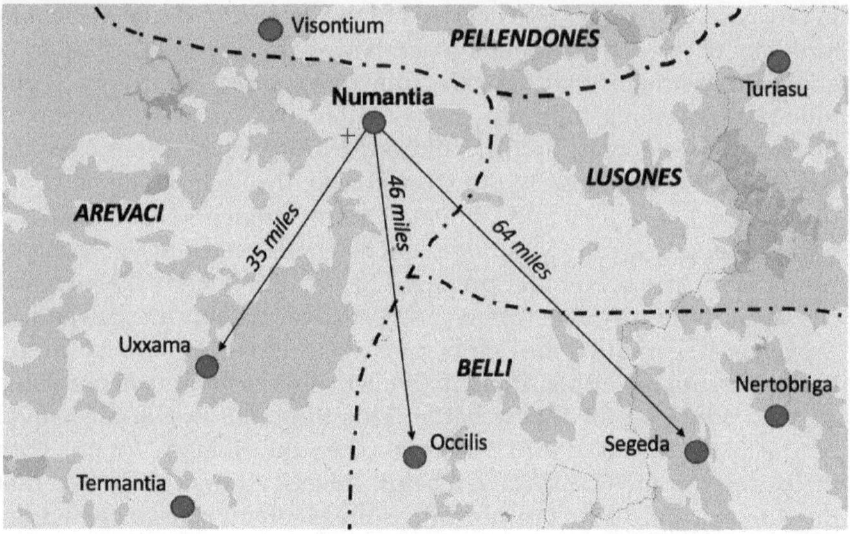

Map 7: Map of the main Celtiberian cities during the Second and Third Celtiberian Wars.

In 152 BC, Ulterior saw the arrival of a new consul, Marcus Claudius Marcellus. But this time, his political and military stature was much stronger than that of his outgoing colleague. He had experience in Hispania, where he had been *praetor* of the two provinces in the period 169–168 BC and was facing his third consulship, after defeating the Ligurians in his two previous terms (166 and 155 BC). Aware of the character of the Celtiberians, Claudius Marcellus began to use diplomacy to try to pacify the territory. He agreed generous pacts to the cities of Occilis and Nertobriga (near modern Calatorao, Aragon). These advantageous conditions soon attracted most of the cities in the area. However, this does not mean that Claudius Marcellus was not forced to fight, and he was victorious on most occasions. Near the end of his term of office, the Arevaci, Belli and Titii were willing to reach a peace agreement to end the war. The consul gave permission for a delegation to go to Rome to ratify the terms of the agreement proposed by Claudius Marcellus and accepted by the Celtiberians. It should be remembered that in the same year, Atilius Serranus, *praetor* of Ulterior, had also reached a peace agreement between the Lusitanians and the Vettones. Being the situation in Celtiberia under control, Claudius Marcellus spent the winter in Corduba, the city he himself had founded as *praetor*. When his *imperium* was over, he returned to Rome to learn that the Senate had not accepted the peace treaty and, consequently, that the war was continuing. This time it was to be carried out by one of the new consuls of 151 BC, Lucius Licinius Lucullus. The first problem the general encountered was that the Romans were reluctant to go to fight in Hispania, especially under his command, as he had a reputation for mistreating his soldiers. However, he was fortunate that Scipio Aemilianus, at that time the leader of the respected *gens Cornelia* and son-in-law of Sempronius Gracchus, a man of great charisma and influence despite being only 34 years old, encouraged the young Romans to accompany him to Hispania, where he himself would serve as military tribune to the controversial consul. When Lucullus' army arrived in Hispania, the situation in Celtiberia was still calm, a peace that, thanks to Marcellus, would be maintained until 143 BC. However, the consul began a campaign of plunder for his personal enrichment. His target was the territory of the Vaccaei, a peaceful people with fertile wheat fields. In this case, the *casus belli* used by Lucullus was that the Vaccaei had attacked the Carpetani, allies of the Romans. He therefore reached the gates of one of their main cities, Cauca (modern Coca, Castilla y Leon), where the Roman consul suspected that an enormous treasure was being kept, and began the siege work, when he was attacked by the Cauquensis. The initial surprise attack was successful for the Celts, but when they ran out of the spears with which they used to attack, they beat a retreat, at which point they were pursued and defeated by the Romans. The next morning, a delegation of Vaccaei left the city to sue for peace. At first, Lucullus seemed a judicious ruler and only demanded reasonable financial compensation and horsemen for their campaigns, to which the Vaccaei agreed. Later, he added the request to leave a Roman garrison inside the city. The Cauquensis, in goodwill, approved it. But following Lucullus' orders, once inside the city, the Roman garrison began to massacre the defenceless population. The rest of the Roman troops joined in the slaughter. Subsequently, Lucullus sacked the city and, as Appian said (*Ib. Wars*, 11, 52) brought infamy upon the Roman name. The few survivors who had been able to flee Cauca took refuge in the city of Intercatia, also a Veccaei city. Lucullus arrived there with his troops. Again, he offered a peace treaty, which the nobles of the town refused, knowing the precedent. Lucullus then ordered work to begin on the siege of the city. Then, a Celtic warrior rode out of the city on horseback challenging any Roman who wanted to fight a duel against him. According to the chronicles, the only one who dared to accept the challenge was Scipio Aemilianus. After a fierce fight, the young Roman ended up killing his opponent. Pliny the Elder (*Nat. Hist.*, 37, 9), explains that Scipio Aemilianus later gave the son of his dead opponent a ring with the image of the combat. But as the days went by, the Romans began to suffer from a lack of food, with some of the troops contracting dysentery. Lucullus did not have much time left, so he ordered an assault on the city. The Roman troops behaved with their usual ferocity. They managed to break down part of the wall and enter the city, but they could not make any further progress. The defence of the Vaccaei was fanatical and casualties on both sides began to be heavy. Finally, a ceasefire was declared, and the representatives of the city reached a peace agreement with Scipio Aemilianus, whom they held in high esteem. They agreed that the inhabitants of Intercatia would hand over to the Romans 10,000 cloaks, cattle and 50 hostages. Lucullus was only interested in gold and silver, but hardly any of these metals were kept in the city, so the Roman general settled for what he was given. From then on, the Roman soldiers would wear the typical black cloaks of the Vaccaei. He then headed for the city of Pallantia (modern Palencia, Castilla y Leon), where he had heard that there was a great deal of wealth, but his legionaries feared the reputation of its inhabitants as good warriors. Ignoring the complaints, Lucullus ordered a siege of the city. But the days passed. The supply problems continued, and, in addition, the Romans were constantly harassed from outside by Celtic cavalry, so Lucullus had no choice but to lift the siege and withdraw for the winter to Turdetania, an allied territory. There, together with *praetor* Galba, he fought the Lusitanians with extreme cruelty. On his return to Rome, the Senate reproached him for the campaign against the Vaccaei, which had been carried out without their consent. However, he suffered no punishment for disobeying the Senate or for the indiscriminate massacre at Cauca.

Numantia and the Third Celtiberian War

> *Numantia quantum Carthaginis, Capuae, Corinthi opibus inferior, ita virtutis nomine et honore per omnibus, summumque, si viro aestimes, Hispaniae decus. Quippe quae sine muro, sine turribus, modice edito in tumulo apud flumen sita, quattuor milibus Celtiberorum quadraginta exercitum per annos undecim sola sustinuit, nec sustinuit modo, sed saevius aliquando perculit pudendisque foederibus adfecit. Novissime, cum invictam esse constaret, opus fuit eo qui Carthaginem everterat.*[28]

28 'Numantia, however inferior in wealth to Carthage, Capua and Corinth, in respect of valour and distinction was the equal of any of them, and, if one judges it aright, was the greatest glory of Spain. This city, without any walls or fortifications and situated on only a slight eminence on the banks of a stream, with a garrison of 4,000 Celtiberians, held out alone against an army of 40,000 men for eleven years, and not only held out but repulsed its foes with considerable vigour on several occasions and drove them to make discreditable terms. Finally, when they found that the city was undefeated, they were forced to call in the general who had overthrown Carthage.' Lucius Annaeus Florus, *The Epitome of Roman History*, 33, 18, 1.

If we follow Appian (*Ib. Wars.*, 15, 66), in 143 BC, Viriathus encouraged the Arevaci, Belli and Titii to take up arms against the Romans again. The Lusitanian victories encouraged the Celtiberian peoples to revolt, and they took up arms again. That year, the consul who received H. Citerior as a province was Quintus Caecilius Metellus Macedonicus. His command was extended for another year, in 142 BC, as proconsul. He was a general of great prestige, who had won several campaigns in Greece. Rome was confident that a military man of his stature, with a consular army of 30,000 men, would be more than enough to crush those barbaric Celtiberian tribes. They were wrong. Nevertheless, his first campaigns were successful. Going up the river Ebro, Caecilius Metellus entered the Jalon valley, practising a subtle policy of warfare and diplomacy, with which he managed to pacify a series of large cities in the territories of northern Celtiberia. The first major battle he had to face was at the city of Centobriga, where resistance was fierce. When the Romans were about to demolish one of the walls, the Celtiberians placed the sons of a king named Retogenes, an ally of the Romans, on it. Retogenes asked Metellus to continue the battle, but the Roman general ordered the attack to stop. He was not going to conquer the city by paying such a price. With that gesture, Metellus gained the trust of many towns and cities in Celtiberia, as well as the eternal gratitude of Retogenes (Valerius Maximus, *Fact. Dict.*, 5, 1, 5). The next city he had to conquer by force was Nertobriga (Florus, *Epitome*, 33, 17, 10), and finally Contrebia Leukade, where he ordered five cohorts who had wanted to desert to lead the assault. The victory over the city brought them the pardon of their general. Caecilius Metellus' next campaign targeted the country of the Vaccaei, at that time allies of the Arevaci, since their lush cultivated fields fed the inhabitants of Numantia with wheat and other foodstuffs. That campaign was a success, but it was slower than expected, so that by the time it was over, his *imperium* was almost at an end, and he had to retire to his winter quarters. As we have seen above, the consul in charge of the province of H. Citerior was Quintus Pompeius Aulus. With his consular army, he immediately set out for Numantia, building a camp on the Castillejo hill, north of the city. There he stayed for a few months, trying unsuccessfully to prepare for the assault. However, constant sorties by the defenders repeatedly wrecked the siege works. Meanwhile, from the outside, the Numantines' allies relentlessly harassed the Romans who thought of leaving their camp to fetch firewood or food. Finally, Pompeius realised that he was wearing out his army in fruitless skirmishes and decided to abandon the siege of Numantia. His new target was the city of Termantia, the second most important of the Arevaci. But the attempted conquest was another disaster. Pompeius then decided to attack a small town, Lagni[29] (Diodorus Siculus, 33, 17), which had a garrison of about 400 Numantine soldiers. When Pompeius arrived, the nobles of Lagni asked to surrender, to which the Roman consul only agreed if they themselves killed the Numantine garrison. When the citizens of Lagni attacked the Numantines, a battle broke out inside the walls, which Pompeius took advantage of to storm the city, killing or enslaving all its inhabitants. Curiously, Diodorus reports that he only showed a certain generosity to the 200 surviving Numantines, letting them go to their city, perhaps in the hope of ingratiating himself with the Arevaci. He then heard that a guerrilla leader named Tanginus was plundering the territory in Sedetania. Pompeius managed to capture his men (we know the story from Appian, but he does not detail Tanginus' fate). But they did not resign themselves to being sold into slavery and began to commit mass suicide or attack their captors. Finally, the Romans were able to reduce them and, tied up, they were transferred to a ship, which would take them to Rome. But during the journey, they mutinied and sank the ships, all drowning. Pompeius then returned to Numantia. But once again, skirmishes and ambushes resulted in heavy casualties for the Romans. In one of these attacks, Appian recounts the death of a military tribune named Oppius, plausibly the Occius Achilles who had fought a duel with Pyresus. But it was not only war that decimated the consul's troops: confined to their camp, they only dared to go out for the most essential activities, so that soon malnutrition, disease and cold were killing Pompeius' army. Finally, the consul asked the Numantines to negotiate peace. The Roman consul's real intention was probably to be able to leave the territory in safety, rather than to sign a lasting peace with the Numantines. It was not necessary to have completed the *cursus honorum* to know that the Senate would never accept such a shameful peace and that, at that stage of the war, it would only accept an unconditional capitulation of the Arevaci or their annihilation. Quintus Pompeius Aulus is generally regarded as one of the worst generals of the Celtiberian Wars.

The year 139 BC saw the arrival of a new consul, Marcus Popillius Laenas. When he planted his army before Numantia, its inhabitants demanded that he respect the peace agreement signed by the previous consul. Prudently, Popillius allowed a Numantine delegation to travel

29 According to García Riaza (op. cit., p. 124) it could be the same city that Appian (16, 77) calls Malia. On the other hand, other authors, such as Jimeno Martínez (2011, pp. 232 and 234) interpret that they were two different cities. In any case, whether they were one city or two, both were destroyed, and it has not been possible to determine where exactly they were located.

to Rome to discuss the matter in the Senate. In the meantime, the new consul went to Hispania Ulterior to fight the Lusitanians. With little success, as we have seen above. In Rome, the Numantine diplomatic delegation was not well received. They were not allowed to reside within Rome and, once in the Senate, they were denied the legality of the agreement reached with Pompeius. The war was to continue. During the second year of his *imperium* in H. Citerior, Popillius devastated the territory of the Vaccaei, but was unable to get close to Numantia. However, the most disastrous consulship was that of Gaius Hostilius Mancinus, elected in 137 BC. A strange choice, given that he was a man with no military experience and little ability. Hostilius arrived in the vicinity of Numantia with few reinforcements, but he had the veteran army that had been fighting in the territory for the past four years. In any case, their situation was far from optimal. The troops were tired, very demoralised and with a very low level of discipline. In his first weeks in the territory, Hostilius locked himself and his men in the camp on the hill of Castillejos, north of Numantia, trying to bring order to the chaos he found. In the meantime, the Numantines were busy harassing the Romans every time they left the camp. The Romans became increasingly discouraged and Hostilius proved unable to reverse the situation. To make matters worse, rumour had it that an army of Vaccaei and Cantabrians was about to arrive in Numantia. This was too much for the panic-stricken troops, who demanded that Hostilius withdraw to a safer place. Hostilius organised the escape. His plan was to march by night to the other Roman camp on the mountain called the Gran Atalaya, and from there to march eastwards. In the morning, however, they were surrounded by an army of Celtiberians. The Romans would have been massacred, except that one of Hostilius' *quaestores* was Tiberius Sempronius Gracchus, son of the eponymous *praetor* who in 179 BC had ended the First Celtiberian War with a peace treaty. Few people could boast a more Roman pedigree than this brave young soldier. If his father had been an excellent politician and military man, his mother, Cornelia Minor, was none other than a daughter of Scipio Africanus. Sempronius Gracchus had already distinguished himself in the Third Punic War, under the command of Scipio Aemilianus, his cousin by adoption as well as brother-in-law. Later, he would go down in history for his attempt to carry out an agrarian reform that pitted him against the aristocratic factions of the Senate which, in 133 BC, organised a revolt in Rome that ended his life and that of hundreds of his followers, a revolt led by Scipio Nasica Serapius, also a cousin of Sempronius Gracchus.[30] His brother-in-law,

30 Nasica Serapius's mother was Cornelia Maior.

Scipio Aemilianus, who, as we shall see, was in Hispania, justified the assassination of Gracchus, since it was against his personal interests and those of his aristocratic class.[31] Let us return to 137 BC, on a cliff near the Gran Atalaya Mountain. There, the name Sempronius Gracchus still maintained prestige and trust among the Celtiberians. Nevertheless, the *quaestor*'s proposal (one might say, plea) had its effect. Moreover, he personally established a *hospitium* bond with the city's rulers. The Romans surrendered their arms and Hostilius named Numantia a city *foedus* of the Romans, which meant that the Arevaci city became part of Rome's allies. This surrender shocked Rome. It was inexplicable that a city with only 4,000 warriors should have held out for so many years against three consular armies. It was shameful, humiliating. As was the pact Hostilius had signed. The Senate was quick to declare it unacceptable. Be that as it may, the continued violations of peace treaties by the Romans scandalised later Latin authors, as Orosius (4, 5).

Later in 137 BC, it seems that Tiberius Sempronius Gracchus returned to Numantia with the aim of retrieving personal documentation that the Arevaci had kept as booty, after the attempted battle on the hill of Gran Atalaya. Honouring the *hospitium*, the Roman was received amicably in the city. A banquet was held, gifts were exchanged, and Gracchus recouped his documents. The next visit was not so friendly. It was Hostilius Mancinus' fellow consul, Marcus Aemilius Lepidus Porcina, who harassed the territory of the Vaccaei. To do so, he asked for help from the *praetor* of H. Ulterior, Decimus Junius Brutus, his brother-in-law. They attacked Pallantia, but the siege was a disaster and they had to withdraw. That action was condemned by the Senate for being carried out without their permission. In 136 BC, a new consul arrived, Lucius Furius Philus, a man from the Scipio circle, and a close friend of Scipio Aemilianus. He was responsible for carrying out the punishment to which Hostilius Mancinus was condemned by the Senate. The former consul was handed over to the Numantines: alone, unarmed, chained, dressed in a simple tunic, and abandoned at the gates of the city of Arevaci. But the Numantines simply ignored him and gave him permission to return to Rome. In 135 BC, the new consul was Quintus Calpurnius Piso, who did not dare to attack Numantia either and limited himself to devastating the Vaccaei camps. But as

31 The mysterious deaths of Scipio Nasica Serapius (132 BC) and Scipio Aemilianus (in 129 BC) were the result of a conspiracy by followers of Tiberius Sempronius Gracchus. In fact, the death of Scipio Aemilianus was blamed directly on his wife, Sempronia, and his mother-in-law, Cornelia Minor. But that is another story.

soon as he thought it decorous, he left Celtiberia to winter on the Mediterranean coast.

But the people of Rome had had enough of this war, plagued by humiliating defeats and inept generals. They demanded that the Senate send the best man of his generation: Publius Cornelius Scipio Aemilianus Africanus Minor. He was the biological son of Lucius Aemilius Paullus Macedonicus, victor of the Third Macedonian War; and adopted by Publius Cornelius Scipio, the eldest son of Scipio Africanus. As we have seen above, he was married to his cousin Sempronia. He was a judicious and intelligent man, as he had shown in his days as a military tribune in Hispania, under the command of the infamous Licinius Lucullus. His first great moment of glory, however, was during the Third Punic War, when he not only defeated but also razed the once-proud Carthage to the ground. However, Scipio Aemilianus had powerful enemies in the Senate who prevented him from recruiting new legions. He had to make do with the troops stationed in Hispania and with those he could recruit himself. He then began an intense campaign to raise funds, arms, and soldiers. Numerous eastern kings provided him with the necessary funding. The king of Numidia, Micipsa, sent twelve elephants and a contingent of soldiers under the command of his nephew, Jugurtha (Appian, *Ib. Wars*, 89; and Sallust, *Jug*. 1, 7-8), a man who in a few years' time would make Rome tremble. Jugurtha, in Hispania, would learn to fight like the Romans and, above all, he would learn how to fight them, taking as an example those Celtiberians who, with a clear numerical and technological inferiority, had been defying Rome for many years. Finally, Scipio Aemilianus recruited from among his clients and friends what was called the *Cohors Amicorum* (Cohort of Friends). Half of his army was placed under the command of his elder brother, Quintus Fabius Maximus Aemilianus, who already had plenty of experience in Hispania, and was the person Scipio Aemilianus trusted and loved the most. His nephew, Quintus Fabius Maximus Allobrogicus (a nickname he earned for his victory over the Allobroges tribe in Transalpine Gallia in 120 BC), was also *praetor* and *propraetor* in Hispania (124 and 123 BC), a period in which he was accused of corruption by Gaius Sempronius Gracchus, who was also part of the *Cohors Amicorum*, as Scipio Aemilianus knew that it never hurt to take a member of the Gracchus family to Celtiberia. In the future, Gaius would be the Tribune of the Plebs who would continue the agrarian reforms of his brother Tiberius, and who would also come to a tragic end. Evidently, he was also joined by friends of his who were part of his intellectual circle such as Gaius Lucilius, the first

Roman writer of satires, and the historians Publius Rutilius Rufus,[32] Sempronius Asellius, of whose works only fragments remain, and, of course, the great Polybius, who was also an expert in poliorcetic. But young men eager to make a career in the Roman army also enlisted, such as Gaius Marius, destined to change the history of Rome in the future. Seven times consul, the great reformer of the army and victor, among others, of the war against his now comrade-in-arms Jugurtha. Plutarch tells us how Marius soon came to the attention of his superiors for his bravery on the battlefield (*Marius*, 2). We cannot fail to mention an anecdote which Plutarch relates about Marius, when he explains that at a dinner which Scipio Aemilius gave to officers of his trusted circle, one of them asked him where the Roman people would find any such chieftain and leader to follow him, Scipio, gently tapping Marius on the shoulder as he reclined next to him, said: 'Here, perhaps.' (Plutarch, *Marius*, 3). As we can see, and if you allow me the sporting metaphor, Scipio Aemilianus took to Numantia a veritable 'Dream Team', which, at its peak, numbered over 60,000 men against the 4,000 Numantine warriors. On his arrival in Hispania, he found the bulk of his troops in Tarraco. His first mission was to re-establish discipline, from which we deduce that Mancinus had not succeeded. To this end, he expelled merchants, prostitutes, quacks, and charlatans from the barracks and imposed an austere and martial lifestyle on his entire army. Then, somewhere in the Ebro valley, he trained his troops in siege work. It seems that he had already planned to reduce Numantia by starvation, instead of taking it by assault. When he thought they were ready, they headed for Arevaci territory. But instead of taking the direct route, they first passed through the territory of the Vaccaei. To prevent the latter from helping the Numantines, he attacked them, taking all the wheat he could gather (meaning he must have arrived to Hispania in July 134 BC), burning the rest. In one of the typical expeditious actions of the Roman general. Finally, as winter approached, he reached Numantia. He immediately began the work of encircling the city. Dividing the troops in two camps: one to the north, at Castillejo hill, under the direct command of Scipio Aemilius; and another to the south, at Peña Redonda hill, under the command of his brother, Maximus Aemilianus; and seven forts: Travesadas, Valdevorrón, Molino, Dehesilla, Peña Julia, Alto del Real and Vega. Between these buildings, he built an impassable wall for the Numantines, on which he placed as many catapults and *ballistae* as possible. Another problem he had to face was

32 His sister Rutilia was the grandmother of Julius Caesar.

to prevent the Numantines from receiving outside help across the river Douro. To this end, he built two small parallel fortifications on either side of the river, between which he placed a series of beams on which he hung cutting weapons to prevent anything from crossing the river without the permission of Scipio.[33]

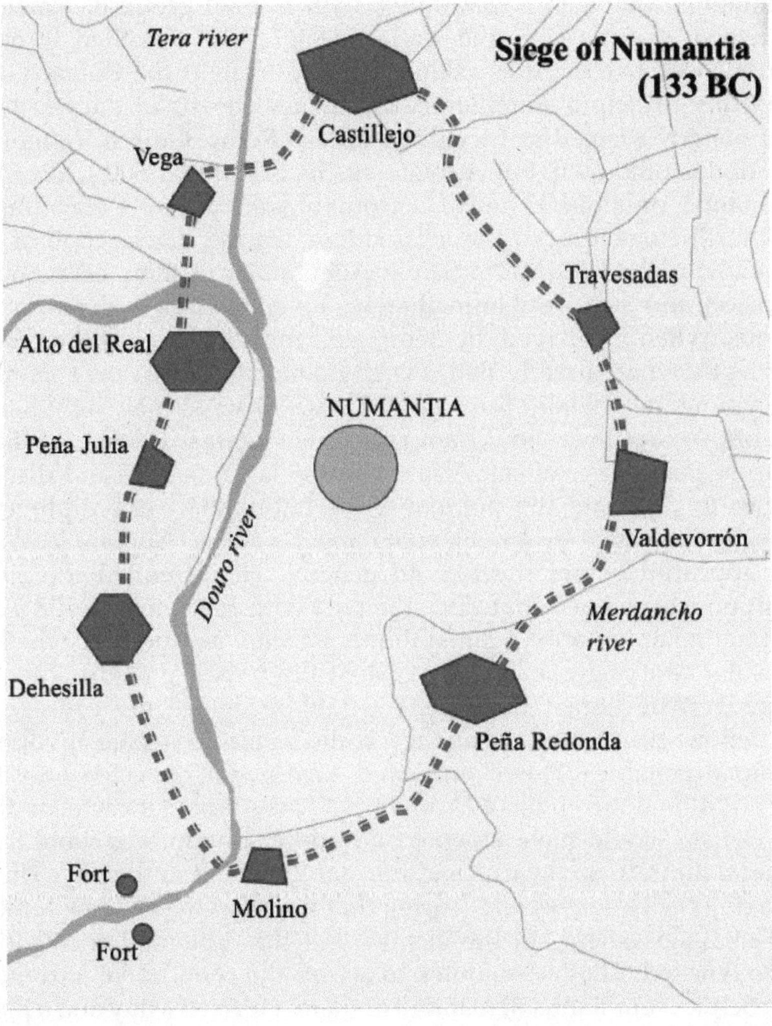

Map 8: Map of Roman camps and fortifications during the siege of Numantia (133 BC).

33 Morillo & Morales (2016).

While all this work was going on, the Numantines did not stand idly by and watch. They made several sorties to attack the Romans, but Scipio Aemilianus had set up an effective communication system which meant that contingents of legionaries moved at full speed to the point under attack. Everything went just as the consul had planned. What he could not prevent was that one of the nobles of Numantia, Rhetogenes Caraunius, with a small group of warriors, managed to jump over the wall one night and travelled through various Celtiberian cities asking for help to fight the Romans. But the army of Scipio Aemilianus caused real terror in the territory, and nobody seemed to be willing to face Rome. Only in Lutia (the location is unknown, but Appian tells us that it was 300 *stadia* from Numantia, or about 35 miles), a group of warriors were encouraged to join Rhetogenes. But the local elders, fearing the reaction of the Romans, rushed to inform Scipio Aemilianus of their neighbours' decision, and the consul immediately moved to Lutia with part of his troops. When he arrived, he demanded the surrender of the rebels, but as they had already fled, the city council handed over another 400 young men, whom Scipio Aemilianus ordered their right hands cut off, so that they would not raise them against Rome. The siege soon began to take effect. A few months later, famine and disease began to decimate the population of Numantia, so a diplomatic delegation headed by a nobleman named Avarus (Appian, *Ib. Wars*, 95) appeared before the Roman general. He defended the city's position. He claimed that since the pact with Mancinus in 137 BC it had not taken up arms against Rome, which was true, since the last consular campaigns had been against the territory of the Vaccaei. Moreover, he hoped that Rome would recognise the courage of his fellow citizens and that they could come to a pact involving minimal penalties. However, Scipio Aemilianus expected only the unconditional surrender of Numantia. At this stage of the war, neither the Senate would have accepted any other option, nor would the general himself. So Avarus and his men returned to the city. There, bringing the bad news and fearing that they had made some kind of personal agreement, all the members of the diplomatic delegation were lynched. They were quick to accept the conditional surrender that Scipio Aemilianus demanded of them. He fixed a day and a place for the Numantines to lay down their arms, and later gave them a reasonable time to allow those who wished to take their own lives to carry out their final task. According to Valerius Maximus, the last to commit suicide was Rhetogenes Caraunius (*Fact.*, 2, 7). The next day, the last survivors left the city. They must have looked ghostly, pathetic. Apparently, during the last few weeks there was nothing left to eat, and they even ate skins, hides and, it is believed, human flesh. Schulten[34] states that there must have been about a hundred of them, of whom Scipio Aemilianus chose fifty to accompany him at the triumph held in Rome the following year. As for Numantia, the inhabitants who had decided to commit suicide set numerous fires inside the city, either to perish in them or to prevent the Romans from appropriating their wealth. And what the fire did not destroy, it was Scipio Aemilianus who ordered to raze the city to the ground, as he had done to Carthage 13 years earlier. Its territory was divided among the tribes allied with Rome and Scipio Aemilianus was given the nickname *Numantinus*. The capital of the Arevaci had ceased to exist, but its name had become a legend.

New Explorations and Conquests

Despite the costly victories against the Lusitanians and Celtiberians, the wars in Hispania continued. In fact, while H. Citerior was entering the final phase of the war against Numantia, H. Ulterior was not exactly idle. In 137 BC, the consul in charge of the southern territory of the peninsula was Decimus Junius Brutus. His mission was to suppress the incursions that, once again, some groups of Lusitanian warriors were carrying out against territories controlled by Rome. In addition, he also intended to conquer or at least explore the territories to the north of the river Douro. This region had already suffered a Roman incursion during the administration of his predecessor Caepio, who had devastated the fields of the Vettones during his campaign in which he pursued Viriathus, as Appian tells us (*Ib. Wars*, 70). Thus, the first thing Junius Brutus[35] did was to pursue the Lusitanian war bands and, as they were extremely elusive, he went to their cities to offer them peace (in exchange for a tax) or their destruction. Once through Lusitania, it reached the territory of its western neighbours, the Turduli Oppidani, on what would correspond today to the central coast of Portugal. In the past, this Celtic tribe is believed to have had some kind of alliance with the Carthaginians. After the Second Punic War, it probably passed into the orbit of the Lusitanians until the assassination of Viriathus, or at least until the arrival of

34 Schulten, op. cit., p. 86.

35 San Vicente (2004) writes a very interesting study of this expedition, especially about the problems of dating in Appian's account.

Junius Brutus, who was the first Roman to set foot in that land. In any case, it seems that the Turduli Oppidani were not nearly as warlike as their Lusitanian neighbours and did not hesitate to ally themselves with the Romans, who fortified several of their cities, such as Olissipo (modern Lisbon), Conímbriga (near modern Coimbra) or Viseu. Later, Junius Brutus crossed the river Douro, which the Romans called Durius, and entered the territory of the Bracari, one of the branches of the Callaeci (or Gallician), the Celtic tribe that dominated the north-west of the Iberian Peninsula. This was a warlike people. Appian (*Ib. Wars*, 72) tells us that even the women were fierce warriors and that if they were taken prisoner, they did not hesitate to kill their own children and commit suicide. It seems that the fighting in this region was fierce, but the Romans continued northwards. Then they came to the river Liamia, which the Romans called Limaeas, which their terrified soldiers did not dare to cross. They were convinced that it was the river Lethe, according to Roman mythology, a river of Hades also known as Oblivion: whoever crossed it forgot everything. To prove his men wrong, Junius Brutus crossed it with a banner and, from the other side, began to call his officers by name, ordering them to cross. As the soldiers saw that their general had not lost his memory, they all crossed it. The Roman troops continued advancing and fighting until they reached the river Minho, known as Nimis by the Romans. But there, they had to stop. The Romans watched as the sun set over the horizon and the ocean seemed to swallow it up (Florus, 33, 17). That was too much for his exhausted soldiers, so Junius Brutus, satisfied with the territory he had explored, returned south. Moreover, news reached him that some cities had revolted against Rome, as was the case of Talabriga (modern Talavera de la Reina, Castilla la Mancha), which the Roman general ordered to be besieged (Appian, *Ib. Wars*, 73). He demanded the immediate surrender of its citizens and the handing over of Roman prisoners and deserters. The Bracari were quick to obey Junius Brutus, thus saving their lives, but not their wealth. Orosius (5, 5, 12) also mentions that he was attacked by an army of 60,000 Callaeci, of whom he killed 50,000 and captured 6,000, the rest managing to flee. No doubt this is an exaggeration, but what is certain is that the fighting in this area was constant and, it seems, usually victorious. Later, on his way back to Rome, he founded for his veterans the city of Valentia Edetanorum (modern Valencia), known as the 'City of the Brave'. His arrival in Rome was an apotheosis, receiving the honours of a triumph and, in addition, a new nickname for having explored a new territory for Rome. From then on, he would be known as Decimus Junius Brutus Callaicus.

The following years were relatively quiet in Roman-controlled Hispania. It was probably a period of economic prosperity. It is likely that the Romans introduced new agricultural techniques and improved infrastructure, but, above all, the allied pre-Roman societies were provided with arable land and a certain degree of sovereignty, so they no longer had any reason to revolt. Moreover, the arrival of Italic settlers and the discharged soldiers (legionaries or auxiliary troops) who stayed in the territory helped to accelerate the process of Romanisation. But Rome had a new military objective: the Balearic Islands, also known as Gymnasiae. Although on a map they may look like a single archipelago, they are two: the Balearic Islands or Gymnasiae, whose most important islands are Maiorca (modern Majorca) and Minorca (modern Menorca); and the Pityussae, whose main islands are Ebusus (modern Ibiza) and Orpheus (modern Formentera).[36] Both archipelagos showed numerous differences, both natural (geological, fauna and flora) and social. As for the latter, the Balearic Islanders came from the Talaiotic culture, while the Pitiusans were Punic, either by origin or by cultural contact, and continued with their way of life even though their metropolis had been destroyed two decades earlier. In 123 BC, one of the consuls chosen was Quintus Caecilius Metellus, who was given the province of H. Citerior, but with the aim of conquering the Balearic Islands. Classical sources are very sparse on details of this campaign,[37] which they justify by the presence of pirates. However, contemporary critical studies[38] provide other possible causes, such as, for example, the control of these archipelagos in order to be able to carry out the trade route by sea between Carthago Nova and Rome, but also to take advantage of their rich natural resources (fruitful salt mines), as Strabo reveals, διὰ δὲ τὴν ἀρετὴν τῶν τόπων καὶ οἱ κατοικοῦντες διὰ τόπων εἰρηναῖοι;[39] not to mention that they could recruit the esteemed Balearic slingers, whom we have already seen fighting so many times on the Carthaginian side. As for the campaign, neither the classical sources detail it, nor has archaeology been able to discover

36 If we follow Strabo (III, 5, 1).

37 Strabo, *Geo.*, 3, 5, 1; Florus, *B. Balearicum* 1, 43; Orosius, 5, 13, 1.

38 For instance, Orfila (2008).

39 'The fertility of these places inclines the inhabitants to peace'. Strabo. *Geo.*, 1, 5, 1.

it. We only know that they limited themselves to attacking the islands of Maiorca and Minorca, where, according to Orosius, they caused thousands of deaths. Although given the length of the campaign, two years, it cannot have been an easy conquest. It was sufficiently successful for Quintus Caecilius Metellus to receive the nickname 'Balearicus'. The archipelago became part of H. Citerior and, in addition, the consul founded two cities, Palma (modern Palma) and Pollentia (modern Pollença), which were inhabited by settlers from Italy, specifically from the Velina tribe of the Picenus region.[40] Curiously, Caecilius Metellus did not attack Ebusus, even though it was a Punic island. Apparently, they reached some kind of peace agreement, so the gradual Romanisation of the territory must have been carried out by non-violent means. An event to note is that in 121 BC, the consul Quintus Fabius Maximus (son of Quintus Fabius Maximus Aemilianus), pacified (conquered) the territory of Gallia Transalpina, earning him the nickname Allobrogicus, for his victory over the Allobroges and the Arverni tribes. This victory allowed the Italic and Iberian peninsulas to be connected by land, thus establishing the trade routes that would allow the fast (and safe) extraction of wealth from Hispania to Rome.

At the end of the 2nd century BC, Rome was in crisis. A crisis that had both an internal and an external nature, but which, as we shall see, were linked. It was caused by the large amounts of money flowing into Rome, which stimulated the greed of many of its political leaders. Social inequalities were causing unrest among the Roman lower classes. Therefore, it was only a matter of time before the first social outbreak occurred. It was on the island of Sicily that the first great slave revolt known as the First Servile War (135–132 BC) took place. And although there were desperate attempts at reforms that would lead to a more equitable distribution of land (and wealth), these usually failed. We mentioned above how the law pushed by Tiberius Sempronius Gracchus led to the death of him and hundreds of his followers. In 121 BC it was his younger brother, Gaius, who tried to carry out his reform. But to do so, he and his ally, Marcus Fulvius Flaccus, had to be elected Tribunes of the Plebs for a third time, which was not permitted by law. This provoked serious riots in Rome, which resulted in Gracchus and Flaccus being killed, along with their followers. According to Orosius

40 Pena (2004). It should be noted that for this reason, other historians claim that the foundation of these cities took place after the end of the *Bellum Sertorianum* and that they were founded by Pompey precisely with colonists from his native region, Picenus, who were part of his clientele.

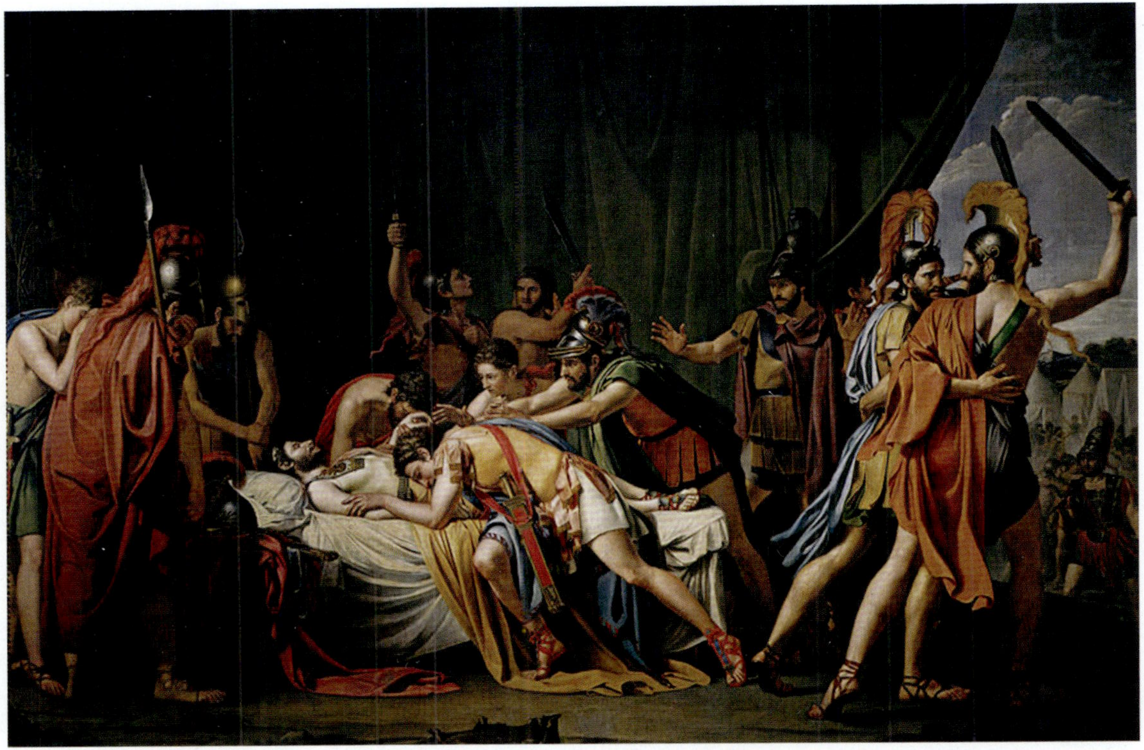

The Death of Viriathus, Chief of the Lusitanians, by José de Madrazo y Agudo. 1807. Oil on canvas. Museo del Prado, Madrid.

The siege of a town by Metellus, by Armand-Charles Caraffe. 1805. Oil on canvas. Ermitage, Saint Petersburg. It represents the siege of Centrobriga by Roman troops under the command of Quintus Caecilius Metellus Macedonicus at the beginning of the Third Celtiberian War.

Numantia's Last Day, by Alejo Vera y Estaca. 1881. Oil on canvas. Diputación Provincial de Soria, Soria.

Minerva and Sertorius, by Juan Andrés Merklein. 1768. Oil on canvas. Museo de Huesca, Huesca. © Gobierno de Aragón

In the Museum of Cádiz we can see two examples of Phoenician sarcophagi: the one on the left, of male anthropoid form; and the one on the right, of female form. Both follow the typical aesthetic model of Sidon, which shows that, after the fall of Tyre, a strong Phoenician influence was maintained on the southern coast of Iberia. (Author's collection).

The Lady of Elche (or Lady of Elx). It is an Iberian artifact which is believed could represent the goddess Tanit, worshiped by the Punic-Iberians. It is held in the Museo Arqueológico Nacional (MAN), Madrid. (Author's collection).

The Lady of Baza is a sculpture found at the site of Basti (modern Baza, Andalusia), with a height of 4.5ft. The archaeological studies have concluded that have formed part of the burial of a priestess-queen of the Iberian tribe of the Bastetani. It is held in Museo Arqueológico Nacional (MAN), Madrid. (Author's collection).

The Roman Villa of Noheda, in Castilla-La Mancha, has the largest collection of mosaics in all of Iberia. Among them, the one known as *Music and pantomime* stands out, which shows a group of musicians and actors together with a *hydraulis*, a Roman hydraulic organ. The rest of the mosaics can be seen at www.cultura.castillalamancha.es. © Viceconsejería de Cultura y Deportes-JCCM-.

Mosaic depicting the Sacrifice of Iphigenia, based on Euripides' tragedy *Iphigenia in Aulis*. Circa 1st century BC. Archaeology Museum of Catalonia, Empúries. (Author's collection).

Mosaic found in the Roman Villa La Olmeda (near modern Pedrosa de la Vega, Castilla y León). It is a lavish rural villa, with a palatial air, which has thirty-five rooms and twenty-six toilets and an extraordinary number of mosaics, from the Late Empire era. It shows incredible luxury and amenities for the time, such as a sophisticated heating system. © Diputación Provincial de Palencia.

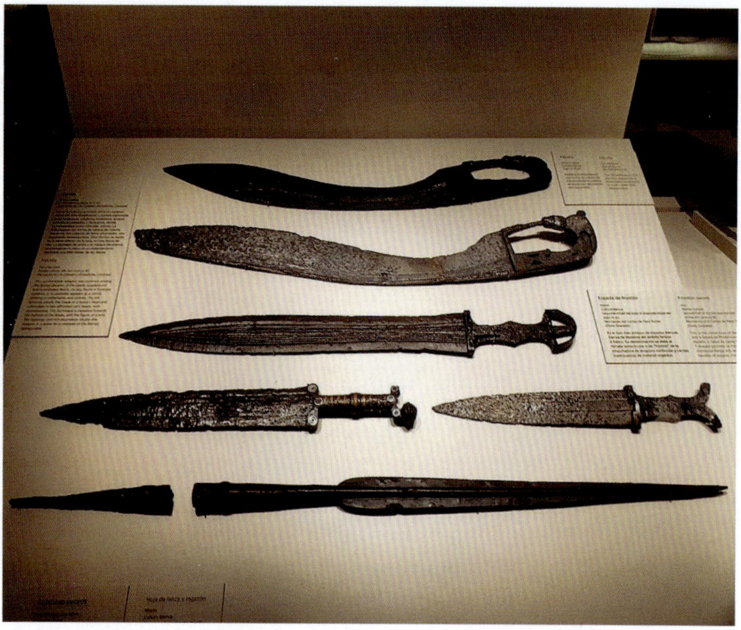

Collection of swords, falcatas, daggers and a spearhead from Iberian societies held in the Museo Arqueológico Nacional (MAN), Madrid. (Author's collection).

The Toixoneres Citadel, located in Calafell, Catalonia, was inhabited by the Cossetani. It is believed to have been devastated during the campaign of Cato the Elder. Currently, on the foundations of the old settlement, the Citadel has been reproduced, being a unique case in Spain. © Ajuntament de Calafell / Gabriel Mestre.

Runes of Emporion. This city of Greek origin (its name literally means 'trading place') was the point through which the Romans entered the Iberian Peninsula in 218 BC. (Author's collection).

Aquis Querquennis. Roman fort in Ourense Province, Galicia. It was constructed circa AD 69–79 and abandoned around AD 120. It housed the Legio VII Gemina. Picture provided by Turismo de Galicia. © Turismo de Galicia.

About 60 miles south of Cadiz lie the ruins of the ancient city of Baelo Claudia. It had its origins in an ancient Bastuli-Punic settlement that achieved great prosperity. Its decline was triggered by a tsunami at the end of the 2nd century. The city was finally abandoned in the 7th century. © Yolanda León.

The Aqueduct of Segovia was built around the 1st century AD and it carried water to the city until 1973. In 1985, it was declared a UNESCO World Heritage Site. It is the most popular aqueduct in Spain, due to its location in the middle of the city. Similar infrastructure can also be found in relatively good condition in Tarragona and Mérida. (c) Empresa Municipal de Turismo de Segovia.

The Amphitheatre of Tarragona. It was built in the 1st century AD. When Christianity became official in the Empire, the building fell into disuse. During the Visigoth period, a basilica was built in the centre to commemorate the martyrdom of the city's bishop, Fructuous. Subsequently, this central building underwent several alterations and became a convent and even a prison. It was abandoned at the beginning of the 20th century.

The construction of the Roman Theatre of Mérida was promoted by Agrippa in AD 15, later being reformed under the orders of emperors Trajan and Constantine I. It was declared an UNESCO World Heritage Site in 1993 and it is also considered one of the twelve Treasures of Spain. © Consorcio Ciudad Monumental de Mérida.

The Roman Circus of Merida. Built in the early 1st century AD, and measuring 481yd in length and 125yd of width, it was one of the most important in the entire Roman Empire. © Jesús Rueda/Consorcio Ciudad Monumental de Mérida.

1. Example of a pre-Roman coin from the mint of Kese, Unity, c. 250–220 BC. 2. Emporion, Drachma, 250–218 BC. 3. Augustus, Denarius, 25–23 BC, from the mint of Emerita Augusta, this coin is remarkable for the reverse, where you can appreciate the trophies captured from the enemy such as helmets, shields, and weapons, probably Astur-Cantabrian. 4. Trajan, Dupondius, AD 103–111. Coins preserved in the Fund of the Numismatic Cabinet of Catalonia. © Museu Nacional d'Art de Catalunya, Barcelona (2023).

The Roman conquest of Iberia has continued to inspire contemporary artists, as we can see in *Decimus Junius Brutus near river Lima* (1957), by Jose de Almada Negreiros. We can find the drawing at Fabrica de Tapetes de Portoalegre (Portugal), while the tapestry is exhibited at Pousada Monte de Santa Luzia at Viana do Castelo (Portugal). (Author's collection)

One of the best-preserved Roman statues in Hispania is to be found in the Archaeological Museum of Empúries (Girona). It is of the famous Aesculapius, probably from the 2nd century BC. (Author's collection)

The triumphal arch at Roda de Berà (Tarragona) is one of four that remain in the territory of ancient Hispania. It was erected by testamentary disposition of Lucius Licinius Sura at the end of the 1st century BC, dedicated to the Emperor Augustus. (Author's collection)

Tombstone of Bishop Optimus from the Late Roman Empire. Museum of Archaeology of Tarragona. (Author's collection)

(5, 12,7), the one in charge of repression may have been the protagonist of our previous story, Decimus Junius Brutus Callaicus. But there were still honest politicians, although they usually only ended up dead or exiled, as was the case of the historian Publius Rutilius Rufus, one of the military tribunes of Scipio Aemilianus during the siege of Numantia, who dared to denounce the corruption of the equestrian order and was condemned to exile.

In Hispania, the situation was no better.[41] Although there was a coastal strip stretching from Emporium to at least Gades and the territory of the Guadalquivir valley and part of the Ebro valley, loyal to Rome, inland the Romans were still viewed with suspicion. Moreover, their relationship with the metropolis was marked by the actions of the *praetores* and tax collectors,[42] whose desire for personal enrichment would lead them to commit all kinds of abuses against the native societies. If we add to this the actions of banditry, endemic in the inland areas of Lusitania or Celtiberia, what is certain is that in 114 BC Lusitanians and Celtiberians were once again up in arms. Classical sources limit themselves to speaking of these uprisings as banditry, and it does not seem that they were given any importance in Rome. The *praetor* who arrived in H. Ulterior that year was none other than Gaius Marius. But it doesn't look like he did anything remarkable. Besides, Rome would soon have other, more serious problems to deal with: the Cimbrian War (113–101 BC), the Jugurthine War (112–106 BC) and, a little later, the Social War (91–87 BC). Marius was replaced by Lucius Calpurnius Piso Frugi. Shortly afterwards, he was killed in a battle against the Lusitanians, and was succeeded by Marcus Junius Silanus, although little is known of his fighting. His successor, Servius Sulpicius Galba, the son of the consul who in 154 BC had perpetrated the massacre of the Lusitanians, seems to have fared better. By 110 BC, Quintus Servilius Caepio[43] was able to celebrate a triumph on his return to Rome in 108 BC. But a year earlier, dark winds were blowing over the metropolis. The Cimbrians, a tribe probably of Germanic origin from the Jutland peninsula (in modern Denmark), reached Transalpine Gaul and asked for permission to settle. Their request was denied by that year's consul in charge of Gaul, Marcus Junius Silanus, the former *praetor* of the Ulterior. This refusal provoked a terrible war

41 Martínez Caballero (2012).

42 On tax collection in Hispania, the work of Blázquez Martínez (1982) is essential.

43 Her daughter, the legendary Servilia Maior, was the mother of Marcus Junius Brutus and one of Julius Caesar's most beloved mistresses.

that made Rome fear for its survival. A period of humiliating defeats of the Roman armies began. One by one, the Cimbrians destroyed all the consular armies that dared to confront them. Junius Silanus and Cassius Longinus, who died in battle, were defeated. But the great disaster for the Roman army came in 105 BC, when the Cimbrians fought against two consular armies, under the command of Servius Sulpicius Galba (another former *praetor* of Ulterior) and Gnaeus Mallius Maximus. In the Battle of Arausius the two consular armies were annihilated. It is believed that 80,000 Romans may have been killed that day. There were hardly any survivors, although one of them, Quintus Sertorius, will be the subject of our next chapters. It seemed that Rome could only be saved by one man, Gaius Marius, who had just defeated Jugurtha. Meanwhile, in 104 BC, part of the Cimbrian tribes penetrated H. Citerior. They sacked Emporium, Tarraco and Ilerda and continued with the greatest impunity through the Ebro valley. They appeared invincible, until they came up against a coalition of Celtiberian tribes. As it was a war between 'barbarians', the classical sources do not specify whether it was in one or many battles, but it is certain that the Celtiberians ended up winning the war. The Cimbrians left Hispania and joined forces with the Teutons in Transalpine Gaul. There they were again defeated by Gaius Marius, who exterminated the Teutons at the Battle of Acquae Sextae (102 BC) and the Cimbri at the Battle of Vercellae (101 BC), becoming the saviour of Rome.

But while Gaius Marius was exterminating the threatening Germanic tribes, in Hispania the Lusitanians and Celtiberians realised the weakness of the Roman army in their territory and took up arms again. The only classic author who could have recounted this new war was Livy, but his books from this period have been lost. In any case, we know that in 102 and 101 BC the *praetor* of H. Ulterior was Marcus Marius, the younger brother of Gaius. It seems that he achieved a great victory over the Lusitanians. For this he was assisted by a Celtiberian contingent, for whom he built the city of Colenda (Appian, *Ib. Wars,* 100). It should be borne in mind that the Celtiberians were not a cohesive group of tribes with the same political interests. Thus, while the more southerly tribes collaborated with the Romans, the more northerly tribes fought against them. Marius' successor in H. Ulterior was Lucius Cornelius Dolabella, who, without further details, is reported to have won victories over the Lusitanians, for which he will celebrate a triumph in Rome in 98 BC. Between 100 and 99 BC, the revolt of the northern Celtiberians was widespread, and the *praetor* Gaius Coelius Caldus was sent to quell it. From some coins that his grandson ordered to be minted, we can deduce that he must have defeated the inhabitants of the Arevaci city of Cluniacus, which later became the Roman city of Clunia. His successor was much more expeditious. He was Titus Didius, consul in 98 BC, who arrived in H. Citerior as proconsul. He was to fight in this territory for the next five years. It would not be a far-fetched hypothesis to think that he had been ordered by the Senate not only to put down the Celtiberian revolt, but also to incorporate that territory once and for all and forever into the dominions of Rome, to ensure its pacification. His campaigns were extremely bloodthirsty, with a particular focus on the Arevaci, of whom he is believed to have killed over 20,000 men, women, and children, as well as reducing thousands of them to slavery. His crucial victory was over the city of Termantia, the most important Arevaci city at the time. Later, he conquered the city of Colenda, which five years earlier Marcus Marius had built for his allied Celtiberian soldiers. Its inhabitants continued to live in the most humiliating poverty, so they turned to brigandage. Didius sold them all into slavery. And in a nearby city, of which the sources do not specify the name, the Roman proconsul offered its inhabitants a new territory in which to settle. He divided them into groups, disarmed them and massacred them all, without distinguishing between men and women, children, young and old, just as Galba had done to the Lusitanians a few decades earlier. From Plutarch (*Sert.*, 3), we know that Quintus Sertorius served as Didius' military tribune. An office for which he was exceptionally young, being only about 20 or 21 years old. In addition, the Greek historian tells us of one of the innumerable achievements of this distinguished Roman, which will be the subject of the next chapter. Plutarch tells us that the troops commanded by Sertorius were stationed in the city of Castulo (modern Linares, Andalusia). It was common for the allied cities to be forced to welcome the Roman soldiers into their homes, which became a serious problem, since the invaders believed they had the right to commit all kinds of abuses and outrages. From time to time, the inhabitants of those cities would get fed up and take up arms against the Romans. And that is precisely what happened in Castulo that night. Its citizens, tired of putting up with the outrages of their occupiers, murdered most of the Roman garrison. Sertorius managed to escape with a small group of survivors. On the outskirts of the city, he reorganised his men and returned to Castulo, where he took his revenge by killing all the men in the city. On being informed that the inhabitants of neighbouring Isturgi had collaborated in the slaughter, he set off with part of his troops, but dressed in Castelunsi garb. On seeing them arrive, the Isturgensis opened their gates and Sertorius ordered his men to kill all the men in the city. The survivors of both cities were sold into slavery. This feat proved that the young tribune had daring, resolution and courage. This earned him enormous popularity in Hispania, but also in Rome, where he was awarded no less than the *Corona Graminea* (the Grass Crown), the highest distinction for heroic valour awarded on only nine times in the entire history of Rome. Little else is known of the deeds of Didius or Sertorius during this period. We only find some reference in Frontinus (*Stratagemata*, 1, 10, 1), who tells us that, after a hard-fought battle, the battlefield was littered with corpses of both Celtiberians and Romans. Nevertheless, when night fell, Didius ordered his men to bury the corpses of the Romans. At dawn, when the surviving Celtiberians saw that the battlefield was littered with the corpses of their comrades, assuming that the Romans had won the previous day, they surrendered. The campaign must have ended with a great victory over the Celtiberians, for on his return to Rome in 93 BC, according to the list of the *Fasti Triumphales*, he celebrated a triumph. Two days later, Publius Licinius Crassus also had his triumphal parade, in this case for his victory over the Lusitanians, whom he had been fighting in H. Ulterior for four years. Although we know practically nothing of the actions he carried out in that territory. From Plutarch (*Cras.*, 4, 1), we are informed that he was accompanied by his son, Marcus Licinius Crassus, the future triumvir, and that he made an expedition to the mythical Cassiterides ('Tin Islands'), whose exact location is not known, which is suspected to be off the coast of Galicia, although it is also thought that it could be the Isles of Scilly in the south-western tip of Cornwall. In Citerior, Didius was replaced by Gaius Valerius Flaccus, who spent an unusually long period of more than a decade in Hispania. Again, hardly any details of his rule in Hispania have come down to us, other than a brief note in Appian (*Ib. Wars*, 100) in which he explains how he exterminated the inhabitants of Belgeda (near modern Azuara, Aragon), who had previously set fire to their local senate and killed the members of their council for refusing to take up arms against the Romans. Flaccus does not appear in the list of the *Fasti Triumphales*, but it is likely that by the end of his rule, the territories belonging to the Arevaci, Vaccaei and Vettones had been definitively conquered. Some of their cities would take sides with Sertorius in the civil war that we will explain below, so it is to be assumed that these were territories that, at least, were already in a phase of Romanisation, at least at an initial stage.

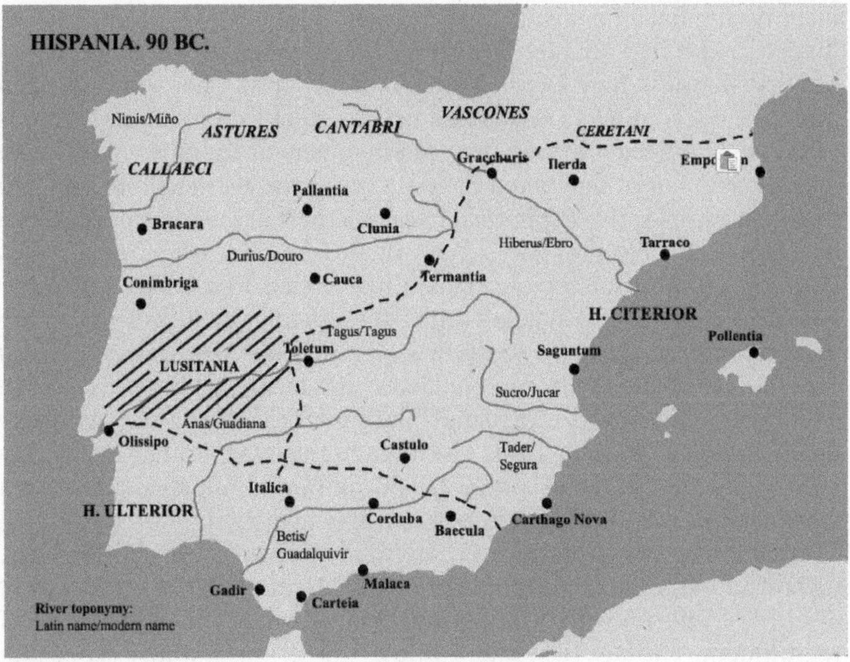

Map 9: By 90 BC, we can say that a large part of the Iberian Peninsula had been conquered. There would be new revolts, especially in the territory of the Lusitanians, but the power of Rome was slowly spreading throughout Hispania.

We must end this chapter with the history of the *Turma Sallutiana,*[44] or at least what we know of it, especially through the so-called Bronze of Ascoli, and which helps us to understand the relations between the Iberian elites and the Romans at the beginning of the 1st century BC. The *Turma Sallutiana* was a squadron of thirty horsemen from different Iberian cities from the Ebro valley, recruited in the city of Salduie,[45] one of the main cities of the Sedetani, and neighbours of the bellicose Celtiberians. It is believed that they must have entered the Roman orbit in the time of Tiberius Sempronius Gracchus, making it a *socii* city of Rome, which contributed decisively to the enrichment (and Romanisation) of its elites. In the context of the Social War, in need of auxiliary troops, the Romans were forced to recruit Gauls and Iberians to fight alongside

44 Amela Valverde (2021), Pina Polo (2008).

45 In the time of Augustus, the city was re-founded under the name of Caesaraugusta (modern Zaragoza, Aragon).

them on the Italic Peninsula. The trade of arms was well known to the Iberians, who had already been hired as mercenaries for more than a century. But now they were no longer mercenaries. They were allies. In this case, the contingent was made up of a squadron of cavalry. That is to say, the horsemen must have been members of the elites of different Iberian cities, since they were the only ones who were able to buy and maintain a horse. The *Turma Sallutiana* took part in the siege of Asculum (modern Ascoli, Picenus, Italy), receiving Roman citizenship from Gnaeus Pompeius Strabo for their gallantry in combat. Receiving citizenship would increase their privileges and, consequently, their prestige within their communities. At the same time, the Romans who granted it also benefited, since those who received it became, tacitly, their clients. And in a world in which it was increasingly important to have many supporters (late-Republican era), this was essential. In this way, Roman politicians such as Gnaeus Pompeius Strabo gained enormous influence in Hispania which, in this case, his son Pompey was able to exploit.

Something was profoundly changing in Rome. And with the city, its army. Under the government of Gaius Marius, the army underwent a series of reforms, of particular importance being the new system of recruitment. The lack of soldiers, due to the serious military crises that had to be faced in those years, led to the recruitment of *capite censi*, i.e., men without any property and who, consequently, were not included in the census. These were the lowest social class in Roman society and could not belong to the army, among other reasons because they lacked the money to buy military equipment. After the Marian reforms, it was the state that lent the money for each soldier to buy his equipment, in addition to paying them a salary. In addition, soldiers could enrich themselves during campaigns, through looting or plundering. This meant that their prosperity depended not so much on the Roman state, but on the general under whom they served. In short, he was directly responsible for their well-being. Hence, their loyalty was no longer to Rome, but to their generals. But in Rome, the generals were also politicians. They therefore also needed a strong client network to help them pass their legislative reforms or support their candidates. And in provinces such as Hispania, a wide client network among the Romanised elites ensured the generals-politicians the loyalty of their tribes, the exploitation of their natural resources and military contingents. In short, the Marian reforms would have the unintended consequence that the generals would become true Lords of War, with civilian (their clients) and military armies, with which to impose their ideas: with which to impose themselves as dictators in Rome. The era of civil wars was about to begin.

Chapter 4

ROMAN CIVIL WARS IN HISPANIA

In the previous chapter, we have seen how an important part of Hispania was already under the control of Rome. Many of the local elites in the valleys of the rivers Ebro, Guadalquivir and Guadiana, and the Mediterranean coastal areas had prospered in the heat of business with the metropolis. But the Iberian Peninsula was also full of new cities founded by the Romans and, moreover, inhabited by settlers from Italy, veterans of the legions and auxiliary troops. It is true that there were some regions, such as Lusitania, which were still up in arms against the invaders, and other regions, such as the coast of the Cantabrian Sea, which remained unexplored. Paradoxically, as Hispania was pacified, the political climate in the *urbs* became increasingly rarefied and tense. It is true that, from practically its foundation, the Republic of Rome had to face social conflict between patricians and plebeians, in which the latter gradually achieved different levels of power through the passing of different laws such as, for example *Lex Horatia Valeria* (494 BC), *Lex Liciniae Setiae* (367 BC, which culminated in the construction of the mythical Temple of Concord in the Forum of Rome to celebrate social peace), *Lex Orgulnia* (300 BC) and *Lex Hortensia* (287 BC). But something changed in 133 BC. While Hispania was trying to subdue the rebellious city of Numantia, Rome was caught up in an unprecedented climate of political violence provoked by Tiberius Sempronius Gracchus when he tried to pass his *Lex Agraria*. From then on, as O'Connell points out, the political violence would become 'the dominant instrument of conflict resolution. This is because violence had greater efficacy than any means of conflict resolution found in the traditional systems of the Roman Republic.'[1] This violence would polarise the political climate into two irreconcilable factions: the *Optimates* and the *Populares*. The former represented the old Roman aristocratic class and defended a centralised power in the Senate. The latter represented the popular classes of Rome and the *homines novi* (in the singular, *homo novus*), the citizens born in the provinces who came to the *urbs* to try to join the *cursus honorum*. It should be made clear that these were not political parties in the contemporary sense and that, in many cases, rather than political ideas, they defended class interests. Thus, for example, the patrician Publius Sulpicius Rufus supported the faction of the *Populares,* while the Cicero brothers or the Pompeii, who were *homines novi,* supported the faction of the *Optimates*. In those days, the inability of the Roman political and economic system to distribute equitably the economic impact of its conquests was evident; moreover, it tended to concentrate land ownership (and thus wealth) in fewer and fewer hands.[2] To this we must add the emergence of a new class of political leaders attached to power, capable of gaining and maintaining it at any price.[3] In fact, the Romans had already for decades been admitting exceptions to the laws governing the awarding of certain military offices. To cite just two, let us remember that to confront the Carthaginians in Hispania during the Second Punic War, Scipio Africanus was appointed proconsul of the Roman troops when he was neither old enough nor experienced enough to hold the post; the same happened a few decades later with Scipio Aemilianus, when he commanded the troops that finally overthrew the city of Numantia. But whereas before these exceptions could be ruled by a Senate free from tutelage, at the beginning of the 1st century BC, a series of generals and politicians accumulated so much power that the foundations of the Republic itself began to be endangered. A poet once said that fishbones were the posthumous vengeance of fish on those who ate them. In this case, we might well think that all the enemies that Rome had defeated and slaughtered over the last few centuries, including Viriathus and his Lusitanians, Hannibal and the Carthaginians, or Rethogenes and the Numantines had become the fishbones with which the Republic of Rome was getting stuck. The metropolis was plunged into an escalation of violence that was reflected in a series of political

1 O'Connell (2022), p. 9.

2 Sun (2001), p. 1164.

3 On this point, the essay *Commentariolum Petitionis* ('Little Handbook on Electioneering'), written by Quintus Tullius Cicero, brother of the legendary Marcus Tullius Cicero, is a gem.

assassinations, such as those suffered by the Gracchus brothers, Glaucia or Marcus Licinius Drusus, but also in cruel proscriptions or forced exiles. We ended the previous chapter by explaining an episode of the Social War. It was precisely in the context of this war that the first Hispanian senator in Rome appeared. He was Quintus Varius Severus Hybrida, described by Cicero as a good orator, but a nasty person. He is often referred to as Sucronensis, as he was born in the city of Sucro (near modern Valencia) and the epithet Hybrida would be since his mother was Hispanian and his father Roman. As Tribune of the Plebs, Quintus Varius promulgated the *Lex Valeria de Majestatis* (aka *Lex Varia*) in 91 BC, which condemned as traitors all those Romans who in the past had supported any legislative reform favourable to the Italic peoples who had taken up arms against Rome. Incidentally, months later his own law would be applied against him and force him into exile. Widespread political violence reached its peak in the struggle for power between Marius and Sulla, leaders of the *Populares* and *Optimates* factions respectively, culminating in the First Roman Civil War (88–81 BC). And it was not to be the last.

Bellum Sertoriarum

To explain the beginning of this story, we must start in the year 82 BC, in the Pyrenees, the gateway to H. Citerior. The protagonist of the following pages is Quintus Sertorius, probably one of the most fascinating (but also controversial) characters in the history of Rome. In that year, Sertorius was not living his best moment, and his life had not been exactly quiet. Months earlier, he had been appointed *praetor* of Hispania and was on his way to his new territory when a political upheaval in Rome changed his personal situation. Lucius Cornelius Sulla had seized power in Rome, declared himself *dictator* and enacted *de facto* death sentences for all his political rivals, for all those who had supported the faction of Gaius Marius and, on his death in 86 BC, in the hands of his successor, Lucius Cornelius Cinna, who would die in early 84 BC, lynched by his own troops as he was about to confront Sulla. Sertorius was on the list of Marians to be eliminated, even though this general had always been very critical of the massacres they had organised.

But who was Sertorius? Our protagonist was born in 122 BC in Nursia, in the territory of the Sabines. Little is known about his childhood. Matyszak[4] indicates that he must have been born into a

4 To explain the life of Sertorius we will rely on several sources, the main ones being Plutarch (*Life of Sertorius*) and Matyszak (2013). Throughout the text, where appropriate, other authors will be cited.

family of the lower nobility. Plutarch tells us that as a teenager he was left fatherless (*Sert.*, 2) and then he moved to Rome, where he studied law and earned a good reputation as an orator. Be that as it may, he must have attracted the attention of the influential Servilii Caepio family, of whom, as García Morá[5] suggests, he must have become a client. Thus, it is likely that at the age of 17 he entered the army as a *contubernalis*.[6] His baptism of fire was no less than in the debacle of Arausio, where he served under the consul Quintus Servilius Caepio. Plutarch tells us how he managed to save his life: 'After the Romans had been defeated and put to flight, though he had lost his horse and had been wounded in the body, he made his way across the Rhône, swimming, shield and breastplate and all, against a strongly adverse current; hence, sturdy was his body and so inured to hardships by training' (*Sert.*, 3). Sertorius did not desert the Roman army in one of its darkest hours and put himself at the service of Gaius Marius to confront the Cimbri and the Teutons, where one of his missions stands out in which he infiltrated an enemy camp disguised as a Celt, having learnt the most rudimentary part of their language, providing valuable information to Marius. We must assume that he took part in the Battles of Aquae Sextiae (102 BC) and Vercellae (101 BC), which definitively defeated the Germanic tribes. Later, as a military tribune, he served in Hispania in the war against the Celtiberians under the command of Titus Didius, which we have already described. Shortly after returning to Rome in 91 BC, he was appointed *quaestor* in Cisalpine Gaul. There, in a battle, he lost an eye, which was a source of pride for him:

> But displayed astonishing deeds of prowess and exposed his person unsparingly in battle, in consequence of which he got a blow that cost him one of his eyes. But on this he always prided himself. Others, he said, could not always carry about with them the evidence of their brave deeds, but must lay aside their necklaces, spears, and wreaths; in his own case, on the contrary, the marks of his bravery remained with him, and when men saw what he had lost, they saw at the same time a proof of his valour (Plutarch, *Sert.*, 4).

5 García Morá (1989).

6 They were a kind of cadets. They were young men belonging to the upper classes of society who, during battles, would stay close to the legates or generals. As the Roman army lacked military academies to train its future officers, they learned in the field. For example, Gaius Marius was *conturbenalis* of Scipio Aemilianus during the siege of Numantia.

But serious events had taken place in Rome. The civil war between Gaius Marius and Lucius Cornelius Sulla has turned in favour of the latter. Marius, old and ill, was forced into exile in Africa. In this new political climate, Sertorius returned from Gaul and stood for election as Tribune of the Plebs, but was opposed by Sulla's powerful electoral machine, which closed the door on him by imposing its candidates. This was an affront that the young Sabine soldier would neither forget nor forgive. In 89 BC, Sulla left Rome to face Mithridates VI Eupator of Pontus in the First Mithridatic War, and he assigned two trusted consuls, Lucius Cornelius Cinna and Gnaeus Octavian. But Cinna began to push through a series of reforms that favoured the popular faction, straining the political situation to such an extent that the Senate removed him from the consulate. With his supporters, including Sertorius, he set out to regain power in Rome. Cinna and most of his followers were in favour of summoning Marius to his side; Sertorius, however, feared that the old general would be an obstacle to his aims. Finally, Cinna imposed his judgement and, with his army, entered Rome, where he carried out a great slaughter among the followers of Sulla. The slaughter, by the way, seems to have been inspired (or ordered) by Marius and tried to be stopped by Sertorius, without success. Among the many victims of Marius' wrath were the consul Gnaeus Octavian, the censor Publius Licinius Crassus, who had been proconsul in Hispania Ulterior, his eldest son, Lucius, and the youngest, Marcus, the future triumvir, was miraculously able to escape and make his way to Hispania, where he found the support of his father's client Vibius Pacciaecus, who, according to Plutarch (*Cras.*, 4-5), allowed him to stay on his estates, provided food for him and his followers (we must understand that someone of his social standing did not travel alone) and even two young female slaves for his amusement. Crassus remained in Hispania until Cinna's death.

Marius died in 86 BC, while the period known as *Cinnanum Tempus* ended abruptly in 84 BC when Cinna was lynched by his own troops as he was about to confront Sulla. Weeks earlier, Quintus Sertorius had been appointed *praetor* in H. Citerior. Presumably, at the time of his departure, Rome was already fearful of Sulla's revenge. Sertorius was therefore joined by important sympathisers of Cinna's faction such as Livius Salinator, Lucius Hirtuleius, Gaius and Lucius Insteius, Tarquitius Priscus, and others. And they were not wrong. Sulla imposed a regime of terror in which he condemned all his political opponents to death. He also dismissed Sertorius, appointing in his place Caius Annius Luscus, who set out for Hispania with a large army. At that time, Sertorius had approximately 9,000 soldiers. Nonetheless, he sent two-thirds of his army under Livius Salinator to defend the Pyrenean passes, to prevent Annius from entering the peninsula. The position that the Sertorians gained was impregnable and the general sent by Sulla seemed to have run aground at the gates of Hispania. However, one of Salinator's officers assassinated him. He was Publius Calpurnius Lanarius, who, it seems, being on Sulla's list of those condemned to death, won a pardon in exchange for handing over his general.[7] Thus, with only 3,000 soldiers, it was impossible for Sertorius to face the reinforced army of Annius Luscus, so he moved to Carthago Nova, where he would embark for Africa. He then embarked on a journey lasting several months, a journey more reminiscent of the Homeric Odyssey than of a history book on Rome. Like a Roman Ulysses, Sertorius arrived in Mauritania, from where he was expelled; he was caught by Cilician pirates, who took him to Ebusus (modern Ibiza) and with whom he ended up forging a solid alliance. Under pressure from the fleet of Annius Luscus, they travelled to the islands that Plutarch cites as Fortunate (thought to be the Canary Islands, although some authors suggest it could be Madeira). In any case, these were islands with a mild climate, abundant natural riches, and a placid life. A kind of new Ogygia for Sertorius, although we do not know if he found his own Calypso there. It was not a bad place to retire and spend the rest of his life. His political faction had no chance of regaining power in Rome, and the Fortunate Isles offered Sertorius and his men everything they could wish for. However, in 80 BC, he was persuaded by his Cilician allies to intervene in the succession crisis in the Kingdom of Mauritania, where a Roman fleet under the command of Vibius Pacciaecus[8] landed. Although Plutarch claims that it was sent by Sulla, it seems to have been a small number of troops, so Manchón Zorrilla[9] believes that it may have been a private initiative by Pacciaecus to win the favour of Annius Luscus. Weeks later, the two armies met, and Sertorius won a crushing victory, in which Pacciaecus was killed in combat and his troops joined the ranks of the rebel general. Sertorius and his allies then occupied the city of Tingis (modern Tangier, Morocco). This victory did not go unnoticed on the Iberian Peninsula. While the Sullans were on the alert, a delegation of Lusitanians arrived in Mauritania. They

7 García González (2023).

8 He was the man who had sheltered M. Licinius Crassus in Hispania, when he was fleeing the massacres promoted by Marius and Cinna. The authors discuss whether he could have been a Hispano-Roman nobleman or a wealthy settler from Italy.

9 Manchón Zorrilla (2016), p. 65.

wanted to revolt against the Romans but lacked an experienced leader to guide them on the battlefield. Sertorius saw the chance of returning to Roman territory and attempting to turn the political situation in the *urbs* around from Hispania. An absolutely audacious objective given that the Sabine had only about 4,700 Lusitanian warriors, 2,600 Roman soldiers and about 700 Mauritanians. With the fleet hired by the Lusitanians and that of the Cilician pirates, the Sertorian army disembarked on the peninsula. Gaius Aurelius Cotta, governor of H. Ulterior, was unable to prevent Sertorius' troops from landing near Baelo Claudia, where a new contingent of Lusitanian troops awaited them. The *Bellum Sertoriarum* began, which can be divided into two phases: the period 80–77 BC in which Sertorius put his forces on the defensive, consolidating his positions in Lusitania, withstanding Metellus' attacks; and a second phase, in 76–72 BC, when he moved into Celtiberian territory, going on the offensive and facing the armies of Metellus and Pompey.

The two armies soon clashed. The first recorded battle was at the river Baetis, where the army of Sertorius defeated that of Lucius Fufidius, the *propraetor* of H. Ulterior, former centurion *primus pilus* and a close friend of Sulla.[10] In 79 BC, alarmed, the dictator had no choice but to send a proconsul to Hispania to crush the rebel leader once and for all. The chosen one was Quintus Caecilius Metellus Pius. But why him? He came from the Caecilius Metellus, one of the most important plebeian families in Rome, who counted more than a dozen consuls in the past and of whom we have already had occasion to speak in this book, as, Quintus Caecilius Metellus Balearicus. However, later historiography is not very kind to this general and stateman, who had occupied the consulship together with Sulla in 80 BC. The later Roman historians will sympathise with Sertorius or Pompey, always leaving Metellus Pius in a secondary position, presenting him as an old man not very inclined to the sacrifices involved in leading an army on the battlefield. However, Simmons, who is surely the greatest specialist on the Metellus family, suggests that he may have been chosen for this position to draw him away from Rome. At the time, Metellus was probably the second most powerful man in Rome, one of the richest and certainly the one with the largest number of clients. Although according to Sulla 'their relationship was not strained, but these two proud aristocrats probably functioned best when not in close quarters'.[11]

10 Manchón Zorrilla, op. cit., p. 67.

11 Simmons (2011), p. 146.

Away from Rome, Metellus could not use his political influence to oppose Sulla. Be that as it may, the proconsul had an absolute material superiority in men and arms for his campaign against Sertorius, as well as a consolidated base in H. Ulterior, blindly loyal to Rome.

Fufidius asked for help from his northern colleague, Marcus Domitius Calvinus, *propraetor* of H. Citerior. For his part, Sertorius sent his faithful lieutenant, Lucius Hirtuleius, who went to meet him in the Carpetania, from where he organised numerous guerrilla attacks, which wore down Calvinus' troops, until he defeated him in a great ambush in a gorge near the river Anas, in which Domitius Calvinus himself was killed.[12] Metellus, who had just arrived in Hispania, sent his legate Lucius Thoranius Balbus to support Calvinus, but he was defeated and killed by Hirtuleius' troops. It is interesting to note that the Carpetanians remained loyal to Sulla's Rome and must have fought against Hirtuleius. Meanwhile, Sertorius consolidated his position in Lusitania. He strengthened his leadership by taking measures that allowed him to increase the number of tribes that agreed to follow him. For example, he levied much lower taxes than those demanded by the Roman authorities and, knowing the local customs, he had his men camp on the outskirts of towns rather than inside them, to avoid an episode like the one Castulus himself had experienced in his youth. Moreover, just as some 120 years earlier Cornelius Scipio had used the religious feelings of his men to conquer Carthago Nova, Sertorius also employed a famous stratagem to gain the confidence of his men and allies. If we follow the story as told by Plutarch[13] (*Sert.*, 11,2) a hunter named Spanus came across a newborn white fawn, which he gave to the general, who declared that it was a gift from the goddess Diana. From that moment on, the little mammal always accompanied him. Before a battle, in front of his troops and in order to be clearly visible, he would pretend that the fawn was whispering the tactics in his ear, which, being divinely inspired, gave his men confidence. Similarly, whenever he received good news from one of the fronts, it was the fawn who 'informed' him of it in front of the leaders of the Lusitanian tribes. Gellius also explains that he used premonitory dreams and that he used lies when it served his military interests. But the fundamental element in understanding Sertorius' military success is to be found in the training of his soldiers: while he trained the Romans in the effective

12 Brennan (2000), p. 506.

13 Sertorius' little pet certainly caught the attention of ancient historians, as we find references to the Artiodactyla in Gellius (*Noctes*, 15, 22) and Frontinus (*Stratagemata*, 1, 11, 13).

guerrilla tactics used by the Lusitanians, he trained the Lusitanians in the tactics of the Roman legions, equipping them as if they were real Roman soldiers.

For his part, Metellus Pius established a series of military camps along the river Anas (modern Guadiana), which was the natural border separating the Lusitanian territory from the Ulterior. Of all these settlements, only Metellinum (modern Medellin, Extremadura) and Castra Caecilia (modern Caceres, Extremadura) were consolidated. His tactic was to surround the Lusitanian territory and cut off their supply lines. But this dispersion of troops meant that his men were constantly harassed by Sertorius' troops. Anyway, the proconsul went ahead with his plan, reaching the territory of the Conii (south of modern Portugal), where he besieged the city of Langobriga[14] (modern Lagos, Algarve), from whose port the Roman suspected that Sertorius was receiving help and reinforcements from Mauritania. As the city had only one well, he intended to reduce it by hunger and thirst, so he only brought enough supplies for five days. Sertorius, however, came to the city's rescue. He devised a plan to move water tanks into the city and evacuate its weakest inhabitants. Therefore, the days passed, and the city did not surrender, while Metellus' men were running out of food. In the end, he had no choice but to send an entire legion, led by his legate Cornelius Aquinus, in search of food. Sertorius foresaw it and ambushed Aquinus' legion, which was virtually annihilated. Almost all the men were killed or captured and went on to reinforce the rebel general's army. Legate Aquinus managed to reach Metellus' camp unarmed and unhorsed, as Plutarch gloatingly recounts (*Sert.*, 13). Faced with this disaster, Metellus had no choice but to retreat to his winter quarters in H. Ulterior and await reinforcements from Rome. The situation was so critical that Lucius Manlius, the *praetor* of Transalpine Gaul,[15] had to come to the support of Quintus Calidius, his colleague in H. Citerior who had replaced Calvinus, killed in action. Thus L. Manlius entered Hispania with three legions, local allies and 1,500 horsemen, i.e., a total of about 20,000 men. Hirtuleius managed to defeat him near Ilerda, and Manlius saved himself with very few men, taking refuge within the walls of Ilerda (Orosius, 5, 23, 4). A passage in Julius Caesar's famous *De Bello Gallico* (3, 20, 1) also mentions the defeat and death of the legate Lucius Valerius Praeconinus, although

14 Not to be confused with Lacobriga (modern Tierra de Campos, Castilla y León), in Vaccaei territory, which will also appear soon in this story.

15 Brennan (2000), p. 507 or Amela Valverde (2016). By the way, Plutarch cites him as *praetor* of Narbonnese Gaul.

it is not clear whether it was in the Battle of Ilerda, in another battle in the same region or in his retreat to Gaul, where, in a difficult journey, the survivors of the army of L. Manlius had to return to their own country. Manlius' army had to return to their territory, probably through parts of Aquitania that had not yet been conquered and had to fight against the Volcae Tectosages. The virtual destruction of the army of L. Manlius would have as a by-product that Transalpine Gaul was plunged into chaos and anarchy. This situation lasted almost two years, until Rome sent, as we shall see, a *carnifex* (butcher) to restore order. In any case, the victory of Hirtuleius at Ilerda tipped the balance in the Ebro valley region in favour of the Sertorians, where they had to apply the same policies that had been so successful in Lusitania to attract the local population. This part of Hispania was soon to play a key role in the great game that pitted Sertorius against Rome.

Meanwhile, in Rome, the situation was far from calm. It all began at the end of 79 BC, when Sulla surprised everyone by announcing his resignation and retirement from public life, dying the following year, and leaving this epitaph which, according to Plutarch (*Sulla*, 38, 4) he wrote himself and which defined him perfectly: 'that no friend ever surpassed him in kindness, and no enemy in mischief'. But when he retired, he left as consuls two men of his closest confidence: Quintus Lutatius Catulus Capitolinus and Marcus Aemilius Lepidus.[16] The first one took command of an army and went to pacify Transalpine Gaul, while Lepidus remained in Rome. There, with his consular colleague hundreds of miles away, Lepidus decreed a series of laws dismantling the legislation passed by the dictator. Faced with these actions, Catullus returned to Rome with his legions and confronted his consular colleague, winning the victory. Lepidus and his troops were forced to embark for Sardinia, where they faced the army of the *praetor* of the island, Gaius Valerius Triarius.[17] The fighting must not have favoured the newcomers, as Lepidus died the following year, in 77 BC (whether from illness or as a result of battle is not known). His legate, Marcus Perpenna Vento, took command of the army and decided to embark with his troops for Hispania. The legate's intention was to fight on his own, bypassing Sertorius' armies, but Sertorius was already a real celebrity among those who opposed Sulla's policies and the Senate, so his men forced him to join the rebel general's army. The

16 He must not to be confused with his son, of the same name, who was to form part of the Second Triumvirate of Rome along with Octavian and Mark Antony.

17 Brennan, op. cit., p. 494.

Senate then turned its attention back to Hispania, where L. Manlius had been defeated (provoking the insurrection of much of Roman-dominated Gaul) and Metellus was calling for reinforcements, holed up in his winter quarters. Thus, the Senate asked the consuls of that year, Mamercus Aemilius Lepidus Livianus[18] and Decimus Junius Brutus,[19] but neither of them volunteered to confront Sertorius. It was at this time that one of the most important figures of this century in Rome appeared: Gnaeus Pompeius Magnus, also known as Pompey. He was a young general of only 29 years of age, but at that time there was no one in Rome as ambitious, efficient, expeditious and courageous a general, as well as immensely rich, heir to the immense fortune of his father, Gnaeus Pompeius Strabo.[20] Young Pompey volunteered to go to confront Sertorius and Perpenna, but there was a problem: he was not even a senator. The solution came from the influential orator Lucius Marcius Philippus, who proposed that a *senatus consultum ultimum*[21] be enacted giving special powers to Pompey. Meanwhile, the young general remained at the gates of Rome with his legions. He had been ordered to discharge them but was delaying the decision with various excuses. The clear pressure manoeuvre had its effect, and he agreed to Marcius' suggestion. The ever-poignant Plutarch (*Pomp.*, 17, 4) adds the anecdote in which 'a certain senator asked with amazement if Philippus thought it necessary to send Pompey out as pro-consul. "No indeed!" said Philippus, "but as pro-consuls," implying that both the consuls of that year were good for nothing'.

But who was this young general? Born in Picenum in 106 BC, he had spent his adolescence accompanying his father in the early stages of the Civil War, supporting Sulla. After his father's death in 87 BC, Pompey, who was only 21 years old, inherited his fortune and his legions. He soon shone on the battlefield, defeating all enemies he faced, displaying a mixture of daring and cunning, but also extreme ruthlessness. However, his great political impetus came from a marriage, when Sulla wanted to consolidate his alliance by marrying

---

18 He was a cousin of the previous year's consul, Marcus Aemilius Lepidus.

19 He was the son of Decimus Junius Brutus Callaicus. His son, Decimus Junius Brutus Albinus, was one of Julius Caesar's assassins and a distant cousin of the most famous conspirator, Marcus Junius Brutus.

20 He was mentioned in the previous chapter when he granted Roman citizenship to the Iberians of the *Turma Sallutiana*.

21 It was a resolution that gave special powers to the Senate, to the detriment of the consuls. It was the opposite of a dictatorship in which one of the consuls was the one with special powers.

his stepdaughter Emilia, who was then pregnant by her first husband, the wayward Manius Acilius Glabrio, to Pompey, in turn forcing the young rising star of Rome to divorce his first wife, Antistia. In any case, this marriage lasted only a few months, as Aemilia died giving birth to her unborn child. In 82 BC, his father-in-law sent him to Sicily with six legions, where he arrested the rebel consul Gnaeus Papirius Carbo. Controversy erupted when the young Pompey, aged just 24, took it upon himself to personally judge and order the consul's execution, which shocked many senators, who began calling him *adulescens carnifex* (teenage butcher). But they were surely relieved to see someone of his ambition and cruelty depart from Rome. Thus, in 77 BC, Pompey set out in command of a considerable number of troops, with approximately 30,000 infantrymen and about 1,000 horsemen, which would correspond to five or six legions, to which he would add the auxiliary troops that he would recruit both in Gaul and in Hispania itself.[22] His first mission, however, was to re-establish order in Transalpine Gaul. Unfortunately, the sources do not detail the activities of the Pompeian army in this region, which was organised around three major cities: Narbo (modern Narbonne), Massalia (modern Marseille) and Aquae Sextiae (modern Aix-en-Provence), which must have remained loyal to Rome; But it is also known that many Celtic tribes, or rather part of the elites of these tribes, such as the Allobroges, the Vocontii, the Helvii or the Volcae Tectosages resisted Pompey who advanced relentlessly amidst a sea of blood, in what Cicero called the *Bellum Transalpinum* (*Leg. Man.* 28). It is no less true, however, that the Roman general also carried out a remarkable diplomatic activity, which resulted, learning from his father, in an army of new clients who adopted the name of Pompeius.[23] All this meant that the arrival of the Pompeian army in Hispania was not recorded until 76 BC.

In the meantime, Sertorius was informed of the arrival of the new army from Rome, so he called Hirtuleius to Lusitania and he moved towards H. Citerior. The journey was not a smooth one, especially when he had to cross Carpetania. The *oppida* of this territory had been conquered by Rome about a century before, but they enjoyed considerable political autonomy, which was combined with great economic development, so that this region remained loyal to the Senate. Consequently Sertorius, to achieve his goal, had to conquer numerous cities, of whose sieges we

22 Amela Valverde (2019), p. 12.

23 On this point, Luis Amela Valverde, *Los Pompeii de la Galia Transalpina. Una reflexión* (in Spanish), which can be consulted at: http://riull.ull.es/xmlui/handle/915/3982

find details in some ancient sources, such as the famous case of Caraca, during the summer of 77 BC, (Plut., *Sert.*, 17), whose inhabitants lived in caves made of clayey mud that was impossible to climb and therefore impregnable. At least in theory. For Sertorius realised that the Caracitians were refreshed by a north wind and that it relieved them from the summer heat. However, the rebel general ordered his men to place all the clayey earth they could find at the foot of that hill. One morning, between the force of the wind and that of the Sertorian soldiers who fanned the earth, it rose to the entrances of the caves, which, with no more vents, suffocated with heat and made it difficult for the Caracitians to breathe. The Sertorians repeated the operation a second day and, the following day, the Caracitians surrendered. Sertorius, as his dedicated Greek biographer emphasised, showed that 'since by his skill he had subdued what could not be taken by arms'. The next city he besieged, according to classical sources, was Contrebeia Leucade, already in the territory of the Pelendonii (modern Aguilar del Río Alhama, La Rioja). The city resisted the siege fiercely, of which Livy (*Hist.*, 91) relates the final stages of the battle, in which the Pelendonii caused great losses in the Sertorian army, even setting fire to a siege tower. However, Sertorius ordered the construction of an identical tower during the night. Thus, the next morning, the inhabitants of Contrebeia Leucade were astonished at the strength of their enemies. Moreover, their main defence tower, which had been undermined, was about to collapse. So they withdrew from the walls and forced the city council to call for surrender. They had held out for 44 days. Sertorius was merciful to the brave Pelendonii, demanding only a small sum of money, hostages, all their weapons and the surrender of their deserters who were free men and to execute any deserters who were slaves, to which the Contrebeians promptly obeyed by throwing them from the city walls. He then left his lieutenant Lucius Insteius in the city with a strong garrison and went to Castra Aelia, at some undetermined point in the middle Ebro valley. From there, he developed a powerful and effective diplomatic policy, managing to attract most of the Iberian tribes of the region to his cause. He likewise sent Perpenna, along with some 20,000 men, to the territory of the Ilercavonians, at the mouth of the Ebro River, with the mission of preventing Pomepius' army from crossing the river and joining his army with that of Metellus. He also ordered Hirtuleius to put pressure on the Roman general by means of ambushes and guerrilla warfare but avoiding a pitched battle. The same tactics were to be used by Perpenna. Finally, having secured loyalty agreements with the tribes of the region, he managed to establish what was to become the nucleus of his most loyal supporters between

Calagurris and Ilerda, turning the Ilergete *oppidum* of Bolskan, which was renamed Osca, into his capital, where he would stay for the winter of 77–76 BC, transforming it into something like a second Rome. He created a new Senate for the Roman senators and citizens who had been exiled. Even he also created a school in which the children of the Hispanian leaders were educated as young Romans, acquiring not only the knowledge, but also the language, customs, and culture of the metropolis. Furthermore, Sertorius ensured that his students were actually his hostages, to avoid any temptation on the part of their parents to join the senatorial army. As a curious fact, and despite the fact that this school had the most tragic of endings, as we will see at the end of this chapter, in the collective imagination it was so important that from the 16th century its university was renamed the Sertorian University of Huesca, a name it still retains today.

In the spring of 76 BC, Pompey penetrated into H. Citerior and, following the via Heraclea (the future via Augusta), managed to take control of the entire coast of what is now the territory of Catalonia, leaving camps at strategic points, such as the one that would become the city of Gerunda (modern Girona), with which to control the main communication route between the H. Citerior and the G. Transalpina.[24] He must have defeated Perpenna's army at some point, as he moved southwards, managing to cross the river Ebro. This caused a few cities on the eastern coast of the peninsula to switch to the senatorial side. Among them was the city of Lauron.[25] Sertorius, fearing that this would lead to general disaffection and in order to prevent the creation of a corridor along the Mediterranean coast that would allow the armies of Pompey and Metellus to join, went to conquer the city. Shortly after his coming, Pompey arrived in command of 30,000 men. The situation was compromising for Sertorius, who, as was customary at the time (we shall see in 52 BC during Julius Caesar's famous siege of Alesia), had placed a palisade in his rear to protect himself from attacks from the outside. However, he devised a plan to attack Pompeian foragers who went to forage near his camp, leaving those who went further afield to fend for themselves. Thus, when he was informed that a large group of foragers had left the Pompeian camp, he ordered Octavian

---

24 Amela Valverde (2018).

25 It is not known exactly where this city was located. Traditionally, and following the suggestions of classical sources, it was positioned to the south of the river Ebro, specifically between the modern Llíria or Alzira; although more recent studies, would place it to the north of the river, in Llerona or Samalús (Catalonia), Guàrdia i Llorens (2014) and Noguera Guillén (2022).

Gracinus to command ten cohorts of legionaries and ten cohorts of Iberian soldiers, and Tarquitius Priscus to command 250 horsemen to ambush the Pompeians when they returned. The plan worked out as Sertorius had planned and his infantry smashed his enemy's infantry, who fled in the direction of their camp, only to find their way cut off by T. Priscus' cavalry, who finished exterminating those who had managed to escape the infantry. Seeing this disaster, Pompey ordered his legate Decimus Laelius to take command of a legion to rescue his men. The legionaries put the cavalry of T. Priscus to flight, who led them to a place where a large part of the rebel army awaited them. It had all been a trap. Nevertheless, the *Optimate* went to the front of his troops and formed a line of battle. But then Sertorius appeared at the top of a ridge in command of the rest of his men. At that moment, the young general was faced with three choices: go to the rescue of Laelius, attack Sertorius, or retreat. The first two options seemed suicidal. In both cases, Sertorius had the upper hand. So he opted for the more bitter option, which was to abandon Laelius, who died in the battle, and his men, who were slaughtered, and then to abandon Lauro. In that battle, Pompey lost about 10,000 men. Moreover, Lauron was left to its own devices. According to Plutarch, its inhabitants surrendered, and Sertorius let them go without further ado, although this account is probably not true, as according to Orosius (5, 23, 6) there was a great slaughter among its citizens, the survivors were sent to Lusitania as slaves and the city was razed to the ground.[26] Incidentally, during the siege, Appian (*Civ. Wars*, 13, 110), tells us that he ordered the execution of a whole cohort of Roman soldiers for their brutality during the sack, something that some historians doubt in a civil war context.[27] After this battle, Sertorius and Pompey retired to their winter quarters.

75 BC was to be a pivotal year during the war. We move to the south of the peninsula. There, following the orders of his general, Hirtuleius had fought Metellus effectively through guerrilla warfare and ambushes during 76 BC and the first months of 75 BC. But at some point, he decided to fight Metellus in a pitched battle with the aim of achieving a decisive victory. So Hirtuleius moved to the vicinity of the senatorial army near Italica and formed up in battle position. The experienced Metellus showed no haste. He took his time in disposing his troops until he was finally ready to fight. Seeing the disposition

---

26 The ancient sources that narrate this battle in more detail are Plutarch (*Sert.*, 18; but in *Pomp.*, 18, 3, he only mentions the defeat of this general) and Frontinus (*Stratagemata*, 2,5, 31).

27 Gendron (2020).

of the Sertorian troops, who placed their strongest units in the centre of the line, Metellus planned a battle by slightly refusing his centre, so that, taking advantage of the fact that Hirtuleius' men had spent several hours in formation under a scorching sun (it must have been summer), his plan was to press the wings of the enemy army and envelop its centre to surround and destroy it, just as Hannibal had developed at Cannae (Frontinus, *Stratagemata.*, 2, 3, 5). Metellus' plan worked as he had envisaged, and Hirtuleius' army was totally destroyed. The most important consequence was that Metellus now had a free hand to move north and unite his troops with those of Pompey. Which materialised Sertorius' worst nightmare. Then, the rebel general decided to march to meet Metellus, while he left his lieutenants Perpenna and Herennius defending the line of the river Turia. Pompey marched on them, and they engaged in a pitched battle that ended with the defeat of the Sertorian army, which suffered about 10,000 casualties, among whom was probably Gaius Herennius. Following this victory, Pompey conquered and razed the city of Valentia to the ground. The archaeological evidence of the massacre that took place is truly horrifying. Numerous skeletons have been recovered with evidence of the atrocious tortures and mutilations suffered by the soldiers who were part of the Sertorian garrison.[28] The city was abandoned until the time of Augustus, i.e., about a century later. Perpenna and his troops retreated southwards to join the army of Sertorius, which was near the village of Sucro, belonging to the Iberian tribe of the Contestanii, situated near the only practicable ford of the river Sucro (modern Júcar), where he hoped to prevent the armies of Pompey and Metellus from joining forces. Shortly afterwards the young Picene general appeared in command of his troops. It was in Sertorius' interest to engage in combat as soon as possible, to avoid being caught between the two senatorial armies; while the ambitious Pompey also hastened to prepare for the battle, not wishing to share the glory of victory with his aged colleague. Therefore, the two armies were disposed as follows: on the right of the rebel army, Sertorius took his place, leaving Perpenna on his left. Pompey stood on his right, leaving the left side to his most trusted legate, Lucius Afranius. At daybreak, the Sertorian army began to advance. Sertorius managed to push Afranius back, but on the other side, it was Perpenna who was retreating. Therefore, Sertorius left

---

28 Alapont Marín, Calvo Gálvez and Ribera and Lacomba (2009) and Ribera and Lacomba (2014).

the command of his wing in the hands of his *legati* and went himself to reorganise Perpenna's army, which was beginning to disband. The general's arrival gave courage to his men, who regrouped to push back the Pompeian troops. In fact, Pompey himself was dismounted and wounded in the leg. But at the other end of the battle, Afranius had managed to turn the tide and eventually defeated the right wing of the rebel army, whose soldiers disbanded. Afranius' men even managed to loot their enemies' camp and the city of Sucro. With Pompey retreating, Sertorius regrouped his troops on the right wing and managed to drive Afranius' men out of the camp and out of the city, inflicting heavy casualties. The fighting continued into the night. The next morning, the two armies prepared for another battle. However, news of Metellus' arrival from the south forced Sertorius to retreat. The general, who during the fighting had been able to defeat both Pompey and Afranius, twice managing to rebuild his front, proved to be a general of extraordinary ability, who had exposed Rome's new shining star for the second time, but had likewise shown that his generals, now Perpenna and formerly Hirtileius, were no match for him. The battle, which ended with no clear winner, saw the death of nearly 10,000 soldiers from each army. Sertorius, disgruntled at his departure, reportedly exclaimed: 'But as for this boy, if that old woman had not come up, I should have given him a sound beating and sent him back to Rome' (Plut., *Sert.*, 19, 6).

Weeks later, the two armies met again, this time in the vicinity of the city of Saguntus, which was still in ruins, in what became known as the Battle of Saguntus or the Battle of the Turia. Sertorius faced Pompey, while Perpenna faced Metellus. While Sertorius was victorious in his sector of the field, Metellus prevailed in his. Losses in both armies amounted to some 10,000 men, with the deaths of Sertorius' lieutenant Hirtuleius and Gaius Memmius, military tribune of and brother-in-law of Pompey, being particularly significant. During the fighting, Sertorius apparently manoeuvred his men to attack the Picene general directly, trying to kill him. Memmius led a counter-attack that saved his brother-in-law's life but paid the price of death. Although the senatorial troops left the battlefield, Sertorius was forced to retreat to Celtiberia, although he ended up spending the winter in Lusitania. Metellus moved to Gaul, while Pompey spent some months among the Vascones, where he founded the city of Pompaelo (modern Pamplona, Navarra). At the end of the campaign in 75 BC, the two senatorial generals made two important decisions. On the one hand, Metellus put a price on

Sertorius' head,[29] offering the fabulous sum of 100 talents of silver[30] and 20,000 *iugera*[31] of land to whoever would bring him the head of the rebel leader. But this offer was only valid for *proscripti* Roman citizens (i.e., those on Sulla's proscription lists) or *hostes publici* (i.e., those declared enemies of Rome by the Senate after the revolt of Lepidus), who were also offered pardons and the possibility of returning to Rome. Neither of these two categories included the soldiers of Sertorius, to whom Metellus offered the possibility of joining his side without fear of reprisal, although they would have to take a *sacramentum* (oath of allegiance) to Metellus and Pompey. This caused a wave of desertions in the Sertorian army. Spoiler: no one would ever collect the reward. For his part, Pompey sent his famous letter to the Senate.[32] In it, he described his personal situation, tired, fed up and ruined by having spent his personal fortune on the war, and demanded immediate reinforcements to end the war once and for all, threatening to march on Rome itself if the Senate did not comply with his demands. The Pompeian ultimatum must have upset the nerves of the venerable senators and that year's consuls Marcus Aurelius Cotta[33] and Lucius Licinius Lucullus,[34]. who sent the requested reinforcements. It must also have been around this time that King Mithridates VI Eupator sent ambassadors to Sertorius to forge an alliance to defeat Rome. It seems that the Sabine general must have reached some kind of agreement with the king of Pontus, although it never materialised, but it did generate some discontent among his followers, who felt that his aim was to regain power in Rome, not to support his enemies. Classical sources, such as Plutarch, also report how Sertorius' character became increasingly obscured. Losses of territory, desertions, and the news of his mother's death, saddened him deeply. The general became more sour, more distrustful, but this is also the period when he lost his proverbial

---

29 Konrad (1988).

30 Approximately GBP 3.48 million or USD 4.3 million.

31 An *iugera* would be the land that one man can cultivate for one day. Thus, 20,000 *iugera* would correspond to 19.48 square miles. For close reference, that would be about the size of Manhattan Island (22.82 square miles) and slightly more than the area currently occupied by Malibu (19.90 square miles) or Oxford (17.60 square miles).

32 The complete letter can be read in: https://elfinspell.com/SallustPompey.html. *De Sallust* with an English Translation by J. C. Rolfe; The Loeb Classic Library; G. P. Putnam's Sons; New York (1920), pp. 414–19.

33 His sister, Aurelia Cotta, was the mother of Julius Caesar.

34 His grandfather had been *praetor* in H. Citerior and was a first cousin of Metellus Pius.

austerity. He began to get drunk and to spend much of his time at parties and banquets.

During the campaign of 74 BC, we could say that the fate of the war was already sealed. Metellus would press his troops into the Sertorian fiefdoms in Lusitania, while Pompey tried to conquer the main Celtiberian cities. For example, he besieged Pallantia, capital of the Vaccaei, but Sertorius appeared just as the city was about to fall, causing Pompey to retreat. But he succeeded in conquering Cauca, among other cities. At the end of the year, he was joined by Metellus to besiege Calagurris, one of the main Sertorian cities. The very hard siege ended with the appearance, once again, of Sertorius, and the senatorial army withdrew. However, the final balance of the year was bad for the rebel general: he had lost control of Celtiberia; on the coast, he only had the cities of Tarraco (modern Tarragona, Catalonia) and Dianium (modern Denia, Valencia); and his allied territories, Lusitania, and the Ebro valley, were exhausted and no longer able to provide him with more soldiers or food. And to this we must add the constant desertions of both Romans and Iberian allies. The end was near. Pompey spent that winter in Gallia Narbonensis, while Metellus went to Corduba, where he apparently held a great parade to celebrate his victories on the battlefield.

The year 73 BC was a prolongation of the previous year: war in the Celtiberian territory, massive desertions of Sertorian soldiers and disaffection of the Hispanian tribes. In addition, the promulgation in the Roman Senate of the *Lex Plautia de reditu Lepidanorum*,[35] which pardoned all the citizens who went into exile after the death of Sulla, caused the Sertorian Senate in Osca to lose most of its members. The insurgent general seems to have lost his head and, in an outburst that is difficult to understand, entered with blood and fire into the school in Osca where the children of his local allies were taught to behave like young Romans, exterminating them all. The news shocked the whole of Hispania. Sertorius was abandoned by virtually all his supporters. His close collaborators, fearing that his bloodlust was not quenched with those young men, began to conspire against him. It seems that it was Perpenna who organised the plot, where a courier arrived at Sertorius' camp announcing a false victory over a senatorial army. The general's lieutenants persuaded him to prepare a banquet to celebrate the victory, and when Sertorius was drunk, he was killed. In this vile and shabby way, one of the most talented Roman generals of his generation

35 García Morá (1992).

died. A man who made up for his lack of means with cunning and intelligence. He was able to keep the armies of the Senate in check for no less than a decade. Did he ever have a chance of victory? Probably not. The means available to Metellus and Pompey were infinitely superior. Moreover, the level of their subordinates, such as Hirtileius, Herennius or Perpenna, was a far cry from Memmius or Afranius.

It did not take Perpenna long to go in search of Pompey. He did not seek pardon, but victory. However, the Picene general defeated him using a very Sertorian tactic. At an undetermined place in Celtiberia, the sources do not give details, Pompey attacked Perpenna's army with a legion. But when the forces clashed, the Pompeians went on the rampage. The new rebel leader's men went in pursuit of their enemies, breaking their formation. At that moment, the rest of Pompey's army appeared and wiped out Perpenna's men, who were captured. In a desperate attempt to save his life, the latter gave the senatorial general the letters listing the politicians and heroes of Rome who were enemies of the Senate. Pompey, in an act that showed his great statesmanship, threw the letters into the fire without reading them. He wanted to end the war once and for all. Perpenna, for his part, was executed. At this point, there was a general disbandment. The surviving Sertorian leaders tried to flee Hispania. Many of them embarked from Dianium for Sicily, while those in H. Ulterior moved to Africa, but they were all captured and executed. Only one of them managed to escape the slaughter. He was Aufidius, one of the conspirators in the assassination of Sertorius, with whom Plutarch ends his *Life of Sertorius* by telling us that he ended up hiding in an Iberian village and that he died old and in the most miserable poverty. Nor do we know the fate of Sertorius' white hind. In any case, it is hard to believe that he had a happy ending. But the war was not over. There were still some cities that remained loyal to Sertorius, despite his death. Hence, Pompey unceremoniously razed Uxama Argaela (modern El Burgo de Osma, Castilla y León), Gracchurris and Clunia to the ground. Finally, he laid siege to Calagurris[36] (modern Calahorra, La Rioja) for the second time, this time by Afranius, by order of Pompey. This siege was extremely harsh, comparable only to that of Numantia. As much as Afranius tried to take the city, its inhabitants resisted to the last consequences, far beyond what might seem logical to contemporary eyes. The Calagurritians died by the dozens from disease, but above all from hunger. So epic must have been the resistance that the expression *fames*

36 Espinosa (1984) and Pina Polo (2006).

calagurritiana became popular in Rome to describe episodes of extreme famine, which some classical authors, such as Valerius Maximus, embellish with episodes of anthropophagy. This spirit of resistance is exemplified by a local legend, known as the Dowager of Calagurris. A woman who, at night, went round the houses whose inhabitants were dead to light lanterns so that the Romans would think that all the Calagarrutians were still alive. Finally, Afranius managed to conquer the city. We do not know how long the siege lasted and whether the Roman victory was achieved by assault or surrender. What was left of the Sertorian army either surrendered or dispersed. However, classical sources (Caes., *BGall.*, 3, 23; or Cassius Dio, *Hist.*, 39, 46), inform us that an unyielding Sertorian contingent moved to Aquitania where, allied with the local tribes, it continued to fight against Rome. But in Hispania, the war was now over.

Map 10: Map of Hispania during the Sertorian War showing where the main battles that have been reliably located were.

Caesar in Hispania

In 72 BC, Metellus, whose mandate expired at the end of that year, returned to Rome to celebrate his triumph, and was replaced by Marcus Pupius Piso Frugi Calpurnianus. For Pompey, however, much work remained to be done. Unlike H. Ulterior, where the war had been largely conducted in Lusitanian territory, H. Citerior had been the scene of great fighting, sieges and scorched-earth policy between the two armies, which left the territory devastated. The young general set to work and, demonstrating his political stature, initiated a policy of reconstruction of the territory that would lead to a period of peace and prosperity for 25 years, that is, until the next civil war. To begin with, he converted his former camps of Pompaelo and Gerunda into cities, merging them with the ancient *oppida* of the Vascones and Iberians respectively. The survivors of the Sertorian wars in the Ebro valley, i.e., those from Gracchurris, Calagurris or Clunia, for example, were deported to Aquitania (modern south-west of France), with whom he founded the city of Lugdunum Convenarum (modern Saint-Betrand-de-Comminges, Haute Garonne), while others were sent to the territory of the Volcos Tectosages. These cities in the Ebro valley were occupied by his Vascones allies. In addition, he colonised these territories with discharged soldiers and citizens from his native region, Piceno. Evidently, this brought him many new clients who consolidated his political position in both provinces. It was the beginning of a new era.

Meanwhile, nothing of note happened in Ulterior, although Pupius, on his return to Rome in 69 BC, celebrated a triumph for his victories in his province, so it is plausible that he fought against the Lusitanians. This triumph, however, was widely criticised in the Senate, given the insignificance of his alleged victories. The passing of his successor, Antistius Vetus, was more notable, not because of his abulic stay, but because he was accompanied by a young *quaestor* who was destined to change the history of Rome. This was a man who, despite his high birth (he came from an old patrician family), suffered a very precarious economic situation. But what he lacked in *denarii* he more than made up for with intelligence, cunning, courage and audacity. The man's name was Gaius Julius Caesar. Although he was taking his first steps in his *cursus honorum*, Caesar had already had an intense political life. Linked to the political faction of Gaius Marius (his aunt, Julia, was Marius' wife) and, later, to that of Lucius Cornelius Cinna, he was appointed by the latter as *flamen dialis* at the age of 16, one of the most important religious posts in Rome, and married to his daughter, Cornelia Cinna, with whom he had a daughter, Julia. But after Cinna's fall, Sulla, the new dictator of Rome, gave him a choice between abandoning Cornelia and exile. Caesar, who seems to have been truly in love with his young wife, chose to leave Rome. He was also removed from his position as *flamen dialis* by legal trickery. The pleas of his mother, Aurelia Cotta, whose three brothers were to be consuls under Sulla's dictatorship, allowed

Caesar to return from exile. Meanwhile, as *Tribunus laticlavius*,[37] he had already taken part in the war against Mithridates VI under the orders of Marcus Minucius Thermus. In this war, he was noted for his bravery and ability to command, and was awarded a *Corona Civica* (Civic Crown), the highest Roman military distinction. He was also sent to make diplomatic representations to the court of King Nicomedes IV of Bithynia. Such was Caesar's success that he was accused of having a homosexual relationship with the king, who had been dazzled by the young Roman. Soon after, he returned to Rome, where he excelled as an extraordinary orator, winning many important court cases in the Forum. In 69 BC, some important events took place in the life of the young Caesar. Firstly, his wife Cornelia died, giving birth to a stillborn child; secondly, he was elected *quaestor*, and in the subsequent lottery he was given the province of Hispania Ulterior. The *praetor* in command of the territory, Antistius Vetus, trusted his subordinate blindly, their relationship was excellent, and he delegated most of the management of the province to him. This would help Caesar to get to know the local elites, and in particular he would form a solid friendship with a citizen of Gadir who would end up becoming one of his closest friends and political allies: Lucius Cornelius Balbus Maior.

It is worth pausing for a moment to talk about Balbus and his family. After all, years later, he would be elected the first consul of Rome born outside Italy. From his name, it is thought that his family might be of Punic origin. It should be remembered that a large part of the Phoenician population in the south of the Iberian Peninsula did not return to the metropolis and remained in what were already their homes, adapting to the new government, but maintaining their religion and customs. The Balbii were extraordinarily wealthy and influential merchants. Lucius Cornelius, born between around 100 BC, so was about the same age as Julius Caesar. During the *Bellum Sertorianum* he joined the army of Metellus Pius, fighting in numerous battles. Subsequently, thanks to the *lex Gellia Cornelia*,[38] he was granted Roman citizenship. Balbus, who would end up having a great influence on Caesar, would come to occupy very important offices in Rome, privileges which other members of his family also enjoyed thereafter.

---

37 *Tribunus laticlavius* (literally 'broad-striped tribune') was the second in command in a legion, and the first step in the *cursus honorum*.

38 The *lex Gellia Cornelia* of 72 BC, officially recognised the status of Roman citizenship of those Hispanians who had been granted such status by Pompey and Metellus for their support in the war.

From Suetonius (*Caes.*, 7) we learn that, apart from his frenetic activity as *quaestor* and in his efforts to obtain new clients, during his stay at this stage the young Caesar visited the Gadir temple of Hercules-Melkart.[39] It was there that the famous scene took place in which Caesar, dejected, laments the few achievements he has made at the age of 32, comparing himself with Alexander the Great, who at his age had already conquered the world. It is likely that at the centre of his envy was also Pompey, only six years his senior, and already the most admired man in Rome, whose youthful achievements were far superior to Caesar's. Presumably that visit was the spur that prompted him to return to Rome and advance his political career, at whatever cost. His first step was to arrange a marriage with Pompeia, the granddaughter of the dictator Sulla, which brought him closer to the party of the *Optimates*. In 65 BC, he obtained the office of *curule aedile* in Rome. And in 63 BC, after the death of the *pontifex maximus* Metellus Pius, he was elected to replace him in office. That vote was marked by controversy, as Caesar apparently spent a fortune in bribes, leaving him with such debts that Suetonius (*Caes.*, 13) tells us that he told his mother that, if he did not get the office, he would never be able to return home. In the election, moreover, he beat two of the most important and influential politicians of the time, Publius Servilius Isauricus (c. 79 BC) and Quintus Lutatius Catulus (c. 78 BC). It was indeed one of the most important religious offices in Rome, which conferred numerous privileges and *auctoritas* on the 37-year-old man. Shortly afterwards, the Bona Dea[40] scandal occurred, and

39 It was located on the island of Sancti Petri, opposite Gadir. It was of Phoenician origin and was dedicated to the god Melkart, whom the Romans related to Hercules. The temple was famous and revered, even guarding a fabulous treasure. Throughout its history, it was visited by great historical figures, who came to worship it, such as: Hannibal (the famous scene in which he swore eternal hatred of the Romans took place there), Pompey, as well as a long list of proconsuls, *praetores*, and philosophers. The arrival of Christianity marked the beginning of the temple's decline. The banning of pagan cults by the emperor Theodosius at the end of that century led to the abandonment of the temple. Soon the despoilment began. Finally, the remains were razed to the ground by the Almoravid army in 1149, and over the ruins they built a castle which, with later modifications. On the history of this temple and the cult of Hercules, Leonor De Bock Cano, *El Templo de Hércules Gaditano. Reality and Legend.* Published by Fundación Vipren. Chiclana de la Frontera (2016).

40 The Bona Dea was a religious celebration exclusively for women that took place in December in the house of the *pontifex maximus* and was organised by his wife, in this case Pompeia. It was attended, disguised as a woman, by Publius Clodius Pulcher, who, according to Plutarch (*Caes.*, 9), had been trying to seduce Caesar's wife. The vigilance of his mother-in-law, Aurelia, seemed to have prevented the flirting. In any case, Clodius was discovered and arrested. He was tried on various charges but was acquitted thanks to bribery. Caesar, surprisingly, did not want to accuse him, claiming he had no evidence. Later, someone

Caesar divorced Pompeia. It was a complicated year, which also saw the conspiracy by which Lucius Sergius Catilina planned to seize power in a coup d'état and assassinate the two consuls. Caesar, who defended some of the conspirators, was accused of taking part in the plot, although it was never proved. In any case, the following year, 62 BC, he was elected to the prestigious office of *praetor urbanus*. His good performance increased his popularity among the Romans. However, the following year, he was elected *praetor*, and was assigned to H. Ulterior, a territory he knew perfectly well. However, Caesar was faced with a serious problem: his enormous debts. His creditors would not allow him to leave the city without settling his accounts. Fortunately for Caesar, all his debits were paid by his friend Marcus Licinius Crassus, who was at that time the richest man in Rome. Caesar would owe Crassus the fabulous sum of 830 talents.[41] Incidentally, the new governor of the province would be accompanied by Gaius Antistius Vetus, as *quaestor* (he was the son of the *praetor* whom Caesar served in 69 BC), his inseparable Lucius Cornelius Balbus, as *praefectus fabrum*,[42] and twenty cohorts. In 61 BC, Caesar took office in Corduba.

But what had happened in Hispania during the time that Caesar had been increasing his political power in Rome? Pompey was able to influence votes so that men from his inner circle were given the positions of *propraetores* in both provinces. However, as the years went by and with Pompey fighting in different wars in the East, he must have lost some influence, where men like Caesar took care to appropriate part of his client networks (the case of the Balbus family is a good example of this), and in Rome itself, where Marcus Licinius Crassus managed to get Gnaeus Calpurnius Piso, a man he trusted, the post of *quaestor propraetore* of H. Citerior in 65 BC. In the same year, Publius Sittius Nucerinus was appointed governor of H. Ulterior. It cannot be a coincidence that both leaders were involved in the first conspiracy of Lucius Sergius Catilina. In fact, it is likely that Calpurnius and Sittius, who could have contributed to political instability, were seen in a favourable light in Rome as having moved away from the

asked him: 'Why, then, didst thou divorce thy wife?' 'Because,' said Caesar, 'I thought my wife ought not even to be under suspicion' (Plut., *Caes.*, 10). A more summarised account of the events can also be found in Suetonius (*Caes.*, 6). P. Clodius Pulcher would eventually renounce his patrician status in order to be elected Tribune of the Plebs, a position from which he would contribute to Rome's unprecedented political instability, but that is another story.

41 Currently, this figure would be approximately GBP 173 million, or USD 216 million, or CAD 290 million.

42 A kind of chief engineer.

metropolis. However, a few months after his arrival, Calpurnius was killed by some Hispanians, probably members of his escort. While some historians argue that this must have been because of Calpurnius' cruel and unjust rule, Sallust (*Cat.*, 19) states that it is more likely that he was killed by clients of Pompey, who, if not the one who gave the order, did approve of this action.[43] The sources do not indicate who replaced Calpurnius Piso. As for P. Sittius, he raised an army in his province. The sources do not say whether he planned to rise against Rome from H. Ulterior, but he was forced to move to Africa, where he received the news of Catalina's defeat in Rome. From then on, he served as a mercenary in various North African kingdoms.

Therefore, we return to Caesar in Corduba. First, he pursued a policy of conciliatory measures to curry favour with the local elites. He abolished taxes created by Metellus and strengthened Ulterior's trade with Rome. The issue that seems to concern him most, however, was the situation in Lusitania.[44] We have already seen above that, at least in theory, these warlike tribes were defeated in the Lusitanian War of 154–139 BC. But in 138 BC, D. Junius Brutus attacked them again, reaching the territory north of the river Douro. However, these tribes never really came to be dominated by Rome, among other reasons, because of the inability of the successive governors of H. Ulterior to impose themselves in those territories. In fact, the *Bellum Sertorianum* began as a new Lusitanian revolt. In 61 BC they were still carrying out raids in H. Ulterior. Caesar's main objective was to pacify Lusitania, the western tribes of the Vettones and the Galatians and incorporate them definitively into Rome. It was a titanic task for which he had only a few months to complete. He recruited new cohorts and 8,000 auxiliary soldiers in Hispania. Together with the troops he had brought from Rome, he had a total of 42,000 men. He again visited the temple of Hercules-Melkart and headed towards Metellium, from where he departed to the north-east. It should be noted that the Lusitanian tribes south of the Tagus River were relatively pacified and did not put up any resistance to Caesar. Unlike his predecessors, the new *praetor* did not intend to simply raze the territory to the ground. Firstly, and whenever possible, he used diplomacy and agreements with the local elites, who had to accept Rome's sovereignty, abandon the *oppida* and found new cities, following the model of the Roman civitas, on flat land; in exchange, they would be granted land on which they could devote

43 Amela Valverder (2002).

44 On Caesar's campaign in Lusitania, Novillo López (2000).

themselves to agriculture, livestock and trade, and where settlers from Italy would also have a place. Caesar encountered more problems in the territory between the rivers Tagus and Douro, where he had to fight against various tribes, which he defeated without difficulty. Once again, he forced them to abandon their *oppida,* setting them up in flat land. In mid-summer, he crossed the Douro to enter the territory of Gallaecia Bracarense, where Caesar again easily subdued the Galician tribes. Returning south, he encountered for the first time a coalition of tribes that put up a battle in the region known in antiquity as *Mons Herminius*[45] (modern Sierra da Estrela, Portugal). Ceasar won the battle, but the survivors fled to the coast, fortifying themselves on an island now thought to be the Portuguese town of Peniche.[46] The *praetor* organised an attack with rafts and small boats, but bad weather meant that many of them failed to reach the island. After this failure, he asked his *praefectus fabrum,* Balbus, to command a fleet of warships from Gadir. When, at the end of August, a fleet of fifteen ships appeared, the Lusitanians of Peniche, terrified, surrendered. In addition, he was informed that to the north there were islands rich in gold and tin, so he took advantage of Balbus' fleet to explore them. It was the Casitérides islands (probably the modern Cíes islands, Galicia), where he was able to confirm the information received. After this campaign, he returned to Gades. He had gained extraordinary booty (not only could he pay off his debts to Crassus, but he had enough gold left over to enjoy fabulous wealth), new client ties, new (and safe) routes for the merchants of the H. Ulterior and, not least, military glory. In fact, it was there that he was first acclaimed as *imperator* by his men, which entitled him to celebrate a triumph in Rome. He then proceeded to Corduba and, after settling several unfinished businesses, ended his stay in Hispania. Caesar's government was a success. He managed to pacify a territory that had been in rebellion for more than a century, opened new trade routes, founded new cities in which Lusitanians, Vettones and Galicians lived side by side with Roman and Italic settlers.

On his arrival in Rome, Caesar won the consular elections. Receiving Gaul as his province, in 58 BC he began the war that would bring him fame and fortune. At this time, he secretly agreed the first triumvirate with Pompey and Crassus, in what was called the Lucan Conference.

45 Literally, 'mountains of Hermes', because he was the god of shepherds. It is believed to be the place where Viriathus was born.

46 In the 17th century, the accumulation of sand and sediment formed a tongue of land that linked the island to the mainland. Peniche is about 52 miles from Lisbon and 155 miles from Porto.

Under this pact, Pompey would marry Julia, Caesar's only daughter. This agreement would be formalised by the *lex Trebonia de provinciis consularibus*, presented in 55 BC by the Tribune of the Plebs Caius Trebonius, which extended the power of Pompey in Hispania, Caesar in Gaul, and Crassus in Syria, giving them the power to declare war and sign peace treaties without the approval of the Senate. As a result, the appointment of the governors of those provinces came to respond to the interests of the triumvirs. Thus, the governors of Hispania were people linked to Pompey, for example, in H. Citerior we find Sextus Quinctilius Varus, father of the infamous Publius Quintilius Varus, the man who commanded the Roman army in the Battle of the Teutoburg Forest, where three legions and numerous auxiliary troops were annihilated in 19 BC. While in H. Ulterior you would see Publius Cornelius Lentulus Spinther or Quintus Caecilius Metellus Nepos. These governors allow us to see how on many occasions they were linked to each other by marriages . . . and unlinked by divorces. For example, Lentulus Spinther was married to Caecilia Metella, Metellus Nepos' niece. On the other hand, Pompey himself had as his third wife Mucia Tercia, daughter of Quintus Mucius Scaevola,[47] who would be the mother of his sons Cnaeus and Sextus Pomepius. Their divorce in 55 BC provoked the triumvir's enmity with the families of the Mucii Scaevolae and the Caecilii Metelli, who were half-brothers of Mucia Tercia. Only Metellus Nepos would remain loyal to Pompey, and remain at enmity with his own family. The events in Rome are so important at this time that, once again, the ancient sources hardly inform us about what happened at this time in Hispania. The only exception is a brief note by Cassius Dio (*Hist.*, 39, 54), which narrates a revolt of the Vaccaei that was harshly repressed by Metellus Nepos. The reason for the new insurrection is unclear but given that the *lex Trebonia* allowed triumvirs to declare wars without the permission of the Senate, it is likely that Metellus Nepos had received instructions from Pompey to begin a new conflict to obtain spoils of war; or, simply, it was the desire of these tribes to try to gain independence from Rome. We know that Metellus Nepos conquered Brigantium (modern Corunna, Galicia), but that he failed in the siege of Clunia (near Peñalba de Castro, Castilla y León). If we consider that between the two cities there is 330 miles, we must suppose that the revolt was widespread along the whole Douro valley. Pompey must have seen that

47 One of the main leaders of the *Optimates* party, killed during the proscriptions of Marius.

the situation could get out of hand, so, the following year, he sent three legates: as governor of H. Citerior none other than Lucius Afranius, his lieutenant during the *Bellum Sertorianum* and, consequently, someone who knew the territory and its people perfectly well; as governor of H. Ulterior Marcus Petreius; while Marcus Terentius Varro would have an army to continue fighting on the frontier of the Vaccaei and the Vettones. All of them would have a five-year term of office and a total of seven legions.

Meanwhile, in Rome the alliance of the triumvirs began to fall apart in 54 BC. The first blow was the death of Pompey's wife Julia in childbirth. The following year, along with most of his army and his son, Crassus died at the Battle of Carrhae, fighting the Parthians. The two ties that bound Caesar and Pompey were broken. Hence, the *Optimates* faction initiated a movement to lure Pompey into their ranks, which culminated in 52 BC with the marriage of the almost sexagenarian general to Cornelia Metella, daughter of Metellus Scipio (adopted son of Metellus Pius) in 52 BC. From then on, the Senate would fight Caesar with all its legal (or illegal) means, to strip him of his command in Gaul with the aim of putting him on trial and, eventually, condemning him to exile. But something had changed in Rome. If two centuries earlier, faced with a similar situation, Cornelius Scipio had resigned himself to being condemned to exile, now Caesar, to paraphrase Dylan Thomas, 'did not go gentle into that good night'. But Cornelius Scipio had no army behind him to support him. As mentioned above, Marius' reforms had created a large mass of soldiers whose loyalty was no longer to the Senate, but to the general who paid them, with whom they shared the spoils of war and who provided them with land to live on after their military service. Thus, in 49 BC, under pressure from the Senate, Caesar decided to cross the river Rubicon accompanied by the Legio XIII Gemina, an act that *de facto* started a new civil war. *Alea iacta est.*

Pompey vs. Caesar

Hispania was to play a fundamental role in this new war, as it was here that the first battles began and where the outcome of the war was to take place. Although it is not the aim of this book to detail the events that led to the end of the Republic, but rather to detail the events that took place in Hispania, this will not be possible without contextualising what happened in other parts of the Mediterranean. Thus, in Italy, Caesar gradually took over cities that came over to his faction, such as Firmun or Castrum Truetium. Meanwhile, the senators of the *Optimates* faction panicked and left Rome. Most of them headed south, to recruit troops, or simply to flee the city. Lucius Domitius Ahenobarbus, who had just been appointed proconsul by the Senate for the province of Gaul to replace Caesar, went to Corfinium, about a hundred miles east of Rome; Cato the Younger, to Sicily; while Pompey and several senators concentrated in Luceria, north of what is now the region of Apulia. In mid-February, Caesar besieged Corfinium. Ahenobarbus received a letter from Pompey informing him that he would not come to his aid, so the proconsul prepared to flee the city. When his soldiers heard of this, they arrested him, surrendered to Caesar and handed Ahenobarbus over to him, who pardoned him and set him free. Meanwhile, Pompey and his allies marched towards Brundisium, with the aim of embarking for Greece, where they hoped to recruit more troops. Caesar arrived at the city gates in early March but was unable to prevent Pompey and his army from embarking. With no fleet to pursue Pompey, Caesar returned to Rome just in time to make some political decisions and march on Hispania. His aim was to dominate all the western Roman provinces, not only to avoid being trapped by the armies of Pompey, but also to be able to dispose of the riches of those territories. He sent Quintus Valerius Orca to Sardinia and Gaius Scribonius Curio to Sicily as legates, who succeeded in getting the islands into Caesar's hands within a few weeks. From Sicily, Cato the Younger escaped, and sailed to Greece to join Pompey and the other *Optimates*. On his way to Hispania, Caesar encountered unexpected opposition from Massilia, leaving Legio VIII, XII and XIII under the command of Decimus Junius Brutus Albinus and Gaius Trebonius besieging the city, which was defended by the obstinate Domitius Ahenobarbus. Paradoxically, these two legates would be among the conspirators who would end up assassinating Caesar five years later.

At the beginning of June, Caesar's army finally reached Hispania. He advanced Legio VII, IX and XI under the command of Gaius Fabius who easily defeated the Pompeian garrisons guarding the Pyrenean passes and moved into Hispania to seek the support of the local tribes. Meanwhile, Caesar waited in Narbonnese Gaul with the rest of his legions, VI, X and XIV. At this time, Caesar must have had about 25,000 legionaries, 12,000 auxiliary troops (mostly Gallic, but during the campaign he would be joined by Hispanian troops) and about 5,000 horsemen (of the same origin as the auxiliary troops). For their part, the Pompeians had seven legions in Hispania, three under Lucius Afranius, two under Marcus Petreius and two under Terentius Varro. While Caesar's troops were mostly veterans of the Gallic Wars, those of the Pompeians had been trained in fighting the Vaccaei and the Vettones. The Pompeian legates agreed that Varro would stay in the rear, while Afranius and Petreius would join their legions at Ilerda to face the Caesarian army. Between the two generals they had some 30,000 legionaries, 18,000 auxiliary troops (Hispanians) and some 5,000 horsemen (Hispanians). They set up camp on a hill known today as Gardeny, in the vicinity of the city, very close to a stone bridge that crossed the river Sicoris (modern river Segre). Days later, a fourth legion joined Fabius' troops, who had already built a camp relatively far from Ilerda and two wooden bridges north of the city over the river Sicoris, one about 11 miles (*pons ulterior*), the second about 6 miles (*pons propior*). The main problem for the Caesarians was the supply of the troops and horses, as opposed to the Pompeians, who had the huge grain stores of Ilerda, as well as many more allies among the Ilergetes tribes in the area. So Fabius was forced to send part of his legions to forage. On 20 June, after heavy rains, the *pons propior* collapsed, just as two of Fabius' four legions had crossed. Afranius and Petreius, who had been following their movements, ordered their three legions to form up and move against the two isolated Caesarian legions under the command of the military tribune Lucius Munatius Plancus, a veteran of the Gallic Wars. Plancus ordered his men to take up a defensive position on a nearby hill and they withstood the Pompeian onslaught. Meanwhile, Fabius crossed the *pons ulterior* with his two other legions and rushed to the rescue of Plancus' men. The arrival of Caesarian reinforcements convinced Afranius and Petreius that it was time to retreat, and they returned to their camp. Thus ended what was known as the skirmish of Alcoletge.

Two days later, Caesar arrived from Massalia. He immediately ordered his men to deploy on a plain in front of Ilerda, but the Pompeians did not come out to fight. Therefore, Caesar ordered the construction of a new camp near the enemy camp. But as the days passed and Afranius and Petreius shunned combat, Caesar decided to take the initiative by seizing a hill between the Pompeian camp and the city of Ilerda, probably Puig Bordell. In doing so, he wanted to cut off the communications and supplies that his enemies were receiving from the city. He therefore deployed three of his legions in the direction of the hill. Afranius and Petreius, noticing the Caesarian movements, sent their troops to occupy the hilltop before the enemy. The Battle of Ilerda had begun. The fighting was fiercely disputed. Surely, many of the Pompeian troops must have been of Hispanian origin, as Caesar himself tells us that their way of fighting disconcerted his legionaries, who began to give ground, so much so that he had to send Legio IX as reinforcements. This ended up tipping the balance in his favour. They took Puig Bordell and caused the Pompeians to retreat to the safety of the walls of Ilerda. But then, in an action difficult to understand in such experienced troops as Caesar's, the legionaries pursued their enemies into the city, where they were met by a hail of arrows and batteries, decimating them terribly. Finally, Caesar ordered his men to return to camp. Puig Bordell was left in the hands of Afranius' men, who hastened to fortify it. Caesar had lost the battle. But the problems for the first man of Rome had only just begun. The thawing of the high Pyrenean basins caused the level of the Sicoris River to rise, turning Caesar's camp into a quagmire, but worst of all, Fabius' two wooden bridges were washed away. Caesar began to suffer from supply problems. He sent numerous convoys of legionaries into Ilergethean territory to get food for his men and fodder for his horses, but they were often attacked by Ilergethean tribesmen allied with the Pompeians. The situation was becoming desperate. Then, Caesar ordered to build a series of coracles, a kind of large Celtic canoe that he must have met in the Gallic Wars, and with them, by night, he crossed part of his men to the other bank of the Sicoris, fortifying a position. From the eastern bank, it would be easier to forage and find food. Luck seemed to change sides. News came of the fall of Massilia, although Domitius Ahenobarbus had managed to flee. In addition, rumour had spread in recent weeks that Pompey and a powerful army would be arriving from Africa. The confirmation that the general of the *Optimates* was not going to move out of Greece demoralised Afranius' and Petreius' men. This news also caused numerous tribes and cities in the territory to change sides. Osca, Calagurris, Tarraco and part of the Ilergetes sent ambassadors announcing their new alliance with Caesar. Now it was the Pompeian foragers who were having trouble getting supplies. It was they who were harassed by the local tribes and Caesar's army. Afranius and Petreius panicked. They did not understand how the tables had turned in this way. The annihilation of a cohort that had gone out in search of food finally convinced the Pompeians to retreat south to Octogesa, an Ilergite town at the confluence of the Sicoris and Ebro rivers, where they hoped to contact Varus' legions. They leave two cohorts of auxiliary infantry at Ilerda and, at night, set out on their march. Caesar did not want to risk going into unfamiliar territory in the dark of night, so he set out the next morning. However, his cavalry constantly harassed the Pompeian rearguard, causing heavy casualties. Finally, in one of their surprising marches, Caesar's troops reached Octogesa before the Pompeians, who were practically surrounded and had to decide whether to march east towards Tarraco or return to Ilerda. A few days passed and many of Afranius' and Petreius' soldiers deserted and joined Caesar. Taking advantage of the fact that Pompey's two legates left their camp to explore possible escape routes, some centurions and even Afranius' teenage son tried to negotiate an honourable surrender. But when their generals heard of this, they refused to surrender and even ordered the execution of the emissaries Caesar had sent to their camp. They then decided to return to Ilerda. But once again, the proconsul stuck to them as if he were their own shadow. The Caesarian cavalry made life miserable for the Pompeian rearguard and their foragers. Afranius and Petreius constantly had to halt the march, losing dozens of men in skirmishes and to desertion. Finally, they were once again trapped in Caesar's army. With hardly any supplies, no wood and morale at rock bottom, the Pompeian generals decide to surrender. The capitulation took place on 2 August. In one of his typical acts of magnanimity, no one was executed. Caesar released Afranius and Petreius and gave his troops freedom to be discharged or to leave with their generals. Approximately one-third of the Pompeian soldiers were discharged, another part went over to Caesar's army, while the remainder, together with their generals, were escorted as prisoners to the banks of the river Var (near modern Nice, France) and there discharged. But the war was not yet over in Hispania. Varro's two legions remained in Ulterior. The *praetor*, encouraged by the news of the victory at Ilerda, probably somewhat exaggerated, which he had received in a letter from Afranius, had prepared a large fleet at Gadir and Hispalis and recruited thirty cohorts of auxiliary soldiers. However, with the final defeat of Afranius and Petreius, he prepared for combat. Caesar had advanced two legions under the command of Quintus Fufius Calenus, who arrived in Corduba with an edict summoning the principal cities of H. Ulterior to send delegates to that city to place themselves under Caesar's command. The summons was a resounding success and all the cities sent ambassadors. Varro began to despair: all the cities closed their gates to him or expelled their garrisons. Unable to reverse the situation, he sent a messenger to the proconsul to offer unconditional surrender. The latter sent his cousin and most trusted confidant Sextus Julius Caesar.[48] Finally, Varro came in person to Corduba to surrender to Caesar, handing over to him all the money he had set aside for his military campaign, as well as a complete list of his troops, warships, and foodstuffs. As he had done with his colleagues, the proconsul pardoned Varro, who were free to leave, and discharged his troops. Hispania was under the control of Caesar. He had wiped out Pompey's

48 In fact, he is believed to have been his heir. His death during a riot in 47 BC meant that his heir became Octavian.

seven legions with just one battle . . . which he didn't even need to win! But then it was time to return to Rome. And to face Pompey. The war continued. And it was approaching its decisive phase. Nevertheless, the proconsul left Quintus Cassius Longinus as legate in Hispania, along with four legions, and headed for Gadir, where he embarked for Rome. But even though the whole province paid obeisance to the proconsul, it did not mean that the old pro-Pompeian sentiment had completely disappeared.

The following year, 48 BC, would be decisive, although not definitive for the development of the war. After being proclaimed dictator, Caesar moved to Greece, followed by the lieutenants who had not been able to accompany him on the first trip, such as Mark Antony. Pompey, who had a huge army and alliances with the cities of the territory, seemed to be able to defeat his enemy. In fact, he defeated Caesar at the siege of Dyrrachium, which boosted the morale of his troops and gave confidence to the leaders of the *Optimates*, who began to pressure Pompey to strike the final blow against the enemy. It seems that the experienced general would have preferred a Fabian strategy to wear down the enemy. He knew Caesar too well not to be afraid of some stratagem that might balance the battle and jeopardise a victory that, on the face of it, seemed likely to be easy in favour of the *Optimates*. But his generals and senators pressed him to act. After all, they had an estimated 50,000 men, including 7,000 horsemen, while Caesar had only 30,000 men, including 1,000 horsemen. Moreover, the Pompeians had on their side the greatest cavalry general of his generation. None other than Titus Labienus, the man who had been Caesar's lieutenant in the Gallic Wars, the only one of his generals who had betrayed him to the *Optimate* side. Labienus had been his closest advisor, one of his best friends. Why did he betray him? There has been much speculation on this point,[49] but surely the fact that Labienus, being from Picene like Pompey, was linked to him as a client or by friendship had a great influence. Be that as it may, and we continue to speculate, it is likely that the *Optimates* also used Labienus as a means of pressure. Given the enormous numerical superiority in cavalry, he would undoubtedly play a leading role in the battle. Consequently, Pompey had no choice but to agree to attack Caesar. As time was against him, the dictator did not shy away from the battle. After all, fighting outnumbered for him and his troops was like 'just another day at the office'. They were all

49 To understand the relationship between the two generals, the work of Majerczyk (2015) is essential.

seasoned from the Gallic Wars and were not going to be intimidated on this occasion either. On 7 June the battle took place on the plains of Pharsalus. The Pompeian camp was divided into four large blocks, from left to right: all the cavalry and auxiliary infantry units under the command of Labienus; to his right, legions under the direct command of Pompey; followed by the legions of Metellus Scipio; and finally, the legions of Cilicia and the Hispanian cohorts of Afranius, under the command of the stubborn Domitius Ahenobarbus (the man Caesar had already defeated and spared at Corfinium and Massilia). The battlefield was enclosed by the river Enipeus. In front of them, the Caesarian army, equally divided into four blocks, but much shallower because of their numerical inferiority. From right to left were the meagre cavalry; the legions under Publius Cornelius Sulla; followed by the troops under Gnaeus Domitius Calvinus; and finally, between him and the river Enipeus, the legions of Mark Antony. The key to the battle was the six chosen reserve cohorts that were placed behind Sulla's legions, and where Caesar himself was also placed. In the first phase of the battle, only the Caesarian legions were put into action. Pompey preferred that, in the heat of the month of June, his enemies should be the ones to wear themselves out going into battle. But halfway through, seeing that the Pompeians were not moving, the Caesarian legionaries stopped in their tracks, giving an astonishing display of order and discipline, showing how well trained those centurions and soldiers were. Fear must have begun to run high in the Pompeian camp, especially among their soldiers, most of whom were novices. Eventually, the front lines of the legionaries broke through, and a close battle ensued. Pompey must have been calm at this point. The battle was going according to plan. And it stayed that way when Labienus set his 7,000 horsemen galloping to meet the 1,000 Caesarian cavalrymen. The plan was simple. It was impossible for his horsemen not to destroy the enemy. It was true that most of the Pompeian cavalry was made up of nobles and notables from the eastern provinces and that the Caesarians were the dreaded Gallic horsemen, but the ratio was 7 to 1! After annihilating the Gauls, Labienus' cavalry would attack the right flank of Sulla's legions and that would be the end of the battle. Nothing could go wrong. But Caesar had an ace up his sleeve. An unpleasant surprise awaited them. At first, the clash between the two cavalries went as planned: the Gauls were overwhelmed and fled. The Pompeian horsemen gave chase, but suddenly, from the Caesarian right flank, they were met with a hail of arrows and *pila*. These were the six cohorts that Caesar had hidden in the rear. This counter-attack brought down many horsemen in the front ranks, who, moreover, suddenly found themselves surrounded by bloodthirsty legionaries and the Gallic cavalry, which had returned to attack them in the rear. They were being exterminated. The second line of Labienus' horsemen panicked and turned and began a disorderly retreat. The confusion among the Pompeian cavalry was total. They began to retreat towards Mount Dogantzis, running over the auxiliary troops to their rear on their way. At this point, Caesar, who was on the right flank among his legionaries, gave the order to Legio X to begin to break through the Pompeian lines. Up to then, they had not been fully engaged. They were simply holding their ground. On Caesar's orders, Legio X slaughtered the Pompeian Legio I and III. It looked like a battle of men against children. The rest of the Caesarian legions imitated their comrades in X and began to push the enemy lines. They were soon flanked on the left. The *Optimates* infantry began to sink. Meanwhile, the Gallic horsemen were slaughtering the enemy horsemen up the hill. Pompey and his staff, including the main *Optimates* leaders, left the battlefield. All was lost. In his *Bellum Civile*, Caesar claims to have lost only 200 men, compared with 60,000 Pompeian casualties. Appian suggests that the figures were significantly different, so that Caesar's casualties were about 1,200 to Pompey' 6,000. The defeat dissolved the group of *Optimates*. For instance, Lucius Domitius Ahenobarbus[50] had lost his life in battle, facing Mark Anthony's legions. Cicero and Marcus Julius Brutus surrendered to Caesar, who pardoned them. He also sought and obtained the magnanimity of the dictator Marcus Terentius Varro, the former *praetor* of H. Ulterior. Less fortunate was Publius Cornelius Lentulus Spinther, who fled to Rhodes and was killed there. The vast majority of the *Optimates*, however, gathered in Africa, although they arrived by different routes. The territory was controlled by the Pompeian legate Publius Attius Varus, who counted the king of Numidia, Juba I, as a loyal ally. Metellus Scipio, who took command of the army because of his consular rank, Cato the Younger, Titus Labienus, Gnaeus Pompeius Magnus (Pompey the Younger, the elder son of the Magnus) and the other two former Pompeian legates in Hispania, Lucius Afranius and Marcus Petreius, among others, arrived there. Thus, the main battlefront shifted to Africa. Pompey, for his part, with a small group of collaborators, travelled to Egypt, where he hoped to find protection at the court of his ally, the young

50 His son Gnaeus was also present at the battle and survived. After Caesar's assassination he sided with Brutus and Longinus with whom he fought in the Battles of Philippi. He later reconciled with Mark Antony, sealing their friendship with a wedding between his son Lucius and Antony's daughter Antonia Maior. One of his grandsons was the emperor Nero.

king[51] Ptolemy XIII Theos Philopator, but shortly before disembarking he was assassinated.

Caesar landed in Africa in 47 BC. Initially, he was in as precarious a situation as he had been in Greece the previous year. However, he managed to receive reinforcements and was able to take the strategic initiative in the campaign, culminating in the siege of the city of Thapsus (modern Ras Dimas, Tunisia). Metellus Scipio could not afford to lose this strategic town, so he decided to engage Caesar in the final battle. The *Optimates* had about 90,000 men to Caesar's 60,000–70,000, as well as a great numerical superiority in cavalry and elephants. The battle took place on 6 April. On this occasion, surprisingly, the strictly disciplined soldiers of Legio VII and X pushed forward more than they should have done, as they were in high spirits and wanted to end the battle quickly. On this occasion, the decisive points were those where Metellus Scipio had ordered his elephants to charge. Those who attacked on the right flank received a hail of arrows and *pila* that so frightened them that they turned and began to charge their own forces, causing chaos among the *Optimates*' army. At another point in the battle, the elephants charged Legio V Alaudae. In a performance that went down in the annals of history, the legionnaires withstood the onslaught of these tremendous war machines and defeated them. From that day on, the emblem of Legio V Alaudae was, deservedly, an elephant. Legio VII and Legio X break through the enemy line. The massacre was unheard of in a battle between Romans. Chaos spread along the line of Metellus Scipio. Juba's Numidian troops retreated in haste without a fight. Once again Caesar was victorious. And once again, the *Optimates* scattered in every man for himself. No one wanted to surrender. No one wanted to give Caesar the satisfaction of forgiveness. It was a fight to the death, and they would continue it wherever they can. Of all the territory of the Republic, the only one in the hands of the Pompeians is Hispania. There, as we shall see in the next paragraph, the despotic rule of the Caesarian legate Quintus Cassius Longinus had led to their expulsion and the territory has changed hands again. In this territory, moreover, Pompey the Younger had begun to operate. Sextus Pompeius (Magnus' younger son), Titus Labienus and Attius Varus, set out there. Others will fail in the attempt. Faustus Cornelius Sulla, the eldest son of the former dictator and son-in-law of Pompey,[52] and Lucius Afranius,

51 During the Ptolemaic dynasty (from 305 to 30 BC), rulers were no longer called pharaohs, but kings and, where appropriate, queens.

52 He was married to Pompeia, daughter of Pompey and Mucia Tercia. He was therefore also brother-in-law to Pompey the Younger and Sextus Pompeius.

were ambushed by the troops of Publius Sittius,[53] who killed them. Metellus Scipio managed to embark but was surrounded by the fleet of Sittius and, before being captured, committed suicide. King Juba I of Numidia and Marcus Petreius were also surrounded and unable to flee. They agreed that an honourable way to die would be in a duel to the death and whoever won would kill himself afterwards. Petreius defeated and killed Juba, and then committed suicide. Finally, upon learning of the Pompeian debacle, Cato the Younger, who was in Uttica, also decided to end his life.

While the campaigns in Greece and North Africa were taking place, in 48 BC Hispania was under the command of a legate of Caesar as *propraetor*, Quintus Cassius Longinus,[54] who established his headquarters in Corduba and had four legions. Two of them came from the Caesarian legions, Legio XXI and XXX, but the other two, Legio II and Legio Vernacula, had been recruited by the Pompeian legates, so Longinus was not convinced of their loyalty. We must bear in mind that the soldiers and officers of the Vernacula were Roman citizens of Hispanian origin (mostly Celtiberians and Lusitanians), and mostly Pompeian clients. According to *De Bello Alexandrino*, Longinus, shortly after taking command, prepared an expedition to Lusitania, a region he knew well since he had served there as *quaestor* in Hispania under Pompey. The anonymous author of this work wonders (*DBA*, 48, 2) whether the motive for the *propraetor*'s offensive was a response to an uprising in the region or simply the result of personal revenge since he had been wounded in battle during his previous stay in Lusitania. He apparently assaulted the city of Meidubriga (modern Castelo de Ranhados, Portugal) and then attacked Mount Herminius, where the survivors had taken refuge. At the end of the campaign, he was acclaimed *imperator* by his men, among whom he distributed 100 sesterces each. He then quartered during the winter in Corduba. There, he began to earn the unpopularity of the Hispanians, as he strangled them with taxes and, if these were not sufficient to satisfy his greed, he arbitrarily confiscated the property of wealthy citizens (*DBA*, 49, 2). Moreover, when he recruited a new legion, following Caesar's instructions to attack King Juba I of Numidia, who supported

53 A former military officer and merchant of the equestrian order who had left Rome when he was accused of participating in Catilina's conspiracy. He went into exile in Africa where with his fortune he bought an army and, as a mercenary, fought for Bocchus II of Mauritania in his war against Juba I of Numidia. During the Civil War, he entered Caesar's service.

54 Brother of Gaius Cassius Longinus, one of Caesar's assassins.

the Pompeian side, many local *equites* refused to fight outside their province, so Longinus gave them the option of buying their release in exchange for a large sum of money. Longinus' rule reached such a level of despotism, abuse and injustice that a plot to assassinate him was soon organised, involving not only Hispanian nobles but also Caesarian Romans who had had enough of his tyranny. It followed a very similar pattern to the assassination of Caesar a few years later. It took place in the forum of Corduba (*DBA*, 52, 2), when he was detained by a Roman citizen with a request. But instead of handing him a document he pulled out a dagger and stabbed him twice. The rest of the conspirators attacked the escort and the *propraetor* himself. However, Longinus survived. When the news spread through H. Ulterior, Legio XXI and XXX mobilised in favour of Longinus. Legio II and V, fearful of the reaction of the Caesarian legions, also mobilised in favour of the *propraetor*. Only Legio Vernacula did not come to the general's aid. Minucius Silon, the man who had accosted Longinus in the first instance, under torture betrayed his fellow conspirators, who were all captured and executed. Prominent among them was Lucius Racilius, who had become a Tribune of the Plebs and was a close friend of Cicero. However, some of the main conspirators, such as Titus Quinctius Scapula and Lucius Munatius Flaccus, escaped death by paying a large ransom. But neither the attack nor the social unrest caused Longinus to change his despotic policies. Yet, finally, there was a revolt. It began in October 48 BC, when Legio II and Vernacula mutinied under the command of Thorius. The *propraetor*, who was in Hispalis, ordered his *quaestor* Marcus Claudius Marcellus Aeserninus to take all available troops and head for Corduba. Claudius Marcellus arrived in the capital of Ulterior before the insurgents and there he met two cohorts of Legio V. After negotiations with the Cordovan elites, he decided to join the rebellion, but without ceasing to belong to the Caesarian side. A few days later Thorius arrived with his two legions, on whose shields his legionaries had written the name Pompey. But when they arrived at the city gates and saw that they had a common enemy with Claudius Marcellus, they decided to unite. After all, they had just received the news of the defeat at Pharsalus and the subsequent death of Pompey. Cassius Longinus soon arrived at the gates of Corduba with the bulk of his troops. Seeing that he could not enter the city, he ravaged the surrounding countryside, causing serious damage. The two armies did not actually clash. They made various tactical moves, feigned to attack each other, but never crossed swords. In early November, Longinus withdrew to Ulia (modern Montemayor, Andalusia), where he hoped to recruit reinforcements. Everything changed with the arrival of Marcus

Aemilius Lepidus, who had been appointed by Caesar as governor of H. Citerior, and who went to Corduba to seek the deposition of the arms of Longinus' and Marcellus' forces. The future triumvir, by skilful negotiation, succeeded in restoring peace and made a pact with his colleague in H. Ulterior that he could return to Rome with all the fortune he had accumulated during his corrupt goverment. But on his way back, his ship was wrecked near the mouth of the river Ebro and Longinus was drowned, surrounded by his riches (*DBA*, 64, 3).

In any case, the situation in H. Ulterior was far from calm. The pro-Pompeian faction was increasingly active, especially when the war moved to North Africa. They organised an effective guerrilla army and, in addition, sent a delegation to Metellus Scipio demanding a leader who would be able to open a new front of war (Plut., *Cass.*, 43, 29, 2). The chosen one was Pompey the Younger, who, from Utica, embarked with a small army of poorly-armed slaves and freemen. His first objective was the Balearic Islands, which he easily conquered, except for Ebusus (modern Ibiza), where he faced stiff resistance. While this campaign was taking place, in Africa the Pompeians were defeated in the Battle of Thapsus. The news of the death of Metellus Scipio convinced the Pompeians of H. Ulterior to take up arms without waiting for the arrival of Pompey the Younger. The insurrection was led by Titus Quintius Scapula, who had as his lieutenant Quintus Aponius, both of whom were wealthy Cordovan equites and high-ranking officers of Trebonius, who was expelled from his province.[55] By September 47 BC, Pompey the Younger finally arrived, and laid siege to and conquered Carthago Nova. In the meantime, most of the cities of H. Ulterior joined the Pompeians either by their own conviction or by force of arms. Corduba, Ucubi, Urso, Hispalis or Carteia proclaimed themselves Pro-Pompeian;[56] Ategua was conquered by Scapula. Only Ulia, Gadir, Obulco and probably Malacca and Sexi remained loyal to Caesar. Although they were few in number, it must be said that some of them were of great strategic importance: Gades, under the influence of the Balbi, had the largest port in the province, while Obulchus (modern Porcuna) was the key to cross the Despeñaperros pass and,

55 Subsequently, Trebonius, despite being favoured by Caesar, who after his time in Hispania appointed him *Consul Suffectus*, was one of the leaders of the plot to end his life. His role in the Ides of March was to detain Mark Antony on the Senate steps, so that he could not help Caesar. After Caesar's assassination, he went to Asia to serve as proconsul. While in Smyrna, he was attacked by the army of Publius Cornelius Dolabella, who captured, tortured, and beheaded him.

56 Rodríguez Mela (2005), p. 345.

consequently, the junction between H. Citerior (still Caesarian) and the Guadalquivir valley, i.e. the heart of the pro-Pompeian resistance. Weeks later, the survivors of Thapsus landed in the province. Titus Labienus was at the head of the senatorial army in Hispania.

In the autumn of 64 BC, on being informed of the delicate situation in H. Ulterior, Caesar decided to go personally into the rebellious province and crush what was left of the senatorial faction, which was managing to raise a colossal army. During the Civil War, this was probably his most difficult campaign. With his famous *celeritas* and accompanied only by a meagre escort, Caesar reached Obulchus in little more than 20 days. There he met a delegation of Cordovans favourable to his faction, who informed him that Sextus Pompeius, the youngest son of the Magnus, was in the capital of H. Ulterior and that, despite the quartered troops, the city could easily be taken by night. While his brother, Pompey the Younger, was besieging the city of Ulia. He sent a detachment of cavalry to that city, which managed to enter the city and aid. Meanwhile, around 11 January,[57] Caesar led a night assault on Corduba, which ended in failure after a heavy battle at the bridge of Corduba over the river Guadalquivir, which the Pompeians fiercely defended. The Caesarian troops were forced to retreat. There was no choice but to attempt to take the city by siege. To do this, he built a temporary bridge with which Caesar could cross his troops to the north bank. Shortly afterwards, Pompey the Younger arrived with his army. His terrified brother, who was only 20 years old, had appealed to him for help. He may have been reluctant to abandon the siege of Ulia when the city's resistance was beginning to give way, but the sons of Pompey could not afford to lose Corduba. Hence, Pompey the Younger established himself on the south bank of the Guadalquivir, controlling the stone bridge. Caesar knew that this was the strategic point on which the city stood. He had to control it and cut off communications between the two brothers. Therefore, for a week, bloody fighting took place for control of the bridge. Both armies lost many men. But the result was that the bridge remained in Pompeian hands. In addition, Caesar had a serious supply problem, which was aggravated by the arrival of Legio VI and X from Italy. Finally, Caesar decided to lift the siege of Corduba and retreat to Ategua, some 20 miles to the south, where were stored huge supplies of wheat, which would be vital for the survival of his troops. The city was under the command of Munatius Flaccus, who had ordered the execution of the

57 Rodríguez Mela, op. cit., p. 348.

Caesarians in the city and put up stiff resistance until he realised that neither Labienus nor Pompey the Younger would come to his aid, so he decided to surrender the city in exchange for Caesarian mercy. Munatius Flaccus was pardoned and marched to Corduba, while Caesar's troops satiated their hunger in Ategua. The situation was now back on an even keel. In addition, delegations from numerous Hispanian cities sent emissaries to Caesar to pay him homage and place themselves under his command. But the army of the *Optimates* still did not dare to put up a fight and the Pompeian troops retreated to Ucubis (modern Espejo, Andalusia), where Caesar's supporters who were unable to flee were executed. The time had come for the final battle, and the place chosen was the city of Munda.[58] The battle would take place on 17 March 45 BC.

There they assembled the largest army ever mobilised during the entire Civil War. Labienus and Pompey the Younger were able to muster thirteen legions (at Pharsalus the senatorial side had nine and at Thapsus eight). But not all of them were of equal quality. Legions II and Vernacula, as well as a new one made up of Italic and Roman colonists and another made up of veterans from Africa who served with Afranius were the most combative. The rest of the units were made up of Celtiberians, Lusitanians, King Bogud's Mauritani, Italic settlers, slaves, and the survivors of the Ilerda campaign of 49 BC. To this should be added some 6,000 Numidian horsemen and some 12,000 auxiliary troops. Normally, the figures calculated by Schulten[59] are taken to be correct. He considers that each legion must have had an average of about 4,000 men (to be complete, at that time they must have consisted of about 6,000), plus the auxiliary and cavalry troops mentioned above, so that they must have amounted to an extraordinary 70,000 men. Most of them had faced Caesarian troops in the past and knew that this time they could no longer count on the dictator's mercy. It a battle of life and death. On the Caesarian side, there were eight legions and about 8,000 horsemen (4,000 Numidians and 4,000 Gauls and Germans), plus about 5,000 auxiliaries, in all some 40,000 men. It would take almost two millennia for Spain to see a battle of such dimensions. The forces were very unbalanced, but this was not Caesar's main problem. As had happened at Pharsalus, he lengthened his lines like the enemies at the cost of shallower lines. But

58 The exact location of Munda is unknown. Some, such as Schulten, place it in the vicinity of modern Montilla, while other authors place it near modern Osuna, both in modern Andalusia.

59 Schulten (1940) (II), p. 137.

on this occasion, the terrain on which he was to fight would also be unfavourable to him, for the troops fighting under Labienus controlled the hill, so the Caesarians had to fight uphill. Their only advantage was their numerical superiority in cavalry, which was also far more combative than that of the enemy.

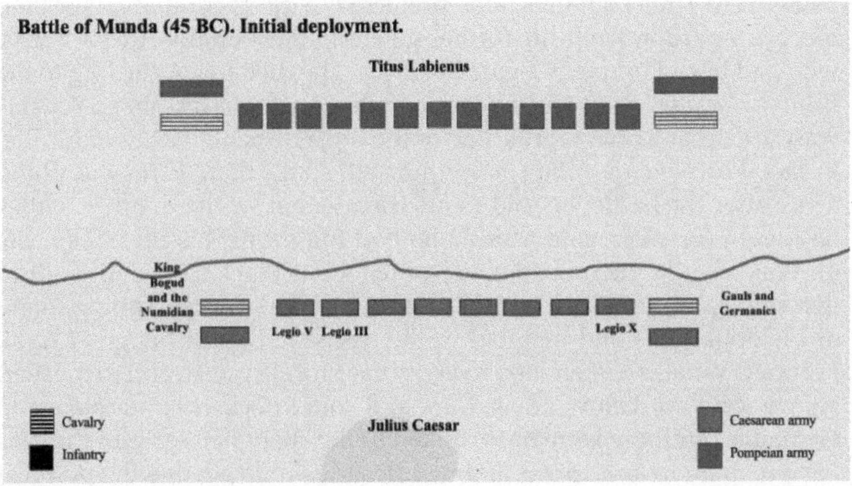

Map 11: After this initial deployment, the greater combativeness of the Caesarian army was compensated by the Pompeians thanks to their numerical superiority. But when Legio X, led by Caesar, began to break the Pompeian left wing, Labienus was forced to reinforce it by moving part of his troops to the right. King Bogud took advantage of this to charge with his cavalry against the Pompeian right wing, which soon collapsed. With both Pompeian wings sunk, the victory went to Julius Caesar.

The battle began with the Caesarian forces crossing the Carchena stream (according to Schulten) and charging the *Optimates* forces. At first, the Caesarian legions could barely contain the counter-attack of Labienus' men. The situation was especially tough on the Caesarian right wing, where Caesar himself had to draw his sword and take up a shield to get close to the battle line where his beloved Legio X, seeing their general in danger, managed to reverse the situation by pushing the Pompeian left wing to the limit. Seeing that the front could unravel in that sector, Labienus took one of the legions from his right wing and sent it to engage Legio X, a counter-attack which he himself led in person. This circumstance was exploited by the wily King Bogud to make a bold manoeuvre in which he managed to envelop the enemy's right wing, which had been momentarily unguarded. This move was accompanied by the experienced Caesarian Legio V and III, which finished off the *Optimates'* front. With their wings down, the legions in the centre of the line began to flee in the direction of Munda, but the Caesarians gave them no quarter and the slaughter was one of the greatest in Roman history up to that point. Schulten puts the number of dead and wounded at over 30,000 men. Among those who died in that battle were Titus Labienus, who preferred to die in combat rather than receive a pardon from his former general; and Publius Attius Varus, who had been Pompey's legate in Africa. The dictator, according to the *Bellum Hispanienses*, would have lost about a thousand men. Yet this was, in Caesar's own words, one of the most difficult battles of his life. In fact, Plutarch, quoting Caesar himself, states that 'as he was going away after the battle, he said to his friends that whilst in other battles he fought for victory; at Munda he had fought for his life' (*Caes.*, 56, 4). Was Munda the crucial battle of the Civil War? This is difficult to determine, since at Pharsalus Caesar succeeded in dismantling many of his opponents and resulted in the assassination of his great rival, Pompey. What is certain, however, is that Munda put an end to the war. As we shall see below, there were still some pockets of resistance in Hispania, but these were more linked to the client networks of the *gens Pompeia* than to an express and manifest desire to change the political regime in Rome. Caesar, who was still a few weeks away from arriving in Rome, was proclaimed dictator for life and celebrated a triumph, which was frowned upon by many senators, since he had won it by fighting other Romans. But his glory (or at least his earthly glory) was short lived, for as fate would have it, Caesar was assassinated almost a year after his triumph at Munda, on the infamous Ides of March.

But if we return to Hispania, after the Battle of Munda we find that the army of the *Optimates* had broken up. Pompey the Younger fled south to Carteia, where he still had some ships. Scapula, accompanied by most of the survivors of the battle, went in the direction of Corduba, where Sextus Pompeius was. While Scapula's troops occupied the stone bridge, Sextus, hearing of Caesar's imminent arrival, fled to Hispania Citerior. The dictator left part of his army besieging Munda and with the rest went to Corduba. Finding the stone bridge occupied, and remembering his previous failure, he built a new bridge a few miles to the south, over which his troops crossed. Scapula, seeing the war was lost, assembled his family and his freedmen, and ordered an opulent dinner, dressing in his best clothes. When the dinner was over, he distributed numerous gifts among his slaves and freedmen, ordered one of them to slit his throat, while the freedwoman who had been his concubine, he asked to be thrown into the bonfire that he had previously asked to be prepared for him (*Bell. Hisp.*, 33). With this spectacular suicide, one of the last Pompeian leaders in Hispania died. The situation in Corduba became desperate. There was too little food and too many refugees, a problem that had been aggravated by the large number of Pompeian refugees and surviving soldiers from Munda. Without a clear leader, tensions soon emerged. Soon voices were raised calling for a surrender to Caesar. In turn, the Cordovan Caesarians took up arms. For several days, the city suffered severe fighting within its walls. Rodríguez-Neila[60] suggests that the defenders may have organised an attack against the Caesarian army, but this failed. The *Bellum Hispaniense* is also unclear what happened next. It is likely that the Caesarians from the inside managed to control a section of the wall and allowed their allies to break through from the outside, or that Caesar's troops simply took the city by assault. What is certain is that the Pompeian Cordovans preferred to die rather than surrender and, seeing their city lost, began to set fire to it. The Caesarians, whether out of revenge, hatred for the Pompeians or because they lost the opportunity for booty with the fire, massacred the Cordovan garrison, a legion that Sextus had formed with manumitted slaves and as many civilians as crossed their path. The *Bellum Hispaniense* (34, 5) states that 22,000 Cordovans were killed during the fighting. The city founded by Marcellus a century earlier had been razed to the ground. Caesar then headed for Hispalis (modern Seville, Andalusia). The city opened its gates, and the general spared them, leaving a garrison inside. But it was not long before one of his Pompeian leaders, named Philon (*Bell. Hisp.*, 35), fled to Lusitania and recruited a small army with which he returned to the city and murdered the Caesarian garrison. When the dictator learned of the treachery, he laid siege to the city. Seeing that its defence was impossible, one night the Pompeians and Lusitanians made a sortie, set fire to some ships in the harbour on the river Guadalquivir and, taking advantage of the confusion, fled. But while Caesar's legionaries tried to put out the fire, the general ordered his cavalry to pursue the enemy, who were all exterminated. Schulten[61] records an anecdote that shows us the character of Caesar, who, although he was besieging Hispalis, had time to write a letter of condolence to Cicero for the death of his daughter Tullia. Also in those days, Caesar also received news of the capture of Pompey the Younger. He was arrested by the authorities of Carteia who hoped to

---

60 Rodríguez-Neila, op. cit., p. 354.

61 Schulten (II), op. cit., p. 101.

ingratiate themselves with the general. But once again, a small civil war broke out inside the city and Pompey the Younger managed to flee with a small fleet. The Caesarian navy commanded by Gaius Didius, which was anchored in Gadir, set off in pursuit. Four days later, the ships of the young Cnaeus Pompey were intercepted when they had stopped on land to get drinking water. Didius set fire to the ships he was unable to capture and Pompey, with a few men, had to continue his flight overland, pursued by Caesarian cohorts and cavalry on the one side and Didius' infantry on the other. Pompey was seriously wounded and had to be carried by litter. He ordered to fortify a hill (probably near Lauro[62]), from which he repulsed several charges from the Caesarian troops, but finding it impossible to resist any longer, he ordered a retreat. His small troop dispersed and the young *Optimate* took refuge in a cave, hoping not to be found. However, he had no luck. He was captured and executed. On 12 April, Caesar at Gadir received the head of his enemy (*Bell. Hisp.*, 37-39). Also in that city, the general was visited by his beloved grand-nephew Gaius Octavian, aged 18, who had been prevented by illness from travelling earlier to take part in the battle. In H. Ulterior, some minor battles continued to take place, most notably the one that ended the lives of Didius and most of his men when he was repairing his ships to return to Gadir. They were surprised by pro-Pompeian Lusitanian troops, and all of whom were ambushed and killed. Caesar, however, considered the war over and decided to return to Rome, where a huge amount of work awaited him. He travelled accompanied by Q. Fabius Maximus, the governor of H. Ulterior that year, leaving in command of all Hispania the governor of H. Citerior, Quintus Pedius[63] together with two legions.

The War of Sextus Pompeius

In the summer of 45 BC, the young Sextus Pompeius Magnus Pius did not seem to be a problem. The Caesarians knew that he had fled Corduba with only an escort of a few horsemen and it would only be a matter of time before he surrendered. However, the youngest son of Pompey was to show far greater determination and command than his elder brother. Little is known of Sextus' activities after his flight from Corduba, but it seems clear that he moved north. Logic would seem to

62 In this case, it is the Lauro found in H. Ulterior. Not to be confused with the Lauro of H. Citerior mentioned in the chapter on the Sertorian War.

63 Although Suetonius (*Caes.*, 83) indicates that he was a grand-nephew of Caesar, it must have been a confusion, since by age he was probably a son of Julia Minor and not her grandson.

indicate that he must have first passed through Celtiberia. There, his father had numerous clients, and it would not be difficult for him to find cities in which to hide and obtain refuge, and even volunteers to follow him in his struggle. Later, he crossed the Ebro. Amela Valverde[64] points out that the classical sources differ as to the destination of the young Pompeius. For example, Cassius Dio states that he went to Lacetania (in the central part of modern Catalonia); while Strabo assures us that he was among the Iacetani, i.e., the citizens of Iacca (modern Jaca, Aragon). In any case, it did not take the young Sextus long to gather around him a large group of followers driven both by loyalty to his father and by anti-Caesarian sentiment. His first small actions took place in H. Citerior. But when he had gathered sufficient forces, he moved into H. Ulterior, where anti-Caesarian sentiment was much stronger because of the high taxes to be paid by the cities that had supported the Pompeian faction during the previous war; moreover, many Hispanians had lost their lands to the dictator's colonists. Thus, Sextus had no difficulty in assembling a growing army, with which he began to conquer the first cities that opposed him. At the time, Caesar still underestimated the problem that Sextus could pose, completely disregarding his skills as a charismatic leader capable of mustering real opposition or as a military man capable of putting his troops in check. However, when he saw that the situation was becoming more complicated, he sent Gaius Carrinas, probably in charge of both Hispaniae and with an army of considerable size, as *propraetor*. But Carrinas was unable to defeat his opponent. Sextus, intelligently, avoided pitched battles and carried out a guerrilla war, like the one Sertorius had waged against his father.[65] In view of Carrinas' failure, Caesar, in early 44 BC, sent in his place Gaius Asinius Pollio, who had been one of his legates in his second Hispanian civil war campaign. But Asinius is unable to reverse the situation. He counted only four legions, while Cicero (*Att.*, 16, 4, 2) states that the young Pompeius totalled seven. Although the sources are not at all clear in determining the exact number of troops in each army or the places where they fought. It does seem certain that Asinius tried to establish new colonies that he could use as a base to attack Sextus' troops, so in 44 BC he re-founded the city of Corduba. In those days, Caesar appointed Marcus Emilius Lepidus (the future triumvir) governor of H. Citerior. But there was a power vacuum that Sextus took advantage of, and he moved to the eastern coast of the peninsula

64 Amela Valverde (2013), pp. 47–8.

65 Amela Valverde, op. cit., p. 65.

where he conquered several cities. During this campaign he must have received the news of the assassination of Caesar in the Senate during the Ides of March, which encouraged him to attack Asinius in the open field. This took place in an undetermined place along the river Guadalquivir, and we have no exact information about the troops who fought or the exact date on which it took place. Only Cassius Dio (*Hist.* 49, 10) tells us that, at a certain point in the battle, Asinius fled from the battlefield, causing discouragement among his men, who began to surrender en masse. The crushing defeat meant that Sextus Pompeius became *de facto* master of the southern Iberian Peninsula. The situation was so tricky that Mark Antony himself proposed in the Senate that an agreement be made with the last son of Pompey. This treaty provided that Sextus would receive from Rome 50 million Attic drachmas, in compensation for the properties confiscated from his father, and the position of *praefectus classis et orae maritimae*, i.e., general of the Roman navy. Sextus accepted the conditions, and in the autumn of 44 BC, he travelled to Massalia to take up his new post. Reconciliation with Rome was short-lived. The young Octavian manoeuvred for the passage of the *Lex Pedia* declaring Caesar's assassins outlawed, including Sextus on the blacklist. The Magnus' son managed to land in Sicily. With the governor of Africa as his ally, he managed to put Rome's grain supply in jeopardy. However, he failed to take advantage of the tactical advantage Octavian gave him by leaving Rome to join Mark Antony in Greece to fight Cassius and Brutus. In 39 BC he signed a new pact with Octavian and Mark Antony at Miseno, but political tensions between the two triumvirs meant that not all the conditions demanded by Sextus were met and he again took up arms against Rome, this time with the islands of Sardinia and Corsica on his side. This caused Rome to stop receiving grain and to suffer a veritable famine and serious unrest (Appian, *Civil Wars*, 5, 67). A new war broke out between Octavian and Sextus, to be decided at the naval battle of Naulochus in 36 BC, where the fleet commanded by Marcus Vipsanius Agrippa crushed that of Sextus, the man who called himself Son of Neptune. The indomitable son of the Magnus fled with a few loyal soldiers and friends. Finally, in 35 BC, he was captured by Marcus Titius, a legate of Mark Antony, and, sent to Miletus (modern Balat, Turkey), was executed. Thus ended the rebellious saga of Pompey.

The Second Triumvirate in Hispania

During the period from 44 BC to 29 BC, i.e., between the departure of Sextus Pompeius and the beginning of the Cantabrian Wars, Hispania played a secondary role in Roman politics, since the great battles that would end up deciding the wars between the triumvirs and Caesar's assassins and, later, the civil war between Octavian and Mark Antony, took place in the eastern Mediterranean. This did not mean that Hispania was experiencing a period of peace and prosperity; on the contrary, there were some conflicts, but of a local nature. Therefore, while Sextus Pompeius set sail for Massalia, the governor of H. Ulterior was still Gaius Asinius Pollio, whom we left shamefully abandoning the battlefield in 44 BC. A man of his political, military and literary stature does not deserve to be left in such an embarrassing situation. His stay in Hispania is considerably detailed through his correspondence with Cicero, who, although not a close friend, certainly had a mutual respect for each other's intellectual gifts. Asinius was a staunch supporter of the Caesarian party. In fact, Caesar regarded him as one of his best friends and stood by his side after crossing the river Rubicon, accompanying him on numerous military campaigns and excelling in the Battle of Munda. However, in his correspondence with Cicero, Asinius was sympathetic towards Brutus and seemed to be able to lean in favour of the Senate in his conflict with Mark Antony. Nonetheless, this support, as in the case of Marcus Emilius Lepidus (governor of H. Citerior), was only apparent, since they were both friends and supporters of Mark Antony. In the summer of 43 BC, in view of the delicate situation in Italy, Asinius decided to leave Hispania and return to Rome, where Lepidus, Mark Anthony and Octavian eventually formed the Second Triumvirate.

The new civil war between the triumvirs and Caesar's assassins was to be decided on the fields of Greece, specifically in the two battles of Philippi, which took place on 3 and 23 October 42 BC. It would be the definitive battle that put an end to the Republic. But it was not just that. It was literally the end of an elite: the two battles of Philippi eliminated a large part of the families that had been at the helm of Rome for the last centuries. For example, Marcus Porcius Cato, the only son of Cato the Younger and brother-in-law of Brutus;[66] Lucius Licinius Lucullus, 21 years old and the last member of the most important branch of the Lucullus, died in battle or by suicide after the battle; Quintus Hortensius Hortalus, the last member of this branch of the Hortensius; Marcus Livius Drusus Claudianus, father of Livia Drusilla;[67] or

66 When Portia, in Rome, learned of the death of her brother and husband, Brutus, she also committed suicide.

67 She was the third and last wife of Octavian. But at the time, she was married to Tiberius Claudius Nero. Octavian fell so madly in love with her that he divorced his second wife, Scribonia, and forced Tiberius to divorce Livia. His son, Tiberius, succeeded Octavian.

Quintus Caecilius Bassus, who had fought against Caesar at Pharsalus and Munda. But many of the conspirators in Caesar's assassination, such as Sextus Quinctilius Varus, Quintus Antistius Labeo, Publius Servilius Casca and Lucius Tillius Cimber,[68] also died at Philippi. In addition, Cassius Longinus and Marcus Junius Brutus, whose head was cut off and sent to Rome, where it was thrown at the feet of Caesar's statue in the Senate (Suet., *Aug.* 13). Few republican leaders were able to escape the wrath and vengeance of the triumvirs. Marcus Tullius Cicero Minor, Cicero's son, obtained Octavian's pardon and joined him in his fight against Mark Antony. While Gnaeus Domitius Ahenobarbus[69] and Lucius Staius Marcus joined Sextus Pompeius in Sicily, but while the former obtained the pardon of Mark Antony,[70] the latter was killed by Sextus, as he suspected that he intended to overthrow him. Once the Republican leaders had been eliminated, the triumvirs divided the Roman world among themselves: Mark Antony took the eastern provinces; Octavian took the government of Italy; and Lepidus took the western provinces, including Hispania. But Lepidus was not to enjoy such a juicy province for long, as Octavian took it for himself the following year. While the Iberian Peninsula lived in a certain calm, the political situation in Rome could not be more tense. The bad relations between Mark Antony and Octavian end up provoking Lucius Antonius and Fulvia, younger brother and wife of Mark Antony, to declare on their own the so-called Perusian War, which Octavian won, showing clemency to Lucius Antonius, but condemning Fulvia to exile. Mark Antony, who enjoyed life at Cleopatra's court, was probably not very interested in the fate of his wife, who, fittingly, died suddenly, paving the way for Octavian and Mark Antony to seal a reconciliation through the marriage of Octavia, sister of the triumvir, to Mark Antony.

In 40 BC Gnaeus Domitius Calvinus and Gaius Asinius Pollio were appointed consuls. However, both resigned a few months later, being appointed *consuls suffectus*[71] by Publius Canidius Crassus, and Lucius Cornelius Balbus Maior. The appointment of this Hispanian as

---

68 All of Caesar's assassins died violent deaths, the last of them being Gaius Cassius Parmensis, who managed to escape after the Battle of Philippi and was pardoned by Mark Antony. However, Octavian ordered his assassination in 30 BC.

69 He was the son of Lucius Domitius Ahenobarbus and nephew of Cato the Younger, both stubborn enemies of Caesar who had died during the previous civil war.

70 He later fell out with Mark Antony because of Cleopatra's influence over him and joined Octavian shortly before the Battle of Actium.

71 Those appointed during the term of office of a resigned consul.

consul is of real significance as he was the first to hold this office born outside Italy. The following year, Gnaeus Domitius Calvinus arrived in Hispania as proconsul of the two provinces. In H. Citerior he took charge of a war against the Ceretani, an Iberian tribe living on the southern slopes of the Pyrenees (Cassius Dio, *Hist.* 48, 42, 1-4). It took the proconsul three years to defeat them, since he celebrated a triumph in Rome in 36 BC. This war probably had its origin in Octavian's desire to definitively control the Pyrenean passes to have a direct means of communication between Narbo and Ilerda. To reaffirm this theory, we must bear in mind that, in the same year, Octavian's right-hand man, Marcus Vipsanius Agrippa, was fighting against the Aquitanians on the northern slopes of the Pyrenees. The *Acta Triumphalis* specify that in the following years, the governors of Hispania celebrated three triumphs in Rome: in 34 BC, Gaius Norbanus Flaccus (c. 38 BC); in 33 BC, Lucius Marcius Philippus (c. suff. 38 BC), half-brother of Octavian[72] and in 32 BC, Appius Claudius Pulcher (c. 38 BC), with whom he had allied himself after his marriage to Livia Drusilla.[73] The fact that four governors with the rank of proconsul were in Hispania for six years and that all four celebrated triumphs on their return to Rome indicates that the situation on the peninsula was far from peaceful. However, the classical sources do not tell us what kind of revolts or wars they had to face.

Meanwhile, the relationship between the triumvirs did not improve. Finally, in 36 BC, the alliance exploded. On the one hand, Lepidus, fed up with being ignored, challenged Octavian from Sicily and Octavian eventually deposed him. On the other side of the Mediterranean, Mark Antony began his Parthian War, whose army included 10,000 Iberian and Celtic horsemen (Plut., *Ant.*, 37). This campaign ended in a great failure for the triumvir, who retreated to Alexandria in search of military support from Cleopatra. But once at the Egyptian court, he finally forgot the Parthians and, madly in love with the Queen, ended

72 His father, also called Lucius Marcius Philippus, was the second husband of Atia Balba Caesonia, Octavian's mother, whose first husband, Caius Octavian, had died in 59 BC. When Lucius Marcius Philippus (Maior) married Atia, Octavian was about 4 years old. Sources indicate that Marcius treated him as a true son, feeling great affection for him. An affection which, by the way, seems to have been mutual. The relationship between the two half-brothers was also very close.

73 Syme (2202), p. 229 and Huntsman (2009), p. 149. These authors suggest that, through his marriage to Livia, also hoped to attract to his party a part of the old Roman aristocracy that had in the past supported the *Optimates*. Livia's father, Marcus Livius Drusus Claudianus, had fought at Philippi on the side of the Liberators (and committed suicide after the defeat).

up repudiating Octavia, which gave his consular colleague the excuse to declare war, presenting it before the Senate and the people of Rome as a conflict against Cleopatra. The great battle of this new conflict took place at Actium in the Ambracian Gulf (Greece) on 2 September 31 BC. It was a naval battle in which Octavian's army was once again led by the pitiless Agrippa. There is no unanimous agreement on the number of warships engaged, but it is believed that Mark Antony had about 250 ships but that they were larger than the 400 at Octavian's disposal. Mark Antony divided his fleet into three large squadrons, leaving a fourth (Cleopatra's) in reserve, ordering the fleets at either end to open, in an attempt to break the encirclement of Octavian's fleet on the Ambracian Gulf and thus make it easier for his larger ships to manoeuvre. Only the Antonian fleet on the left, commanded by Gaius Sosius, seemed to be able to succeed over the enemy. The centre and right wing were clearly losing. At one point, taking advantage of a large gap between the Antonian left wing and the centre of the battle, Cleopatra's fleet slipped through and fled. Mark Antony switched to a smaller, faster ship and followed the queen of Egypt. Octavian's (well, Agrippa's in his name) victory was total. A few months later, in Alexandria, Mark Antony and Cleopatra, with the city surrounded by the Octavian army, had no choice but to commit suicide. Rome belonged to Octavian.

Chapter 5

BELLUM CANTABRICUM ET ASTURICUM: AUGUSTUS' WAR

Sub occasu pacata erat fere omnis Hispania, nisi quam Pyrenaei desinentis scopulis inhaerentem citerior adluebat Oceanus. Hic duae validissime gentes, Cantabri et Astures, inmunes imperii agitabant.[1]

Lucius Annaeus Florus (*The Epitome*, 2, 33)

If we were to paraphrase the first sentence of the adventures of the famous Asterix, we could say that 'a territory north of Hispania of indomitable Celts still holds out against the invaders'. Curiously, Goscinny & Uderzo's phrase is not very far from Florus'. In the north of the peninsula there were two great societies of Celtic origin: the Cantabrians and the Asturians. From west to east, they were bordered by the Galleacii, the Vaccaei, the Turmodigi and the Austrigones, all of Celtic origin. Except for the last ones, all of them had been incorporated relatively few decades ago to H. Citerior. Probably the most Romanised were the Austrigones, who must have entered the Roman orbit shortly after the conquest of Numantia in 133 BC; the Turmodigi were then conquered around 73 BC by Pompey during the *Bellum Sertorianum*; the Gallaecii were definitively subdued by Julius Caesar around 60 BC; and the Vaccaei

1 'In the west almost, all Spain had been subjugated, except that part which adjoins the cliffs where the Pyrenees end and is washed by the nearer waters of the Ocean. Here two powerful nations, the Cantabrians and the Asturians, lived in freedom from the rule of Rome.' Translation from *The Epitome of Roman History* by Lucius Annaeus Florus published in the Loeb Classical Library (1929).

were pacified by Metellus Nepos around 56 BC, although the Vaccaei were never fully integrated into the Roman system and continued to rise up from time to time and, in fact, complete pacification would take place during the first stage of the war described in this chapter. We must bear in mind that we cannot consider these societies as a group of homogeneous citizens of a tribe, but that their ethos would probably be marked by belonging to a particular clan. Thus, if we take the case of the Vaccaei as an example, there were clans that would accept Roman domination under Metellus Nepos, while other clans would maintain their struggle with Rome. The same would happen with the Cantabrians and Asturians during the war, especially in the later stages of the conflict, as we shall see.

Although the historiography marks the beginning of the war in 29 BC, we must bear in mind that war in this territory was endemic and that it was part of the life of its inhabitants. The geography is determined by the rugged Cantabrian Range, whose overwhelming landscapes forced its inhabitants into a poor economy based on transhumant livestock and poor agriculture, which they were forced to supplement by plundering neighbouring peoples, especially the cereal-rich Vaccaei and Turmodigi. War was so closely linked to these societies that in the past Cantabrian mercenaries had already been hired by both Punics and Romans. Silus Italicus tells us how they took part in the Second Punic War on the Carthaginian side (*Punica*, 3.306, 5.178, 9.211, 10.15, and, 15.400) and, recently, had formed part of the army of Sertorius, some of whom passed to Aquitania after his defeat; just as, according to Julius Caesar (*BCiv*, 1,38), they took part in the Battle of Ilerda in 49 BC under the orders of Afranius on the Pompeian side. Lucan (*Phars*., 8, 4) is the only one who mentions the Asturians also in that battle together with the Pompeians. This leads us to deduce that these Celtic societies were perfectly familiar with the Roman way of fighting. Moreover, it is likely that some of the triumphs reflected in the *Acta Triumphalis* of the last Roman proconsuls in Hispania mentioned at the end of the previous chapter (G. Norbanus Flaccus, L. Marcius Philippus and A. Claudius Pulcher) were to celebrate a victory over Asturians or Cantabrians. An example of this can be found at the archaeological site of Andagoste (near Cuartango, Basque Country). These are the remains of a half-built *castra aestiva* (Roman field camp) that was attacked by neighbouring tribes. From the artefacts recovered, it can be deduced that the Roman troops were totally or partially annihilated. Coins found allow us to date this battle to the 30s BC.

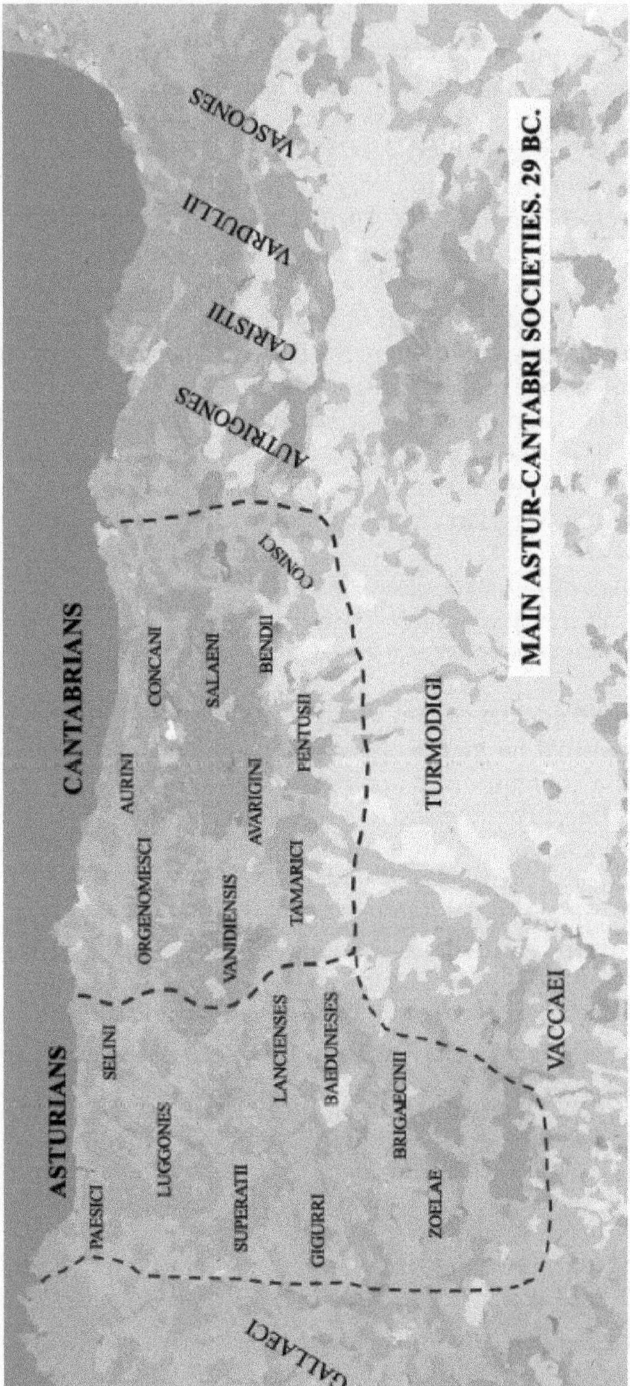

Map 12: Map showing the main Asturian and Cantabrian tribes.

In Rome, after his victory over Mark Antony, Octavian needed to consolidate his power to carry out his reform plan. And one of the measures he took to legitimise himself in power was to become, in the eyes of the people, a guarantor of peace.[2] Thus, the *Pax Augusta* became the axis of his foreign policy. As Cassius Dio tells us (*Hist*. 51, 20), one of his first decisions was to order in 29 BC the closure of the doors to the Temple of Janus in the Forum, which meant that the wars in the territory under Roman domination were over, after 200 years of being open. But the *Pax Augusta* was not only for Rome. Peace was to be brought to all the territories dominated by Rome. They were to be pacified so that they could enjoy the benefits of Roman civilisation. In practice, this meant that Rome considered as its own territories those that had not yet been annexed, such as the Cantabrian coast in Hispania or the frontier marked by the Rhine River in Gaul. But pacifying those territories was merely a euphemism for waging war on them. This is clearly stated by Virgil in *The Aeneid:*[3]

tu regere imperio populos, Romane, memento;
hae tibi erunt artes; pacisque imponere morem,
parcere subiectis, et debellare superbos[4]

It cannot be a coincidence that Virgil began writing this work precisely in 29 BC and that he had been, for years, a close friend of Octavian. To put it in a contemporary analogy, the concept of bringing the *Pax Augusta* or, later, *Pax Romana* to sovereign territories would have the contemporary equivalent of bringing democracy to South American, Asian or African countries by Western powers through invasions or military interventions, either by allied third countries or by the Western powers themselves. As long as the democratic results are convenient for these powers. Otherwise, democracy can be bypassed, as has happened in recent decades in numerous countries such as

2 Solana Sanz (2004).

3 Vergil. *Bucolics, Aeneid, and Georgics Of Vergil*. J. B. Greenough. Boston. Ginn & Co. (1900).

4 'But thou, O Roman, learn with sovereign sway
To rule the nations. Thy great art shall be
To keep the world in lasting peace, to spare
humbled foe, and crush to earth the proud.'
Translation from: Theodore C. Williams. trans. Boston. Houghton Mifflin Co. 1910. In: http://www.perseus.tufts.edu/hopper/text?doc=Perseus%3Atext%3A1999.02.0054%3Abook%3D6%3Acard%3D801. Accessed August 7th, 2023.

Indonesia (1959), Chile (1973) and Algeria (1991), to not mention more recent examples.

The Astur-Cantabrian Wars are usually divided into three stages, depending on who commanded the military operations: from 29 BC to 27 BC, the stage of the proconsuls; from 26 BC to 22 BC, when Octavian took command of operations; and from 21 BC to 19 BC, with the final offensive under the command of Agrippa. It was an extremely complicated war because, in addition to the irreducibility of the Hispanian tribes and a battle front of more than 250 miles, in this case we must add an extreme orography, a tremendously rugged and mountainous landscape, in which the local tribes moved perfectly and in which the Romans were not used to fighting. According to Roman sources, such as Cassius Dio, the *casus belli* of this war was a revolt of Asturians, Cantabrians and Vaccaei, and the proconsul Titus Statilius Taurus was sent from Rome to put it down. The fact that the Vaccaei are not mentioned again in the chronicles of this war leads us to suppose that Statilius at least managed to defeat them. The proconsul was replaced in 28 BC by Gaius Calvisius Sabinus, a man famous in Rome for his friendship with Caesar and later with Augustus. In fact, according to Nicolaus of Damascus (*Aug.*, 26) during the Ides of March assassination, Calvisius was the only one, along with Lucius Marcius Censorinus,[5] who tried to defend Caesar. For this reason, the triumvirs granted them both the consulship in 39 BC. Although ancient chronicles tell us that he did not fare well commanding a fleet against Sextus Augustus, he did effectively carry out Augustus' order to cleanse Italy of bandits. Unfortunately, we know nothing of his time in Hispania, except that on his return to Rome he celebrated a triumph. Calvisius was replaced by Sextus Appuleius, a nephew of Octavian being the son of his half-sister Octavia Maior. He was consul together with Octavian in 29 BC and that, the following year, his uncle sent him to Hispania, but we do not know how he conducted the war against Asturians and Cantabrians.

The year 27 BC is an important year in the history of Rome. Continuing with his political reforms, Octavian carried out a territorial reorganisation, creating new provinces, leaving the Senate to manage the territories at peace and keeping for itself the territories that were still at war. The gates of the Temple of Janus were reopened. In the case of Hispania, the territory was divided into three provinces:

5 Velleius Paterculus (*Hist.*, 2, 14, 3) tells us that Marcius Censorinus acquired Cicero's mansion on the Palatine after his death. Later, the house was acquired by Statilius Taurus.

H. Ulterior was renamed Baetica, while H. Citerior was divided into the provinces of Lusitania and Tarraconensis, both under the direct command of Octavian. In addition, the *princeps* took the initiative of personally leading the army to definitively conquer the Asturians and Cantabrians. History has shown us that Octavian was not a great general, but he was an extraordinary statesman. He knew that he needed to gain prestige as a conqueror. So far, Octavian had only won one war against other Romans, so he needed a war of conquest to boost his public image. He therefore hoped that a quick victory against the Cantabrians would give him the longed-for triumph. That year, the Senate also granted him the title of Augustus,[6] so that his official name became Caesar Augustus and by which, following the Roman chronology, we will call him from now on.

Map 13: In 27 BC, Octavian Augustus promoted a new territorial organisation in all the territories under Roman rule.

6 It was a purely symbolic title, but it was later associated with the emperors, since they accumulated several political magistracies (consul, first senator . . .) and religious offices (*pontifex maximus*).

Caesar Augustus made thorough preparations for the Asturian-Cantabrian campaign, arriving with seven legions and two *legati Augusti propraetore*: that of Lusitania was Publius Carisius, who had fought in the past under the orders of the *princeps*; and that of Tarraconensis, Gaius Antistius Vetus, whom we have already mentioned in the previous chapter. He was the *quaestor* who accompanied Julius Caesar when the latter was appointed *praetor* of H. Ulterior. While Caesar lived, he was loyal to him, but at his death he aligned himself with Brutus. After the Battle of Philippi, he reconciled with the triumvirs. He seemed a suitable general for the job, given that in 35 BC he had fought the Salassi in Transalpine Gaul, though admittedly without much success. The initial plan was to advance through Asturian-Cantabrian territory with three columns in a spectacular encircling manoeuvre that would destroy villages, conquer *oppida*, raze crops and kill livestock, leaving the enemy with nowhere to take refuge and no means of subsistence, so that they would be forced to ask for the Roman *Pax*. The classical sources do not make it clear where these three columns advanced, nor do modern historians agree on the routes they must have used, although there is a certain consensus in following the interpretation of events given by Syme,[7] according to which two of them would attack the Cantabrian territory towards the sea: one of the columns must have taken the course of the river Pisoraca (modern Pisuerga) looking for a way to reach the sea, in the direction of Portus Blendium (modern Suance) or Portus Victoriae Iuliobrigensium (probably modern Santander, Cantabria), where a fleet from the coast of Aquitania landed and also attacked the Cantabrians from the rear; while another would move close to the border between the Cantabrians and the Autrigones to open a way to get wheat from Aquitania; while the third column would enter Asturian territory. Once again, there is often some confusion about the chronology. But if we continue to follow Syme, it was the first column that was the most successful. A Cantabrian army faced Legio III Macedonica (and perhaps also Legio X Hispana) under the orders of Caesar Augustus himself at Vellica (probably modern Olleros de Pisuerga, Castilla y León). The Roman victory was clear, and the surviving Cantabrians were divided: one group went to Aracillum, where they were again defeated; while another group fortified themselves in the *oppidum* of *Mons Vindius*, whose location is unknown, and there they were besieged until their inhabitants died of hunger and cold. No information has come down to us about the other

7 Syme (1934).

two columns since the sources have concentrated on narrating only the activities of Caesar Augustus.[8] However, the result of the campaign was not positive. A few victories were won, but the price paid for them was extremely high. The Cantabrian troops were engaged in a guerrilla war that prevented Augustus from advancing as he had planned. His troops were constantly harassed, his food convoys looted, his soldiers starved, and some of his camps suffered from epidemics and a plague of rats. The situation was very precarious. In fact, Augustus, who suddenly became so ill with liver disease that even in Rome rumours of his death spread, retired to Tarraco, where he spent two years, and where he was cured by the famous Antonius Musa[9] (Suetonius, *Aug.*, 81). To convince him to abandon the campaign, he also suffered a bad omen, for, during a night march, one of the slaves who carried his litter was struck by lightning. The impression on Augustus was such that, on his return to Rome, he dedicated the shrine to Jupiter the Thunderer (Suetonius, *Aug.*, 29). He left the command of the troops to Vetus.

The campaign of 25 BC was particularly important in Asturias. There, at the beginning of spring, a confederation of Zoelas and Lancian tribes prepared to make a surprise attack on the three camps into which Carisius had distributed his legions. According to classical sources, the Asturian and Roman armies would have had a similar number of soldiers on the battlefield, which would have been around 20,000 men each, if we count that Carisius' army would already have that number if we add his three legions (we know that they were Legio V Alaudae, Legio VI Victrix and Legio X Gemina), the cavalry and the auxiliary troops. But shortly before the attack began, the Roman general was warned by the inhabitants of Brigaecium[10] (near

8 The chronology of the events is not clear. Thus, for example, Peralta Labrador (2009) places these events in the year 25 BC and carried out by Antistius Vetus.

9 Considered to be the best physician of his generation, he soon after failed to save the life of young Marcus Claudius Marcellus, Augustus' promising nephew and son-in-law, whom he had adopted as his son. Everything seemed to indicate that he might become his successor. His untimely death, due to a septicaemia, was a heavy blow for the emperor, who built the Theatre of Marcellus in his honour, near the Forum, which can still be visited today in Rome.

10 The attitude of the Brigaencii may be considered by some as treason and by others as pragmatism, but the fact is that the alliance with the Romans was very beneficial for this Asturian tribe. In any case, the crisis in Hispania in the 3rd century and the subsequent collapse of the Roman Empire led to the abandonment of the city. Today, historians and archaeologists argue about the exact place where Brigaecium may have been located. Peralta Labrador (2009) suggests that it could be in Fuentes de Ropel or Valderas; Santos Yaguas (2004), states that it was in Santa Cristina de la Polvorosa; and Martino García (2015), in his monograph dedicated to this town adds Villabrázaro as a possible location.

modern Benavente, Castilla y León), neighbours of the Zoelas and Lancians, so the Asturians lost the element of surprise. The ensuing battle ended with a clear Roman victory and the flight of the Asturians towards the *oppidum* of Lancia.[11] The fighting was fierce, but it seems that the Asturians accepted Carisius' offer of surrender in exchange for their lives. The campaigns of these last two years ended with many Asturian and Cantabrian cities subdued, their inhabitants were forced to destroy their *oppida* and settle in plains near the Roman camps, and a large number of prisoners were sold as slaves and sent out of Hispania.

It was particularly important for the Roman economy that they began to exploit the mines which, especially in Asturian territory, were exceptionally rich in minium, malachite and, above all, gold. In fact, the flourishing mines of Las Médulas became the largest open-pit gold mine in the whole Roman Empire, from which 15,432lb of gold were obtained annually, which for three centuries represented at least 5 per cent of the total income of the Roman state or, in other words, some 1,500,000,000 sesterces a year.[12] As for the Cantabrian front, the sources hardly mention it in this year. However, archaeological evidence indicates that there were also several battles. An example of this is the site of the *oppidum* of Las Lomas[13] (modern Santibáñez de la Peña, Castilla y León), where the largest collection of arrows in all of Europe has been found, as well as remains of all kinds of weapons: swords, *pila*, siege weapons, etc. And the coins found allow it to be dated to this period. A similar case takes place at *Mons Bernorius*[14] (Pomar de Valdivia, Castilla y León), some 30 miles to the east. Here, remains of a pitched battle have been found in a nearby plain, in which the Cantabrians must have been defeated and took refuge in their *oppidum*. Archaeological excavations have recovered a city wall that must have been a mile long and about 10ft thick, and three fortified gates. Archaeological evidence seems to show that the city was conquered and razed to the ground by the Romans. The appearance of systematically shattered household mills demonstrates a thorough destruction and the intention that the *oppidum* should never be inhabited again. In fact,

---

11 Once again, archaeologists do not agree on its location. Peralta Labrador (2009) indicates that it was in Castro de Villasabriego, Castilla y León, while Santos Yagua (2004), 50 miles away.

12 Cuervo Álvarez (2014).

13 Peralta et alt. (2022).

14 Torres-Matrínez et alt. (2012).

it is likely that the adult men were exterminated, and the rest of the population sold into slavery. Finally, Augustus ended the war and returned to Rome. The gates of the temple of Janus were closed again. The *Pax Augusta* was established.

After completing his commission, Antistius Vetus also returned to Italy. It seems that he died shortly afterwards in Puteoli (modern Pozzuoli, Italy) in the villa which had previously belonged to Cicero, and which had been confiscated and sold by the triumvirs. Carisius stayed three more years in Lusitania. In fact, during the winter of 25 BC he founded the *Colonia Iulia Augusta Emerita* (modern Merida, Extremadura) where the legionaries of V Alaudae and X Gemina settled. Considering the years of service of the legionaries, some members of V Alaudae could have been veterans of battles such as Thapsus, Philippi, or Actium. As for X Gemina, it had its origins in the mythical X Equestris, Caesar's favourite legion, the one that had distinguished itself in the battles of Pharsalus and Munda. Like V Alaudae, at Actium had fought on the side of Mark Antony; however, after Octavian's pardon, the X rebelled against the *princeps* who, as punishment, disbanded it, renaming it X Gemina and recruiting legionaries from other units.

There is some confusion about the *legatus Augusti propraetore* who replaced Antistius Vero on the Cantabrian front. Cassius Dio (*Hist.*, 53, 29) affirms that it was Lucius Aemilius and Syme[15] establishes that it was Lucius Aemilius Lepidus Paullus, nephew of the triumvir; while Cassiodorus (*Chron.*, 730), maintains that it was Lucius Aelius Lamia.[16] Whoever it was, he suffered a new revolt from the Cantabrians. The Cantabrians sent an emissary to summon him to give him grain and various gifts. But when the Roman troops arrived at the appointed place, they were ambushed, and all the legionaries were massacred. Augustus' legate responded by cruelly suppressing various Cantabrian tribes, but was unable to quell the revolt, which continued the following year. In 22 BC, it was the Asturians who, fed up with Carisius' abuses, took up arms. On the Cantabrian front, Augustus' new legate was Gaius Furnius, who responded expeditiously to the Cantabrian revolt, taking numerous prisoners who were deported from Hispania to be sold into slavery. As Carisius' situation on the Asturian front was complicated, Furnius had to come to his aid. It is believed that this was the year

15 Syme (1934), p. 315.

16 Syme (1989), pp. 44 and 49.

in which the *oppidum* of Mons Medulius was besieged, where the Asturians resisted the Roman attacks until, let Orosius (6, 21, 8) tell us the end:

> *itaque ubi se gens hominum trux natura et ferox neque tolerandae obsidioni sufficientem neque suscipiendo bello parem intellegit, ad uoluntariam mortem seruitutis timore concurrit. nam se paene omnes certatim igne ferro ac ueneno necauerunt.*[17]

I cannot end this episode without citing the work of Fernández Vázquez,[18] in which he tries to prove his theory about the location of Mons Medulius on the current border between León and Galicia and in which he transcribes a popular song from the 13th century in which he states that the Astures who took refuge in Mons Medulius did not commit collective suicide but were massacred by the Romans. A different point of view between the victors and the vanquished. At this time, Gaius Furnius managed to conquest a few strategic ports of the coast.

In 22 BC, Carisius was replaced by Lucius Sestius Quirinalis Albinianus. It seems that one of his main missions was to organise the so-called Transdurian Province. There is no record in official documents of its existence. It is only mentioned in the Bembibre Bronze or Bierzo Edict, and it would mention an ephemeral province that must have existed between 22 BC and 15 BC, approximately, and which would have covered the territory of the Asturians and Cantabrians. The sources do not give specific information about the events that took place until 19 BC. In that year there was a revolt of Cantabrian slaves in Gaul! These slaves revolted against their masters and decided to return home. Along the way, they clashed with Legio I Augusta, slaughtering many of their soldiers and keeping their banners and eagle. It was only the fourth time in history that a Roman legion had lost its eagle.[19] When the former Cantabrian slaves

17 'When this group of men, by nature wild and fierce, realised that they were neither able to withstand a siege nor strong enough to fight it out, they agreed to take their own lives because of their fear of slavery. Almost all unhesitatingly killed themselves by fire, sword, or poison.' Translation from Adapted from the translation by I.W. Raymond (1936) in http://www.attalus.org/translate/orosius6B.html. Accessed on August 8, 2023.

18 Fernández Vázquez (2003).

19 Previously, only the eagles of Crassus at the Battle of Carrhae (53 BC), those of Decidius Saxa in Cilicia (40 BC) and those of Mark Antony in his campaign against the Parthians (36 BC) had been lost. However, all of them were later recovered. The eagle was

arrived in their home territory, the insurrection became widespread. Rome was once again losing control of the territory. This was a tremendous humiliation for Augustus. He had no choice but to send Marcus Vipsanius Agrippa, his best general, his best friend and, for the past two years, his son-in-law. The man who solved all his military problems. And what he found in Cantabria was a disaster. According to Cassius Dio (*Hist.*, 54, 11), the legionary troops were totally demoralised. Most of them had been fighting in the territory for ten years, suffering extreme weather, constant ambushes and a war that seemed to have no end. Agrippa had a clear mission to end it by every means at his disposal. He was joined in his titanic task by the new propraetore of Tarraconensis, with consular rank, Publius Silius Nerva. As for his soldiers, he imposed an iron discipline that was not without its punishments. For example, he forbade Legio I to continue using the name Augusta.[20] As for the Cantabrians, he decided to literally exterminate them mercilessly. They knew what awaited them if they surrendered: slavery. And they were unwilling to lose their freedom. Now the fight would be to the death. It is Strabo, in his third book on Hispania, who gives us more details of the genocide. Agrippa ordered the right hand of all men of military age to be cut off, later he ordered their murder. 'It is a proof of the ferocity of the Cantabrians, that a number of them having been taken prisoners and fixed to the cross, they chanted songs of triumph.' For them, death in freedom meant victory. Mothers therefore preferred to kill their sons rather than hand them over alive to the Romans. In the numerous sieges fought in the last episodes of this war, collective suicides were common. And the few who decided to surrender were forced to abandon their *oppida,* which were also razed to the ground, and were forced to settle in the plains near the Roman camps. After three years of heavy fighting and an outrageous number of indigenous dead, Agrippa declared the war over, and the Cantabrian territory pacified. He also managed to recover the eagle of the Legio I and the rest of the insignia that the Romans had lost during the ten years of war, depositing them in the Temple of Mars Ultor (*Res Gestae,* 29). During this campaign, Agrippa obtained a *corona muralis* (mural crown), but

20 Shortly [illegible] had been a handful (*manipulus*) of straw fixed to the top of a spear or pole.

the sources do not reveal the reasons why it was granted to him.[21] He was also granted a triumph at Rome, which he rejected in favour of Augustus. However, three legions were left in the territory. It was still feared that the few Asturians would revolt again. Near the mines of Las Médulas, Legio X Gemina was encamped in an area where in 14 BC the city of Asturica Augusta (modern Astorga, Castilla y León) was founded, while Legio VI Victrix was placed in what is now the city of León. The Cantabrian territory was controlled by Legio IV Macedonica, located in Pisoraca (modern Herrera de Pisuerga, Castilla y León). They were accompanied by numerous auxiliary troops who had also taken part in the war. The Cantabrians and Asturians did not take up arms again. It is true that there was an attempted uprising in 16 BC and another even in the time of Emperor Nero, but they were not widespread and were quickly put down. In the following years, the governors of Hispania founded new cities with the veterans of these wars. Besides the two mentioned above, this was the origin of Lucus Augusti (modern Lugo, Galicia); Bracara Augusta (modern Braga, Portugal), on a previous Lusitanian settlement; and Caesaraugusta (modern Zaragoza, Aragon), on Saludie, a previous Sedetan settlement. In any case, the Romanisation of Astur-Cantabrian territory was much slower than in the rest of Hispania. The pre-Roman tribes continued to practise their way of life, although it is true that they abandoned the attacks over the southern territories. In fact, despite the laws of Theodosius that forced the demolition of pagan temples, the Christianisation of this territory was very late, and it was not until the 6th century that we can begin to find a gradual abandonment of the Celtic religion in favour of Christianity. Since then, all the invaders that have passed through Spain, from the Muslims in the 8th century to the Napoleonic invaders in the 19th century, have been unable to dominate these lands of fierce warriors jealous of their freedom.

Many questions remain unanswered about the Astur-Cantabrian wars. As the classical sources have already been extensively studied, it will be archaeology that in the future will have to continue to reveal more information about the battles that took place and even about the leaders of this revolt. Of these we have only the vague reference by Cassius Dio (*Hist.*, 56, 47) to a certain Corocotta for whom Augustus offered a stratospheric reward of one million sesterces. Corocotta

21 Bestowed upon the soldier who first climbed the wall of a besieged city or fortress to successfully place the standard (flag) of the attacking army upon it.

reacted by personally presenting himself at Augustus' camp to claim it. The *princeps*, recognising his courage, handed over the money. This story opens up new questions, but common sense seems to indicate that Corocotta would have agreed to go over to the Roman side in exchange for such a tempting bribe. This concludes the story of one of the longest and bloodiest wars of conquest, considering the small size of the territory, which Rome had to face at the beginning of Augustus' government. Augustus ordered the construction of the Ara Pacis to celebrate the fact that peace had come to Rome after his victories in Gaul and Hispania. Peace, as political propaganda, was embodied in a marble altar.

Chapter 6

THE *AMPHORAE* AND THE EMPEROR

In AD 98, Trajan was proclaimed emperor. He was the thirteenth emperor and the first one born outside Italy.[1] He was a native of Italica, in the province of Baetica. And it was not by chance or improvisation or the impulse of his aged predecessor, Nerva, that he appointed a Hispanian successor. In fact, so was the other candidate, Marcus Cornelius Nigrinus Curiatius Maternus. Ever since Julius Caesar appointed the first Hispanians as senators, a powerful lobby had been growing in Rome during the first century, a lobby that would see its great explosion during the first half of the second century. In no sense was it a 'Hispanian nationalist party': they felt themselves to be Romans, they were Roman citizens, they fought in Rome's wars, they decreed its laws and, in short, they could not conceive of a Hispania that was not integrated into Rome. The long process that led a group of Hispanians not only to influence Roman politics, but also to have several emperors (some of them considered to be the best in the history of Rome), began from the moment when, in 218 BC, Gnaeus Cornelius Scipio landed in Emporion to fight Hannibal's brothers. From that moment on, Rome's ruling class saw that the Iberian Peninsula was not just a battlefield on which to fight the Punics. It was a land full of natural riches. It had vast fields of crops that could provide Rome with the classic Mediterranean triad (olive trees, vines, wheat) and inexhaustible mines from which they could extract tremendous wealth (gold, silver, tin, malachite . . .). But it also had an indigenous population with an iron will to maintain

1 It is true that the Emperor Claudius was born in Gaul, but he came from the most Roman of families, the *gens Julia-Claudia*. His birth in Lugdunum (modern Lyon, France) was entirely circumstantial.

their sovereignty. As we have seen throughout this book, some regions were particularly jealous of their freedom, such as the Celtiberians, the Lusitanians or the Cantabrians, for example. Others quickly understood the impossibility of confronting Rome and adapted to the new circumstances. It was on the Mediterranean coast and along the valleys of the Ebro and Guadalquivir rivers that the Romans found it easier to reach amicable agreements with the local tribes, while in the mountainous regions of the centre and north of the peninsula they had to bring their legions into play. Rivers unite, mountains separate. The coasts and waterways had allowed many Hispanian tribes to contact each other or foreign powers (such as the Greeks or Phoenicians), but the arrival of the Romans was to result in a real conquest of the territory. For Rome, the best way to exploit the wealth of a territory was to Romanise it, to make the indigenous peoples (obviously their elites) understand the benefits of integrating into the Roman orbit. But this is a controversial term that deserves to be qualified. From the insightful critique of Syme,[2] the term 'Romanisation' has undergone a profound revision. Today, it seems indisputable that the Romans did not carry out a systematic process of cultural assimilation. In fact, the closest project to Romanisation in the classical sense (i.e., an acculturation of Hispanian society to adopt Roman customs and mores) was the one that Sertorius attempted to carry out in Bolskan among the sons of the elites of his allied tribes. But in neither case did the Romans pursue a policy in which local languages were replaced by Latin,[3] or a religious policy in which local gods were replaced by the boisterous Roman pantheon. The new conquerors were tolerant of local language, religion (until Christianity was declared the official religion, a foreign one, by the way) and customs. And while it is true that there was a gradual language shift in favour of Latin, this process lasted for centuries. For example, Ferrer Albelda[4] tells us how various mints in southern Hispania adapted the Punic language that their inhabitants continued to speak to the Latin alphabet. Thus, the pre-Roman languages coexisted alongside Latin while a process of diglossia caused them to

2 Syme (1983).

3 We may recall, for example, how some of the Roman elites saw it as a sign of culture and distinction to express themselves in Greek rather than Latin, much to the chagrin and disapproval of the traditionalists.

4 Ferrer Albelda (2012), p. 678. An example of this can be found in the Museu de Badalona, which displays a tombstone written in the Iberian alphabet but whose syntax is Latin.

disappear almost completely.[5] In the religious field, Hispanians and Romans added or exchanged hundreds of gods to their respective pantheons. But in many parts of the peninsula, customs, local traditions, forms of urban planning and manufactured products specific to each territory (such as pottery or *amphorae*) persisted, as long as they were in accordance with the laws of Rome. For example, as Andreu Pintado reminds us, in 61 BC Julius Caesar abolished the Phoenician custom in Gadir of burning alive criminals condemned to death, and Crassus in 95 BC prohibited the Lusitanians from practising human sacrifice. As for urban planning, during the book we have found numerous examples of the Romans forcing the indigenous people to leave their *oppida* to move into cities built under Roman planning rules, but there were many cities that maintained their form from before the Romans arrived.[6] The case of the *amphorae* of Gadir[7] is the definitive example of how Romanisation may have actually worked. It was around 60–70 BC when archaeologists noticed a gradual change in the way *amphorae* were made in this city, moving from the typical Punic typology to the manufacture of Roman models, motivated by the greater commercial success that these, made by Italic settlers, had over those traditionally made in Gadir. However, pottery for domestic use would follow Punic patterns until well into the Augustan era, when we assume that the gradual social impact of Rome affected all aspects of society. Obviously, these social and cultural changes were not uniform throughout society. There were regions of Spain that were practically impervious to the influence of Roman society. Thus, within the territory of the warlike Asturians and Cantabrians, no Roman city has been found, nor is there any trace of buildings typical of Roman culture, such as theatres, amphitheatres and circuses, which are very common in the rest of Iberia. Also in this region, some customs that Strabo himself recounted (*Iberia*, 3, 4, 17), such as the couvade, survived until the beginning of the 20th century.

Thus, we have that, in the middle of the 1st century, Rome began to have a problem that could be alleviated in the transalpine provinces: finding a new ruling elite. Finding 'new Romans'. Civil wars had decimated the traditional Roman and Italic elites and the new strongmen of Rome, first Julius Caesar and then Augustus, would

5 In the Basque Country, the Basque language still survives as a rare example of a pre-Roman language.

6 Ferrer Albelda, op. cit., p. 681.

7 Ferrer Albelda, op. cit., p. 682.

surround themselves with loyal 'provincials' who would help them carry out their reforms. But many others would also come to work as state officials or to open schools of rhetoric, oratory, and grammar. In this period of the High Empire, the *gens Annea*, a family of the equestrian order from Corduba, stands out. At the beginning of the 1st century, Lucius Annaeus Seneca (Seneca the Elder) moved to Rome with his three sons, still children, where he worked as imperial procurator and where he excelled as a good dramatist and historian. His eldest son was Lucius Junius Gallio Annaeanus, who was later adopted by Lucius Junius Gallio, a Hispanian rhetorician living in Rome. Gallio Annaeanus had a brilliant political career that led him to become consul in AD 56 and proconsul of the province of Achaea (in the Peloponnese peninsula, Greece). His middle brother was the famous philosopher Lucius Annaeus Seneca (also known as Seneca the Younger), who became one of the greatest exponents of Stoic philosophy, considered the best orator of the Senate of his generation, was the tutor of the young Nero at the behest of his mother Agrippina Minor, as well as holding numerous public offices, such as consul, and going down in history as one of the best and most influential philosophers of antiquity. Finally, the younger brother was Marcus Annaeus Mela, who devoted himself to the family business, amassing a huge fortune, was the father of the great poet Lucan, the author of *Pharsalia* and the object of the jealousy of Nero. Seneca the Elder's three sons, as well as his grandson Lucanus, were suspected of having participated in a conspiracy against Nero and were forced to commit suicide. Although the Annaeus are the most famous, it was many other Hispanian *gens* that achieved wealth and political power in Rome, such as the *gens Pedania* from Barcino (modern Barcelona), for example, with one of its members, Lucius Pedanius Secundus, consul in AD 43, the first one of Hispanian origin since Balbus, almost 70 years earlier. During this period, Caius Julius Hyginus, whom Julius Caesar brought from Hispania as a slave and later, as a freedman, was appointed by Augustus as director of the Library of Palatine Apollo, the most important library in Rome, and the writers and orators Caius Turranius Gracilis and Marcus Porcius Latro also stood out in the intellectual sphere. The extension of the *ius Latii* (Latin citizenship) to Hispania in AD 74, which is believed to have benefited some 350 municipalities and thousands of Hispanians, who acquired Roman citizenship.

But the most important moment of Hispanian influence in Rome came during the Antonine dynasty (AD 96-192), coinciding with Rome's famous Golden Age. After the assassination of Domitian, it seems that the group of Hispanian senators supported the candidacy of Nerva, who was soon elected. However, the elderly emperor did not have the support of either the army or the Praetorian Guard, who literally kidnapped him, suggesting that he adopt a prestigious general to calm the nerves of the military establishment. Nerva, who had no biological children, had two clear candidates as heir, both of whom were the most prestigious military men of their generation and both of whom were Hispanian: the first was Marcus Cornelius Nigrinus Curiatius Maternus. He was an extraordinary military man. In fact, he is considered one of the most decorated Roman soldiers in history.[8] Not only had he personally taken eight banners from the enemies of Rome, he also had two *coronae vallaris* (for being the first to storm an enemy camp), two *coronae muralis* (for being the first to jump over the wall of an enemy city), two *coronae aurea* (for victory in single combats), two *coronae castrensis* (the first man who penetrated into an enemy camp or field during combat) and eight *hastae purae* (silver spears, a decoration for heroic deeds or for saving the lives of fellow citizens). He began his career as a military tribune of Legio XIV Gemina legion in Britannia, had risen to the consulship, had distinguished himself in the Dacia wars and was at that time the governor of Syria. The other candidate was Marcus Ulpius Traianus (Trajan), born in Italica (modern Santiponce, Andalusia), the son of a prestigious general of the same name who had won imperial favour in command of Legio X Fretensis during the first Judeo-Roman war between AD 67–68. But if the father had been a prestigious general, the son was even more so. At the time, Trajan was governor of Germania and was fighting against the Bructeri tribe on the Rhine frontier. In making his decision he listened to the advice of Lucius Licinius Sura, a senator who had been *consul suffectus*, as well as that of other Hispanian senators such as Lucius Minicius Natalis, or Marcus Annius Verus, a *homo novus* from Ucubi (modern Espejo, Andalusia) who would end up being related to three emperors.[9] To understand the importance of these senators, it should be borne in mind that two of them were consuls on three occasions during their public life, a very unusual fact. Nerva followed the recommendation of his advisors and the chosen one was Trajan, whom Nerva adopted as Marcus Ulpius Nerva Traianus. To prevent Cornelius Nigrinus from any revolutionary temptation, he

---

8 It is believed that the most decorated Roman soldier was Lucius Siccius Dentatus, who lived in the 5th century BC and won twenty-six *coronae*.

9 His daughter Faustina Maior was the wife of Antoninus Pius. And through his son Marcus Annius Verus he would be the grandfather of Marcus Aurelius and, consequently, great-grandfather of Commodus.

was removed from his post as governor of Syria and returned to his birthplace in Edeta (modern Llíria, Valencia) where he spent the rest of his life. Trajan adopted his cousin to succeed him, another Hispanian from Italica, Publius Aelius Hadrianus (Hadrian). His successor, Antoninus Pius, although an Italian born in Lanuvium (about 20 miles from Rome), had a Hispanian for a wife, Faustina Maior. Incidentally, during his government, Gnaeus Papirius Aelianus was appointed governor of Britannia, the only one born in Hispania, specifically in Municipium Florentia Iliberris (modern Granada, Andalusia), and Antoninus Pius' successor, Marcus Aurelius, although a Roman, came from an Ucubian family, as mentioned above. The end of the Antonine dynasty was marked by the assassination of Commodus on 31 December 192. For some years now, the influence of the Hispanians in the government of the Empire had been waning. Decades of a multitude of consuls, *praetores*, and governors of the provinces from Hispania were left behind. It would be almost two centuries before the empire would again have a Hispanian emperor or to find senators with as much influence or power as, to cite one last example, Lucius Iulius Ursus Servianus, three times consul, close friend and brother-in-law of both Trajan and Hadrian.

But the Hispanian influence was not only seen in politics. The Romans also adapted the sword of the Iberians and Celtiberians with whom they fought for the first time during the Punic Wars and copied it, making it the sword of the Roman legions for centuries. Not only did they adopt this sword, but some also cavalry tactics. For example, after the end of the Astur-Cantabrian Wars, the Romans adopted two tactics used by their enemies during the conflict: the '*Cantabricus Densus*' or '*Cantabricus Impetus*', in which the heavy cavalry would hit an enemy infantry point; and the '*Cantabricus Circulus*', in which two columns of horsemen advanced on the flanks of the enemy infantry and instead of charging them, threw a javelin at them and returned to their formation, all in a circling manoeuvre. But the Roman army not only drew on Hispanian weapons, tactics, and generals, it also recruited huge numbers of soldiers from the peninsula. At first, as auxiliary troops, but later also as legionaries.[10] Many of the legions that passed through Hispania drew on local recruits to make up for casualties, so it is logical to think that in almost all the legions there would be soldiers from different provinces. For example, there were three legions with a high percentage of Hispanian recruits who took

10 Peralta Labrador (2018).

part in the invasion of Britannia. One of these was Legio XX Valeria Victrix, which arrived in Hispania during the Astur-Cantabrians Wars and drew on many Hispanian recruits to replace the heavy casualties they suffered. The nickname Valeria Victrix was earned for their victories during the Boudican revolt. Similarly, a *vexillatio* of the all-Hispanian Legio VII Gemina or the mythical Legio IX Hispana, whose strange disappearance near Hadrian's Wall around AD 118 has excited the imagination of novelists and filmmakers, who have favoured an epic battle in which the legionaries were annihilated and lost their eagle.[11] However, there is no archaeological evidence of this massacre, so historians tend to believe that the legion was simply relocated elsewhere in the imperial *limes*. For example, there is evidence of the presence of this legion at Noviomagus, a city of the Batavi (modern Nijmegen, the Netherlands) on the Germanic border near the mouth of the Rhine. There, for example, an inscription of Lucius Latinius Macer, the *Primus pilus* and *Praefectus castrorum* (third in command) of Legio IX Hispana, has been found. In any case, it is certain that the legion was subsequently annihilated or at least suffered a disastrous defeat in some eastern territory, either in Judea under Hadrian or in Armenia under Marcus Aurelius. Incidentally, at Hadrian's Wall, IX Hispania was replaced by another legion whose members were mostly of the same origin. In fact, Griffiths[12] makes an interesting point given the habit of Rome's legionaries to form families and settle in the places where they were garrisoned, it would not be unusual to find traces of DNA of those Hispanians among today's inhabitants of York.

Of great importance to the Roman armies were also the auxiliary units.[13] For many men from the provinces, they were a way of earning a living, in many cases by doing what they were best at: fighting. They usually came from poor regions and at the end of their military service they knew that they would be rewarded with Roman citizenship and land to settle on. In the 1st and 2nd centuries, numerous auxiliary units were recruited in the north-east of the Iberian Peninsula. Some of them were destined for Britannia. Examples include Ala II Asturum,[14] which

11 There are many novels and films that deal with this subject. We will highlight the novel *The Eagle of the Ninth*, by Rosemary Sutcliff (1954) which was adapted into a film as *The Eagle*, by Kevin Macdonald (2011). A year earlier, the same theme was dealt with in another film, *Centurion*, by Neil Marshall (2010).

12 Griffiths (2014).

13 Morillo Cerdán (2003).

14 Santos Yanguas (2006).

had a first camp at Bremetenacum (modern Ribchester, Lancashire) and was later moved to Hadrian's Wall at Cilurnum (modern Chesters, Northumberland) where, incidentally, the ruins of a fort and an interesting museum can be visited. Ala I Hispanorum Asturum had its headquarters at Condercum (modern Benwell, Tyne and Wear) where they were based in the late 2nd or early 3rd century until the end of the Roman occupation of the area. The Ala Vettonum, recruited from the Vettones, took part in the conquest of the island in the time of Claudius. It was initially garrisoned in the south at Cicucium (modern Brecon, Powys), but was soon moved north to Vinovium (modern Binchester, County Durham) where it remained until the early 3rd century. Cohors I Hispanorum accompanied Hadrian on his visit to Britannia in AD 122, staying in the fort of Maryport (Cumbria). In the same region, they would later occupy forts at Netherby and Stanwix, up to the early 5th century. Cohors I Fida Vardullorum was made up of recruits from the Varduli tribe (modern Basque Country). Inscriptions attesting to their presence have been found at Corstopitum (modern Corbridge, Northumberland), Lanchester (Durham) and High Rochester (Northumberland). Cohors II Asturum Equitata,[15] made up of Asturians and Galicians, was garrisoned at Aesica (near modern Haltwhistle, Northumberland), and was probably stationed until around AD 400. Cohors III Bracaraugustanorum, with recruits from the town of Bracara Augusta in Lusitania, maintained two forts near Manchester and in the nearby town of Castleshaw. And finally, Cohors I Celtiberum had a barracks at Caersws II (modern Montgomeryshire, Powys), although Costa García[16] does not rule out that it participated in the construction of Hadrian's Wall. As we can see, most of these units were stationed on the northern frontier. And as was the case with the legions, it is very likely that many Hispanians from these units ended up settling in those territories once their military service was over. Incidentally, it is striking that numerous auxiliary troops were recruited from the territories of the Asturians, Lusitani and the rest of the tribes of northern Hispania, while there is only record of the existence of two Cohors of Cantabrian origin. Though we do not know whether this was due to the tremendous genocide to which they were subjected by Agrippa, which meant that there was no 'surplus' of men who were forced to join the army or, simply, as the territory was not very Romanised, they had no interest in meddling in 'Roman affairs'.

15 Santos Yanagua (2007).

16 Costa García (2009).

The contribution of Hispanians to Roman culture was also notable. In addition to the aforementioned Seneca and Lucan, many others also stood out. Curiously, in the time of Nero, while in the world of politics a generation of Hispano-Roman politicians disappeared after Pison's conspiracy was discovered, at that time a group of artists of the same origin flourished, among whom Marcus Valerius Martialis stands out. Known as Martial, he was born in Bílbilis (modern Calatayud, Aragon) in AD 40. Around AD 64 he travelled to Rome, where he hoped to study law with Seneca. But shortly afterwards he saw his teacher forced to commit suicide, the same path being taken by his friend Lucan. Martial found friendship and financial support in a circle of Hispano-Romans, many of them notable writers such as the poetess Pola Argentaria, widow of Lucan, and from a wealthy family of mine owners in Corduba. And the writer Julius Canius Rufus, from Gadir, whose work is largely lost, and which included satires, elegies, and a *Res Gestae* of the governments of Claudius and Nero. What little we know of Canius is through the *Epigrams* of Martial,[17] who tells us that he was a jovial man, always smiling and a terrible womaniser. The other member of the Hispanian circle was the famous lawyer and rhetor Marcus Fabius Quintilianus, born in Calagurris (modern Calahorra, La Rioja) and the son of a lawyer who sent him to study in Rome. In AD 61 he was sent to Tarraco to practise law, where he met and befriended Servius Sulpicius Galba, with whom he returned to Rome in AD 68 when the latter was proclaimed emperor. Quintilianus soon gained great prestige as a lawyer and as a rhetor. Vespasian gave him the first official and public chair of rhetoric, which he held for two decades, where Hadrian and Pliny the Younger, among many other young Romans, were educated. He was also responsible for the education of the sons and nephews of Vespasian and Domitian. Of his work, *De institutione oratoria* is considered to be the best encyclopaedia of the ancient world for training a good orator. He ended his life surrounded by honours and prestige. Among Martial's group of friends were also Pliny the Younger and Silius Italicus, author of *Punica*, the work we have followed in previous chapters. During Trajan's rule, Martial returned to Bilbilis where he spent the rest of his days in the villa given to him by an admirer. His *Epigrams* are considered to be one of the great poetics works of antiquity and have come down to us practically in their entirety.

---

17 Lagioia (2020).

But Hispanians also excelled in sports. One of the cases takes us to one of the Hispanian families who were favoured by the emperors in the early 2nd century, the Minicius Natalis. Originally from Barcino, Lucius Minicius Natalis was a military tribune of the Legio III Augusta and behaved heroically during the Dacian Wars. He was appointed Tribune of the Plebs, consul in AD 106 and went on to hold important public offices in Rome. His career was the impetus for his son Lucius Minicius Natalis Quadronius Verus to also enjoy a successful career in Rome, being tribune *laticlavio* of Legio I Adiutrix in Dacia, Legio XI Claudia in Moesia and Legio XIV Gemina in Pannonia. His heroism was rewarded by Hadrian who appointed him as his legate of Legio VI Victrix in Britain. His career culminated when he was appointed *consul suffectus* in AD 139. But before that, in addition to being an excellent military man, he proved to be an extraordinary charioteer by being the first Hispanian to win the Olympic Games in AD 129. But if we are talking about sport, we can't fail to mention Gaius Appuleius Diocles. He would surely be among the GOATs of all history. He was a charioteer, and his career was extraordinary. He competed in 4,257 races and won 1,462 races, which means that he won 34 per cent of the races he competed in and came second in a similar percentage. That means he competed for more than 23 years, which is truly unheard of, given the very high percentage of riders who died during races. This earned him 35,863,120 sesterces, which Professor and Chair of Classical Studies at the University of Pennsylvania, Peter T. Struck[18] has calculated to be about $15 billion, making him by far the highest-paid athlete in history.

During the following decades, Hispania experienced a period of peace and prosperity, although Rome's political influence gradually waned. The legions stationed in Hispania gradually left the territory and were transferred to war zones such as Germania, Pannonia and Britannia. The first great crisis began at the end of the 2nd century and continued throughout the 3rd century, and was caused by an economic crisis, the first barbarian invasions (by the Mauritanians from North Africa and the Franks from Gaul), and a plague that decimated the population, especially the most populated cities of Tarraconensis, such as Ilerda, Bilbilis and Calagurris, which were practically depopulated. During the last third of the 4th century, we find a flourishing of Hispanian influence in the affairs of Rome. On the one hand, we could start with Flavius Theodosius, a prestigious Hispanian general

18 Struck (2010).

who in AD 368 was appointed *Comes Britanniarum,*[19] and took his son Theodosius with him to Britannia, where they coincided with another successful Hispanian general, Magnus Maximus, a relative of his. In AD 378, the Battle of Adrianople took place, in which the Eastern Roman Emperor Valens was killed. The Western Roman Emperor Gratian, only 19 years old, was faced with a colossal challenge. To begin with, he had to choose a new colleague to replace Valens as ruler of the East. Gratian would listen carefully to the advice of two men,[20] both of them from Hispania. One was his *Comes Sacrarum Largitionum,*[21] Flavius Eucherius, and the other Pope Damasus I, who convinced him to choose Theodosius, who had a brilliant military record in Britannia and was living in Hispania away from politics after the execution of his father following a palace conspiracy that followed the death of Emperor Valentinian I in AD 375. Gratian accepted the proposal of his advisors and Theodosius was designed emperor. He was an energetic, effective and reformist statesman. In AD 384, he had to mediate a revolt in Britannia by Magnus Maximus, who sought to seize the Western Roman Empire from Valentinian II, who was only 13 years old, although it was his mother, Justina, who ruled. At Verona, Justina, Magnus Maximus, and Theodosius agreed that Valentinian II and Maximus would divide the western territory. But three years later, Maximus invaded Valentinian II's territories. Justina and the young emperor went to the court of Theodosius and offered Galla, Justina's daughter (and Valentinian II's sister), as his wife, in exchange for fighting Maximus. In the war between the two, Theodosius eventually won and received Maximus' head as a trophy. Incidentally, there is a close link between Magnus Maximus and Britannia, especially in Wales, where he is known as Macsen Wledig, and who, according to the *Mabinogion,*[22] would have married Helen of Caernarfon, and they would have had several children, among them Sevira who, according to the Pillar of Eliseg (*Croes Elisedd* in Welsh, near Valle Crucis Abbey, Denbighshire, Wales), would marry Vortigern (*Gwrtheyrn* in Welsh) and they would start the Gwerthrynion dynasty that would found the Kingdom of Powys which was independent until its conquest

19 Latin for 'Count of Britains', it was a military post with command over the mobile field army from the mid-4th century onwards.

20 Canto (2006).

21 Latin for 'Count of the Sacred Largesses', a sort of 'Finance Minister', with many nuances.

22 A collection of prose stories from medieval Welsh manuscripts.

by Edward I of England in 1283. If we return to Rome, Theodosius carried out a huge programme of political reforms, although he will go down in history for the Edict of Thessalonica (380) which proclaimed Christianity as the official religion of the Roman Empire, while Pope Damasus I was still Pope. He also promoted a policy of persecution against paganism, which included the destruction of many temples. In AD 394, he unified the two branches of the Empire after defeating the new Emperor of the West, Eugenius, and his general, Arbogast, at the Battle of the Frigidus, who had been involved in the mysterious death of Valentinian II. As in the time of Trajan, the Roman administration was filled with high-ranking officials from Hispania, such as the brilliant general Flavius Timasius, or the statemen Flavius Sallustius or Maternus Cynegius, among many others. Theodosius died in 395, dividing the Empire again between his two sons: Honorius in the West and Arcadius in the East.

But while all this was taking place among the upper echelons of the empire, Hispania was undergoing a great transformation. The threat of barbarian invasions caused the increasingly depopulated cities to wall themselves in. Christianity spread rapidly, with prominent figures such as Orosius, Prudentius and Melania the Elder. In the field of culture, we cannot fail to mention Egeria, a writer and traveller from the 4th century who came from a noble family in Gallaecia, probably related to the emperor Theodosius. Her book *Itinerarium ad Loca Sancta* narrates her long pilgrimage to the Holy Land and is a real delight in its description of the places she passed through and the people she met, as well as being written in Vulgar Latin, which is a gem for linguists studying the transition from Classical to Late Latin. But political instability was constant. In the early 5th century, the cousins of Honorius and Arcadius, Flavius Didymus and Verinianus, defended the Pyrenees against the Germanics tribes until AD 408, when they were unable to stop a new wave of 'barbarians' (Suebi, Alans, Vandal Asdingi and Silingi) led by Gerontius, a general of Constantine III, a usurper who had rebelled against Honorius and succeeded in having himself recognised as co-emperor of the West. The imperial cousins were finally defeated somewhere in Lusitania. Shortly afterwards, Gerontius revolted and proclaimed Maximus (probably his son) emperor, who established his capital at Tarraco. In those years, the situation in the Western Empire was total chaos. In fact, in AD 410 the city of Rome was sacked by the Visigoths led by their king, Alaric, who took several hostages, including Galla Placidia, the youngest daughter of Theodosius. Around AD 411, Maximus reached an agreement with the Germanic settlers in Hispania, offering them land and a *foedus* (a federation with Rome, in this case Tarraco) in exchange for their participation as auxiliary troops in his army. Hydatius tells us that the Germanics shared out the land by means of a kind of lottery:

> *Subversis memorata plagarum grassatione Hispaniae provinciis, barbari ad pacem ineundam, Domino miserante conversi, sorte ad inhabitandum sibi provinciarum dividunt regiones. Gallaeciam Wandali occupant et Suebi, sitam in extremitate Oceani maris occidua. Alani Lusitaniam et Carthaginiensem provincias, et Wandali cognomine Silingi Baeticam sortiuntur. Hispani per civitates et castella residui a plagis, barbarorum per provincias dominantium se subjiciunt servituti.*[23]

Thus, the Suebi and the Vandal Asdingi settled in Gallaecia, the Alans in Lusitania and the Vandal Silingi in Baetica, leaving Tarraconensis in the hands of the Hispano-Romans. Three years of anarchy came to an end and the Germans exchanged the sword for the plough. But in the same year, Gerontius died, and Maximus renounced the imperial throne. In Italy, Alaric died of a short illness, and was succeeded by his brother-in-law Athaulf as king of the Visigoths, who made peace with Rome in exchange for the rule of Gaul. Once there, however, he was attacked by Honorius' Roman troops and retreated to Hispania, where he conquered Tarraconensis and established his capital at Barcino (modern Barcelona), and married Galla Placidia, Honorius' half-sister, with whom he hoped to reach a peace agreement. But this rapprochement turned his nobles against him, who ended up assassinating him. However, his successors were forced to make a pact with Rome, so the Visigoths agreed to a *foedus* for which they would receive large quantities of wheat in exchange for fighting the Vandal Silingi and the Alans, who were exterminated. Meanwhile, the Vandal Asdingi moved to North Africa, where they established a powerful kingdom. By now, Rome had lost control of the situation. In Italy, Ricimer, whose father was Suebic and mother Visigothic, served as *magister militum* of the emperors, but in reality, it was he who ruled. Hispania was divided into several territories: that of the Suebi, that of the Vascones (who moved from the Pyrenees to

23 'After spreading these plagues over the provinces of Spain, the Lord had pity and the Barbarians were forced to peace, dividing up the territories of the provinces to settle there. The Vandals occupied Galicia and the Swabians the western part on the edge of the ocean. The Alans took over the provinces of Lusitania and Cartagena, the Vandals Sillings, Betica. In the cities and fortresses the Spaniards spared by misfortunes submitted to the domination of the Barbarians who directed their provinces.' Translation by the author.

what is now the Basque Country and northern Navarra), that of the Asturians and Cantabrians, who regained their independence, and that of the Visigoths, whose territory was included in the Kingdom of Toulouse, ruled by King Euric. In AD 475, Emperor Julius Nepos recognised the independence of the Kingdom of Toulouse. Hispania was definitively separated from the Western Roman Empire. An empire that would only exist for one more year, as in AD 476 Odoacer deposed the last Roman emperor, Romulus Augustulus, and proclaimed himself king of Italy. From that moment on, another story begins.

It had been 688 years since the first Roman had set foot on the Iberian Peninsula. At that time, for them it was an unknown territory where they only intended to fight the Carthaginians. But there they discovered its extraordinary riches in mineral resources and agriculture, which they soon began to exploit. However, beyond the coastal societies, which were more accustomed to trade and contact with foreigners, they encountered fierce opposition from the inland tribes, who fanatically defended their independence. The names of Viriathus or Numantia would make even the bravest of Romans tremble, and they were forced to send their best legions and generals to fight them, even forcing them to change their calendar! To subdue them, they had to resort to murder, treachery, and genocide. Hispania was the territory where the careers of many of history's greatest Romans were forged, such as Scipio Africanus, Aemilianus Scipio, Marius, Pompey, Caesar . . . In return, the Hispanians who allied themselves with the Romans and the survivors of the conquest were able to enjoy the benefits of belonging to the great civilisation of the West. They adopted its language, its religion, its customs, became richer thanks to its trade networks and infrastructure, and went from living in austere *oppida* to increasingly opulent cities, in which circuses, theatres, amphitheatres, temples and victory arches were built. And not only that, the Hispanians reciprocated by giving Rome many of its best men: emperors, senators, and thousands of soldiers, but also historians, scientists and poets. Hispania was Rome, but Rome also had something of Hispania. A common past that will live on forever.

Map 14: Among the numerous reforms undertaken by the emperor Diocletian was a new provincial organisation, which left Hispania divided into five provinces. Later, in the time of Constantine I, the islands of the Balearics were separated from Tarraconensis.

BIBLIOGRAPHY

Primary Sources

ANONYMOUS: *Bellum Hispanienses,* in: https://latin.packhum.org/author/430 (accessed 1 June 2023).

ANONYMOUS: *De Bello Alexandrino,* in: https://latin.packhum.org/author/428 (accessed 10 June 2023).

APPIAN: *The Civil Wars.* Horace White, ed. In: https://www.perseus.tufts.edu/hopper/text?doc=Perseus%3Atext%3A1999.01.0232 (accessed 23 March 2023).

APPIAN: *The Iberian Wars,* in *The Foreign Wars.* Translated by Horace White. New York. The MacMillan Company (1899). In: https://www.perseus.tufts.edu/hopper/text?doc=Perseus%3Atext%3A1999.01.0230%3Atext%3DHisp (accessed 5 May 2023).

CASSIUS DIO: *Roman History.* Herbert Baldwin Foster. William Heinemann, Harvard University Press. London; New York. (1914). In: https://www.perseus.tufts.edu/hopper/text?doc=Perseus:abo:tlg,0385,001:1/ (accessed 20 February 2023).

CICERO, Quintus Tullius: *Breviario de campaña electoral.* Published by Cuadernos del Acantilado. Translated by Alejandra de Riquer (2011).

DIODORUS SICULUS: *History.* Loeb Classical Library, 12 volumes, Greek texts and facing English translation: Harvard University Press (1933 thru 1967). In: https://penelope.uchicago.edu/Thayer/E/Roman/Texts/Diodorus_Siculus/home.html (accessed 12 March 2023).

FLORUS: *Epitome of Roman History.* Loeb Classical Library edition, published in 1929. In: https://penelope.uchicago.edu/Thayer/E/Roman/Texts/Florus/Epitome/home.html (accessed 15 February 2023).

FRONTINUS: *The Strategemata.* Loeb Classical Library, edition 1925 by Charles E. Bennett. In: https://penelope.uchicago.edu/Thayer/E/Roman/Texts/Frontinus/Strategemata/home.html (accessed 15 February 2023).

GELLIUS, Aulus: *Noctes Actiae.* Translation by J. C. Rolfe, first published in 1927 in three volumes as part of the Loeb Classical Library. In: https://penelope.

uchicago.edu/Thayer/E/Roman/Texts/Gellius/home.html (accessed 12 April 2023).

HERODOTUS: *History*. Editor: Godley, Alfred Denis; Publisher: W. Heinemann & G. P. Putnam's sons (1921–4). In: https://www.perseus.tufts.edu/hopper/text?doc=Perseus:text:1999.01.0126 (accessed 12 May 2023).

HORACE: *Odes and Epodes*. Paul Shorey and Gordon J. Laing. Chicago. Benj. H. Sanborn & Co. 1919. In: http://www.perseus.tufts.edu/hopper/text?doc=Perseus%3Atext%3A1999.02.0024 (accessed 18 April 2023).

HYDATIUS: *Chronicon*. In: https://www.thelatinlibrary.com/hydatiuschronicon.html (accessed 30 May 2023).

JULIUS CAESAR: *Comentarios de la Guerra de las Galias*. Ed. Espasa Calpe. Col. Austral. Madrid (2001).

LIVY: *History of Rome*. English Translation by. Rev. Canon Roberts. New York, New York. E. P. Dutton and Co. 1912. 1. Livy. History of Rome. English Translation. Rev. Canon Roberts. New York, New York. E. P. Dutton and Co. (1912). In: https://www.perseus.tufts.edu/hopper/text?doc=Perseus:text:1999.02.0026 (accessed 3 February 2023).

LUCAN: *Farsalia*. Ed. Cátedra. Madrid (2003).

NICOLAUS OF DAMASCUS: *Life of Augustus*. Translated by Clayton M. Hall (1923) in https://www.csun.edu/~hcfll004/nicolaus.html, California State University Notrthridge (accessed 4 August 2023).

OROSIUS: *Historiae Adversum Paganos*. Based on the edition by C. Zangemeister (1889). In: https://www.attalus.org/latin/orosius6B.html (accessed 8 August 2023).

PLUTARCH: *The Parallel Lives: The Life of Marius*. Published in Vol. IX of the Loeb Classical Library edition (1920). In: https://penelope.uchicago.edu/Thayer/E/Roman/Texts/Plutarch/Lives/Marius*.html (accessed 5 September 2023).

PLUTARCH: *The Parallel Lives: The Life of Sertorius*. Published in Vol. VIII of the Loeb Classical Library edition (1919). In: https://penelope.uchicago.edu/Thayer/E/Roman/Texts/Plutarch/Lives/Sertorius*.html (accessed 7 September 2023).

PLUTARCH: *The Parallel Lives: The Life of Crassus*. Published in Vol. III of the Loeb Classical Library edition (1916). In: https://penelope.uchicago.edu/Thayer/E/Roman/Texts/Plutarch/Lives/Crassus*.html (accessed 8 September 2023).

PLUTARCH: *The Parallel Lives: The Life of Caesar*. Published in Vol. VII of the Loeb Classical Library edition (1919). In: https://penelope.uchicago.edu/Thayer/E/Roman/Texts/Plutarch/Lives/Caesar*.html (accessed 30 September 2023).

SALLUST: *The War with Jugurtha.* Published in the Loeb Classical Library (1921, revised 1931). In: https://penelope.uchicago.edu/thayer/e/roman/texts/sallust/bellum_jugurthinum/1*.html (accessed 3 October 2023).

SALLUST: *The War with Catilina.* Published in the Loeb Classical Library (1921, revised 1931). In: https://penelope.uchicago.edu/Thayer/e/roman/texts/sallust/bellum_catilinae*.html (accessed 26 March 2023).

SILIUS ITALICUS: *La Guerra Punica.* Akal Clásica. Madrid (2005).

STRABO: *Geography.* Edition Loeb Classical Library, 8 volumes, Greek texts with facing English translation by H. L. Jones: Harvard University Press (1917 thru 1932). In: https://penelope.uchicago.edu/Thayer/E/Roman/Texts/Strabo/home.html (accessed 17 March 2023). SUETONIUS: *The Lives of the Twelve Caesars;* An English Translation, Augmented with the Biographies of Contemporary Statesmen, Orators, Poets, and Other Associates. Suetonius. Publishing Editor. J. Eugene Reed. Alexander Thomson. Philadelphia. Gebbie & Co. 1889. In: https://www.perseus.tufts.edu/hopper/text?doc=Perseus:text:1999.02.0132 (accessed 3 September 2023)

THUCYDIDES: *The Peloponnesian War.* Translator: Richard Crawley. In: https://www.gutenberg.org/files/7142/7142-h/7142-h.htm (accessed 1 May 2023)

VIRGIL. *Bucolics, Aeneid, and Georgics of Vergil.* J. B. Greenough. Boston. Ginn & Co. (1900).

VIRGIL. *The Aeneid,* Translation from: Theodore C. Williams. trans. Boston. Houghton Mifflin Co. (1910). In: http://www.perseus.tufts.edu/hopper/text?doc=Perseus%3Atext%3A1999.02.0054%3Abook%3D6%3Acard%3D801 (accessed 7 August 2023).

Secondary Sources

ALAPONT MARTÍN, Llorenç; CALVO GÁLVEZ, Matías; and RIBERA I LACOMBA, Albert: 'La Destrucción de Valentia por Pompeyo (75 a.C.)' in *Quaderns de Difusió Arqueològica,* vol. 6. València (2009).

AMELA VALVERDE, Luis: 'Cneo Pompeyo hijo en Hispania antes de la batalla de Munda' in *Espacio, Tiempo y Forma,* Serie II, Historia Antigua, Vol. 13 (2000), pp. 357–90.

AMELA VALVERDE, Luis: 'La emisión 'Hispanorvm' de Morgantina' in *OMNI* N°7 – 12/2013, pp. 34–44.

AMELA VALVERDE, Luis: 'El asesinato de Cn. Calpurnio Pisón' in *Gerión,* Vol. 20 Núm. 1 (2002), pp. 255–79. ISSN: 0213-0181.

AMELA VALVERDE, Luis: 'Un Pasaje del *De Bello Gallico* (3, 20, 1). La Participación de L. Manlio en el Conflicto Sertoriano' in *Anuari De Filologia. Antiqva Et Mediaevalia* (6/2016), pp. 23–40. ISSN: 2014-1386.

AMELA VALVERDE, Luis: 'Sobre la fundación de Gerunda (Girona, prov. Girona). Unas notas' in *Tiempo y Sociedad,* 30 (2018), pp. 9–31.

AMELA VALVERDE, Luis: 'Pompeyo Magno y la Galia Transalpina. La guerra sertoriana' in *Helmantica: Revista de filología clásica y hebrea* Vol. 70, N° 204 (2019), pp. 9–52. ISSN 0018-0114.

ANDREU PINTADO, Javier: 'Imperium del magistrado provincial: límites administrativos, réditos políticos, conquistas territoriales. El caso hispano' in Juan SANTOS YANGUAS, Juan; and Gonzalo CRUZ ANDREOTTI (eds), and M. FERNÁNDEZ CORRAL and l. SÁNCHEZ VOIGT (col.): *Romanización, fronteras y etnias en la roma antigua: el caso hispano.* Published by Servicio Editorial de la Universidad del País Vasco. Vitoria/Gasteiz (2012).

BELLÓN RUIZ, Juan Pedro; RUEDA GALÁN, Carmen; LECHUGA CHICA, Miguel Ángel; MORENO, María Isabel: 'An archaeological analysis of a battlefield of the Second Punic War: the camps of the Battle of Baecula' in *Journal of Roman Archaeology* Vol. 29, N°. 1 (2016), pp. 72–104. ISSN 1047-7594.

BLÁZQUEZ MARTÍNEZ, José María: 'El sistema impositivo en la Hispania romana' in *Historia de la Hacienda Española (épocas antigua y medieval).* Instituto de Estudios Fiscales, Madrid (1982), pp. 67–125.

BRAVO JIMÉNEZ, Salvador. 'Lucio Canuleio y la romanización del Campo de Gibraltar' in ALMORAIMA, *Revista de Estudios Campogibraltareños* 45 (octubre 2016). Algeciras. Instituto de Estudios Campogibraltareños, pp. 321–33.

CANTO, Alicia M.: 'Sobre el origen bético de Teodosio I el Grande, y su improbable nacimiento en Cauca de Gallaecia' in *Latomus*, Tome 64, Fascicule 2 (2006).

COSTA GARCÍA, José Manuel: 'Tras los pasos de la Cohors I Celtiberorum: Evidencias arqueológicas' in *BSAA Arqueología* LXXV, 2009, Universidad de Valladolid, pp. 201–22. ISSN: 1888-976X

CUERVO ÁLVAREZ, Benedicto: 'La urbs Asturica Augusta' in *Historia Digital* XIV, 24, (2014).

CUI, Siwen: 'The Marian Military Reform and Its Effects on the Roman Republic' in *Advances in Social Science, Education and Humanities Research*, volume 586. Published by Atlantis Press SARL (2021).

DOMÍNGUEZ MONEDERO, Adolfo J.: 'Libios, libiofenicios, blastofenicios: elementos púnicos y africanos en la Iberia Bárquida y sus supervivencias' in *Gerián* 3 (1995). Servicio de Publicaciones. Universidad complutense. Madrid.

DOREY, T. A.: 'The treaty with Saguntum' in *Humanitas*, Number 11, Year 1959, pp. 1–10. Published by Faculdade de Letras da Universidade de Coimbra, Instituto de Estudos Clássicos. Coimbra. URL: http://hdl.handle.net/10316.2/6946 (accessed 22 October 2022)

DUFF, J. D.: *Silus Italicus. Punica.* Harvard University Press. Cambridge, Massachusetts (1961).

ECKSTEIN, Arthur M.: *Mediterranean Anarchy, Interstate War, and the Rise of Rome.* University of California Press. Los Angeles (2006).

ESPINOSA, Urbano: 'Calagurris y Sertorio' in *Calahorra: bimilenario de su fundación. Acta del I Symposium de Historia de Calahorra.* Madrid (1984), pp. 189–99.

FERNÁNDEZ RODRÍGUEZ, David: 'La toma de Carthago Nova por Publio Cornelio Escipión: ¿leyenda o realidad?' in *POLIS. Revista de ideas y formas políticas de la Antigüedad Clásica* 17 (2005), pp. 31–72.

FERNÁNDEZ VÁZQUEZ, Vicente: 'Localización del Monte Medulio en la sierra de la Lastra (León/Orense)' in *Argutorio*, 5 (2003).

FERRER ALBELDA, Eduardo: 'El sustrato púnico en las urbes meridionales: Persistencias culturales e identidades cívicas' in Juan SANTOS YANGUAS, Juan; and Gonzalo CRUZ ANDREOTTI (eds), and M. FERNÁNDEZ CORRAL and I. SÁNCHEZ VOIGT (col.): *Romanización, fronteras y etnias en la roma antigua: el caso hispano.* Published by Servicio Editorial de la Universidad del País Vasco. Vitoria/Gasteiz (2012).

GARCÍA GONZÁLEZ, Juan: 'P. Calpurnius Lanarius, A New Name on The Sullan Proscription Lists' in *The Classical Quarterly* 1-8 (2023). doi:10.1017/S0009838822000593

GARCÍA MORÁ, Félix: 'Lex Plautia de reditu Lepidanorum' in *Florentia Iliberritana* 3 (1992).

GARCÍA RIAZA, Enrique: *Celtíberos y lusitanos frente a Roma: Diplomacia y derecho de guerra.* Vitoria-Gasteiz: Servicio Editorial. Universidad del País Vasco / Euskal Herriko Unibertsita-tea (2002).

GENDRON, Juliana: 'Violaciones y sanciones en el ejército romano: ¿el ejemplo de Sertorio?' in *Revista Universitaria de Historia Militar* Vol. 9, n. 19, year 2020, pp. 56–76. ISSN: 2254-6111.

GÓMEZ DE CASO ZURIAGA, Jaime: 'Amílcar Barca, táctico y estratega. Una valoración' in *Polis. Revista de ideas y formas políticas de la Antigüedad Clásica.* Number 13, year 2001, pp. 33–68.

GRIFFITHS, Mike: *Roman York's Spanish connection* in BBC York & North Yorkshire. October 29, 2014. In: https://www.bbc.co.uk/northyorkshire/content/articles/2005/09/28/spanishlegion_ilny_feature.shtml (accessed 16 August 2023).

GUÀRDIA I LLORENS, Marc: 'Lauro y el poblado ibérico del Puig del Castell de Samalús (Cànoves i Samalús, Barcelona): hacia una nueva propuesta de la localización de la ceca' in *XV Congreso Nacional de Numismática* Madrid (28–30 octubre 2014), pp. 863–86.

HOZ, Javier de: *Historia lingüística de la Península Ibérica en la Antigüedad. I: Preliminares y mundo meridional prerromano.* Editorial CSIC - CSIC Press. Madrid (2010).

HUNTSMAN, Eric D.: 'Livia Before Octavian' in *Ancient Society* vol. 39, 2009, pp. 121–69. JSTOR, http://www.jstor.org/stable/44079922 (accessed 31 July 2023)

KONRAD, C.F.: 'Metellus and the head of Sertorius' in *Gerión*, 6. Published by Universidad Complutense de Madrid. Madrid (1988), pp. 253–61.

KORNEMANN, Ernst: *Die neue Livius-epitome aus Oxyrhynchus*. Dieterich'sche Verlagsbuchhandlung T. Weicher, Leipzig (1904).

KROLL, John H.: 'Early Iron Age Balance Weights at Lefkandi, Euboea' in *Oxford Journal of Archaeology* 27(1) (2008), pp. 37–48.

LAGIOIA, A.: 'Il Risus di Canio Rufo e il Lusus di Marziale (3.20)' in *Lexis* 38 (n.s.), 1 (2020), pp. 251–66.

LATORRE MOLINA, Guillermo: 'Estudio de un acontecimiento de la Segunda Guerra Púnica: Ilorci y la muerte de Cneo Cornelio Escipión' in: CONESA, MARTÍNEZ, SÁNCHEZ, MOLINA, GARCÍA (coord..).: *Antigëdad in progress . . . Actas del I Congreso Internacional de Jóvenes Investigadores del Mundo Antiguo (CIJIMA I)*. Published by Centro de Estudios del Próximo Oriente y la Antigüedad Tardía. Universidad de Murcia. Murcia (2017).

LECHUGA CHICA, M. A., QUESADA SANZ, F., BELLÓN RUIZ, J. P. y PÉREZ GARCÍA, J. L. (2021): 'Datos sobre el más antiguo empleo de artillería romana en Iberia: el asedio a Iliturgi (Mengíbar, Jaén) (206 a.n.e.)', *Spal* 30.2, pp. 158–88. https://dx.doi.org/10.12795/spal.2021.i30.21 (accessed 29 November 2022).

MAJERCZYK, Michael R.: 'Fractured Friendship at the Battle of Munda 45 BC: Julius Caesar and Titus Labienus' in *Saber and Scroll* (2015), pp. 37–56.

MARTÍN CÓRDOBA, Emilio; RECIO RUIZ, Ángel; RAMÍREZ SÁNCHEZ, Juan de Dios; y MACÍAS LÓPEZ, Milagros: 'Enterramiento Fenicio en Las Chorreras (Vélez-Málaga. Málaga)' in *Mainake*, nº XXIX, year 2007, pp. 557–81.

MARTÍNEZ CABALLERO, Santiago: (2012). 'La ciudad fundada por M. Marius, Termes y Colenda (App., Iber. 99-100). La guerra de 104-93 a.c. en territorios arévacos, vacceos y vettones' in *Studia Historica. Historia Antigua*, year 2012, number 29, pp. 119–51. In: https://revistas.usal.es/uno/index.php/0213-2052/article/view/8806 (accessed 1 December 2022)

MARTINO GARCÍA, David: 'Apuntes sobre Brigaecium de los Astures: Hacia un modelo de la ciudad hispanorromana de la cuenca media del Duero' in *oppidum. Cuadernos de Investigación* n.11 (2015), pp. 79–97. Universidad, Segovia. ISSN: 1885-6292.

MATYSZAK, Philip: *Sertorious and the Struggle for Spain*, Pen & Sword Military; (2013)

MORILLO CERDÁN, Ángel: 'Hispania en la estrategia militar del Alto Imperio: Movimientos de tropas en el Arco Atlántico a través de los testimonios arqueológicos' in *Unidad y diversidad en el Arco Atlántico en época romana I. Hombres, territorios y fronteras*. Gijón (2003), pp. 19–33.

MORILLO CERDÁN, Ángel; MORALES HERNÁNDEZ, Fernando: 'Campamentos romanos de la guerra de Numancia: La circunvalación

Escipiónica' in *Los Escipiones. Roma Conquista Hispania*. Published by Museo Arqueológico Regional. Alcalá de Henares (2016), pp. 275–98.

MUÑIZ COELLO, J.: 'El proceso de Galba, las quaestiones y la justicia ordinaria (Roma, siglos II/I a.C.)' in *L'Antiquité Classique* n. 73 (2004), pp. 109–26.

NOGUERA GUILLÉN, Jaume: '¿Dónde está la ciudad de Lauro, destruida durante las guerras sertorianas?' in *Studi di Letteratura e Storia dell'Antichità* Vol. 110. I. Università di Pavia (2022), pp. 28–47.

NOVILLO LÓPEZ, Miguel Ángel: 'La propertura cesariana en la Hispania Ulterior: La II Guerra Lusitana' in *Gerión* Vol. 28, n. 1 (2000), pp. 207–21.

O'CONNELL, Jack Thomas: *Political Violence in the Late Roman Republic*. A thesis submitted to the History Department, College of Liberal Arts and Social Sciences University of Houston (May 2022). In: https://uh-ir.tdl.org/bitstream/handle/10657/10489/OConnell_Jack_PoliticalViolence_2022.pdf?sequence=1&isAllowed=y (accessed 28 March 2023).

ORFILA, Margarita: 'La intervención de Q. Cecilio Metelo sobre las Baleares' in *Pyrenae* 39/2 (2008), pp. 7–45.

PANIEGO DÍAZ, Pablo: 'Los túrdulos del occidente peninsular' in *Revista Historia Autónoma* 5 (2014), pp. 27–41.

PENA, María José: 'La tribu Velina en Mallorca y los nombres de Palma y Pollentia' in *Faventia* 26/2 (2004), pp. 69–90.

PERALTA LABRADOR, Eduardo: *Los cántabros antes de Roma*. Real Academia de la Historia. Madrid (2003).

PERALTA LABRADOR, Eduardo: 'Los auxiliares cántabros del ejército romano y las maniobras de la caballería romana' in *Hispania Antiqua* N°. 42 (2018), pp. 123–98. ISSN 1130-0515, ISSN-e 2530-6464

PERALTA LABRADOR, Eduardo; F. TORRES MARTÍNEZ, Jesús and DOMÍNGUEZ SOLERA, Santiago D.: *Asedio de La Loma* (Santibáñez de la Peña, Palencia). Campaña de 2003 a 2018. Clan Editorial (2022).

PÉREZ VILATELA, Luciano: 'Ilercavones, Celtíberos Y Cartagineses en 218-217 a.C.' in *Caesaraugusta* 68 (1991), pp. 205–28. I.S.S.N.: 0007-9502

PINA POLO, Francisco: 'Calagurris contra Roma: De Acidino a Sertorio' in *Kalkorikos* 11 (2006), pp. 117–29.

POWELL, Lindsay: *Marcus Agrippa: Right-hand Man of Caesar Augustus*. Pen and Sword. London (2015).

RIBERA I LACOMBA, Albert: 'La Destrucción de Valentia (75 A.C.) y la Cultura Material de la Época de Sertorio (82-75 A.C.)' in SALA SELLÉS, Feliciana and MORATALLA JÁVEGA, Jesús (ed.): *Las Guerras Civiles Romanas en Hispania. Una Revisión Histórica desde la Contestania*. Published by Diputación de Alicante and Universidad de Alicante. Alacant (2014).

SALINAS DE FRÍAS, M.:'Sobre la memoria histórica en Roma: los escipiones y la traición de los celtíberos', *Studia Historica: Historia Antigua* 29 (2012), pp.

97–118. In: https://revistas.usal.es/index.php/0213-2052/article/view/8805 (accessed 18 November 2022)

SAN VICENTE, José Ignacio: 'La Victoria de Décimo Junio Bruto Sobre los Galaicos y la Retirada de Emilio Lépido de Pallantia: Algunas Consideraciones sobre su Cronología' in *HISPANIA ANTIQVA* XXXVII–XXXVIII (2013–2014), pp. 41–68.

SANTOS YANGUAS, Narciso: 'Lancia de los Astures: Ubicación y significado histórico' in *Historia Antigua* vol. XXVIII (2004), pp. 71–86.

SANTOS YANGUAS, Narciso: 'El Ala II de los Astures en el Ejército Imperial Romano' in *Historia Anticua* XXX (2006), pp. 87–100.

SANTOS YANGUAS, Narciso: 'La cohorte II de caballería de astures y galaicos' in *Cuadernos de estudios gallegos* T. 54, Nº. 120 (2007), pp. 35–44. ISSN 0210-847X.

SCHULTEN, Adolf: *Fontes Hispaniae Antiquae. Las Guerras de 154-71 a. de J.C.* Published by Librería Bosch. Barcelona (1937).

SMITH, William: *A Dictionary of Greek and Roman biography and mythology*. Little, Brown, and Co. (1867). Publication info: Ann Arbor, University of Michigan Library. URL: http://name.umdl.umich.edu/ACL3129.0002.001 (accessed 12 May 2023).

SOLANA SANZ, José María: 'La pacificación de los pueblos del norte de España' in *Historia Antigua* vol. XXVIII (2004), pp. 25–70.

STRUCK, Peter T.: 'Greatest of All Time' in *Lapham's Quarterly*. Monday, August 02, 2010. In: https://www.laphamsquarterly.org/roundtable/greatest-all-time (accessed 16 August 2023)

SUÁREZ PADILLA, J., RAMON TORRES, J., MORA SERRANO, B., SALVAGO SOTO, L. and CHACÓN MOHEDANO, C.: 'La cronología fundacional de la Malaka fenicia: investigaciones en el solar del Rectorado de la Universidad de Málaga' in *Spal* 29.1 (2020), pp. 41–77. DOI: http://dx.doi.org/10.12795/spal.2020.i29.02 (accessed 12 November 2022)

SUN, Zefu: 'The Causes and Development of Political Violence in the Late Roman Republic' in *Advances in Social Science, Education and Humanities Research*, volume 615. Proceedings of the 2021 4th International Conference on Humanities Education and Social Sciences (ICHESS 2021)

SYME, Ronald: 'Rome and the Nations' in *Diogenes* 31 (124) (1983), pp. 33–46.

SYME, Ronald: *The Roman Revolution*. Oxford University Press. Oxford (2002).

SYME, Ronald. 'The Spanish War of Augustus (26-25 B. C.)' in *The American Journal of Philology* vol. 55, no. 4 (1934), pp. 293–317. JSTOR, https://doi.org/10.2307/290141 (accessed 7 August 2023)

SYME, Ronald: *The Augustan Aristocracy*. Clarendon Press (1989).

TORREGARAY, Elena: 'Legatorum Facta: La ejemplaridad de los embajadores romanos' in *Veleia* 26 (2009), pp. 127–52.

TORRES-MARTÍNEZ, Jesús Francisco; MARTÍNEZ VELASCO, Antxoka; and LUIS MARIÑO, Susana de: 'El Oppidum de Monte Bernorio en la Cantabria Histórica. Nueve siglos de historia' in *Kobie Serie Paleoantropología* no 31 (2012), pp. 137–56. Bizkaiko Foru Aldundia-Diputación Foral de Bizkaia Bilbao – 2012. ISSN 0214-7971. In: http://www.bizkaia.eus/kobie (accessed 9 August 2023)

VALIANI, Laura, 'Carthaginian Casualties: The Socioeconomic Effects of the Losses Sustained in the First Punic War.' Thesis, Georgia State University (2016). DOI: https://doi.org/10.57709/8898041 (accessed 18 December 2022).

WILLIAMS, Richard S.: *Ilarcus Porcius Cato. A Conservative Stateman in the Second Century B. C.* Michigan State University Press (1969).

INDEX